T0386645

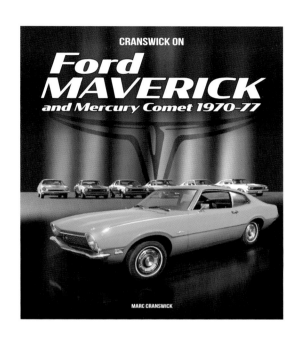

CRANSWICK ON

Ford
MAVERICK
and Mercury Comet 1970-77

MARC CRANSWICK

First published in September 2021 by Veloce Publishing Limited, Veloce House, Parkway Farm Business Park, Middle Farm Way, Poundbury, Dorchester DT1 3AR, England.
Tel 01305 260068 / Fax 01305 268864 / e-mail info@veloce.co.uk / web www.veloce.co.uk or www.velocebooks.com
ISBN: 978-1-787116-69-6 UPC: 6-36847-01669-2

CRANSWICK ON

Ford
MAVERICK
and Mercury Comet 1970-77

MARC CRANSWICK

Contents

Introduction

The 1970 Ford Maverick was a horse of a different color: four different colors, in fact. It could claim to be the most versatile model that FoMoCo has made in its history.

For starters, it was America's first modern subcompact, at a time when foreign small car competition was really heating up, and Detroit had no answers … until Maverick! As 'The Simple Machine,' Maverick turned 'simple style' from an oxymoron into reality. It combined the rugged reliability Ford was known for, with looks that belied its bargain basement starter sticker.

Secondly, in the American idiom, Maverick was an attainable junior supercar. When the Mustang was slipping out of reach due to price, insurance and gas mileage, the Maverick Grabber stepped in to fight inflation. And if Mustang had Cougar as an upscale cousin, the Grabber could have Comet GT as its partner in crime. With the 1971 Mercury Comet, Ford announced that its new small car, wouldn't be limited to econoland. With a power dome hood, Lincoln grille and plush interior, even *Car and Driver* was forced to recount its earlier assessment of the Maverick.

Indeed, it was in this third area of small car luxury that Maverick LDO (Luxury Décor Option) and Mercury Comet with Custom Option were truly innovative. Ford was the first domestic to break the heretofore accepted tenet that luxury went with size. Then, too, by making its handling pack standard on such small, luxurious cars, the Maverick LDO and Mercury Comet Custom Option were Detroit's first responses to the upscale European sedans, which were quickly getting a stranglehold on the new definition of luxury.

Still, all plush and no sport makes Henry a dull lad. In drag racing, Ford's new small cars were utilized by legends of the sport. That sport was Super Stock and Pro Stock. In numerous match races, the Ford Maverick was raced by Dyno Don Nicholson, Fast Eddie Schartman and Gapp & Roush to victory! In South America, the Maverick was also quite a force in road circuit racing. Overall, the Ford Maverick was a winner on the track, and in the showroom. Thanks a couple of million, Henry!

Marc Cranswick

Ford Model T and Model A

In keeping with Henry Ford's practical thinking, there were common elements employed on his cars from 1908 up to 1980. Straightforward, rugged designs that were economical to manufacture over a big production run. Indeed, value for money cars that would keep accumulating miles when other, fancier hardware had bitten the dust. It began with Ford's immortal Model T, affectionately known as the Tin Lizzie, or when hot-rodded, the T-bucket. You would generally be considering a passenger car with a separate chassis and 20-horsepower in-line four-cylinder engine, displacing 177 cubes. The all-up weight was under 1500lb.

Have any color you like, said Henry Ford ... as long as it was black! While the Model T was a rudimentary device, the way it was made and the tools used to make it were revolutionary. Advanced production facilities and techniques, plus a greatly mechanized assembly process, put private car ownership within the hands of the masses for the first time.

In 1916, the purchase price was $360 – much less than that previously asked for motor cars, which had placed such devices solely in the realm of rich folk. Permitting this achievement were the aforementioned advancements, not least of which was Ford's invention of the moving assembly line, with piecemeal assembly of the motor car. A relatively small task for each worker. The Model T, Ford's only car, was cheap to make, strip down and repair. It fulfilled the need for basic, affordable and reliable transport, heretofore beyond the reach of the average man.

Between 1908 and 1927, 15,007,033 Model Ts were manufactured, with peak sales achieved in 1923. [1] Unfortunately, the Model T's basic design had gone relatively unchanged for too long. Henry Ford, a man from a practical agrarian background, thought the Model T was all anyone would ever need. However, rivals GM and Chrysler had other ideas and designs.

Greater style, comfort and convenience became desired by the people. How were you going to keep them down on Henry's farm, once they had seen gay Paris? The answer was the more advanced Ford Model A. Ford's tardiness in coming up with a modern successor had cost it the number one sales position. Even worse was Ford's need to shut

From the days of the Model T to the Ford Pinto, simple, rugged designs brought success to Ford. (Courtesy Ford Motor Co)

down for retooling to make the Model A, whose own development had to be rushed to make up for lost time. A similar fate befell the automaker and model that surpassed the Model T's all time best-seller record: Volkswagen with its VW Beetle.

As well as low price and dependability, Ford's reach was immense. It had a huge dealer network at home, and overseas operations in many countries. These qualities were continued with the Model A which, from 1932, brought a seminal development in the life of the American automobile, the affordable V8 engine. Ford, Chevrolet and Plymouth, the one-time low cost three, had in-line four-powered family cars until the late 1920s. The latter two moved onto in-line sixes thereafter. However, it wasn't until the mid-1950s that such companies joined Ford with a V8 for the family man.

Ford's new 1930s motor was the 90-degree,

The Ford Model A popularized the V8 engine, with the Flathead motor becoming a favorite with hot rodders. (Courtesy *Hot Rod Deluxe*)

three-bearing 221cu in (3622cc) Flathead V8. This new side-valve V8 was fed by a single, one-barrel downdraught Detroit Lubricator carburetor. Upon its 1932 debut, it made a respectable 65bhp gross at 3400rpm. This made the 2580lb, 166in-long Model A a great performer. Bonnie and Clyde liked such V8 power, as did moonshine runners, and even public enemy number one John Dillinger. Dillinger wrote a letter to Ford in praise of the excellent V8-powered Model A. Internationally, the Model A enjoyed a sporting image. A successful rally car in Europe, it even won the prestigious Monte Carlo Rally in 1936.

Ford's family car rivals stuck with straight sixes; in arch-rival Chevrolet's case, the OHV Stovebolt Six. Henry offered a smaller version of the Flathead, but the larger 221cu in edition proved far more popular.

For all its sporting success, and trailblazing budget V8, the Ford Model A was still a simple car. Ultimately, the V8's side-valve nature, plus the vehicle's transverse front and rear leaf springs, proved to be technical limitations as the Model A aged. By 1953, the Flathead V8 was making 110 horsepower, which marked its demise in Ford family car usage. It was replaced by the OHV 239cu in Y block V8, which raised power to 130 horses at 4200rpm in 1954, utilizing a 7.2:1 comp ratio. By 1954, the family Ford could have the fully automated Ford-O-Matic three-speeder with torque converter. [2] It was an advancement on the three-speed column shift manual

with non-synchro first that was found in the 1932 Ford Model A V8. Indeed, Ford's latest 223cu in OHV in-line six was 14bhp up on the final Flathead.

The new age of consumerism

Even before the Y block V8, the 1949 family Ford was seen as an ideal vehicle of its type in terms of its size, handling, ruggedness and cost. Even so, postwar America wanted more: more than just basic transportation, and especially something new compared to prewar designs, which had lingered on thereafter. Ford, and Detroit in general, jumped to accommodate such desires with larger, fancier and more powerful new models. They satisfied a rising demand for more automation in controls or gadgets.

An historical highpoint of such burgeoning consumerism came in the form of the 1955-57 Ford Thunderbird. In short, it was when Ford got it right, and Chevrolet did not – a Dearborn response to the plastic Chebby, Ford's two seater included vital ingredients that buyers wanted. Apart from rakish, low-to-the-ground styling, there was the Y block OHV V8 making 225bhp in 312cu in form, and even more with the optional blower.

To this dream on wheels could be connected a manual gearbox. In contrast, the Corvette commenced as a six-cylinder only, whose sole gearbox was the two-speed Powerglide slushbox. Not really sports car material. Naturally, early Vettes couldn't hold a candle, let alone a blue flame, to the mighty Baby Bird. More than this, Ford's two-seater had the comforting conventionality of a steel body.

The Thunderbird outsold the Corvette 24 to

The 1955-57 two-seater Thunderbird was a Ford success story, critically and commercially, to the tune of 53,277 sales. (Courtesy Marc Cranswick)

one! This was handy, given the T-Bird was, for a time, Ford's performance flagship and image leader. Strong sales were good for Ford, and for the economy. The President was of the same opinion.

Well, it seemed like the public were ready for a little more, and the 1957 Ford 500 Skyliner was it. It made its debut at the 1956 New York Auto Show, and was advertised on TV by America's favorite housewife, Lucille Ball, and her husband, Desi Arnaz. With the 'Retractible' it seemed like not even the sky was the limit for Ford and America. A 1957 Retractible was even presented to President Eisenhower, and ol' Ike was an advocate of '50s consumerism. [3]

In spite of such rampant consumerism, Ford was a company founded on thrift. Nothing was wasted, not even the packing crates containing CKD Model T parts for overseas assembly: the wood from the crates served as floorboards for the completed Model Ts. When asked why Ford factories in sunny climes still had roofs capable of dealing with heavy snow, Henry Ford said he didn't wish to pay an architect twice for the same job! Good horse sense also prevailed with the Ford Thunderbird. While the two-seater did possess a new, pressed steel body on a separate chassis, most mechanicals came from Ford's parts shelf. It contributed to the T-Bird's commercial success. While Chevrolet was considering axing the slow-selling Corvette, it was certain the Thunderbird would continue beyond 1957.

Similarly, thrift had helped Ford's successful reintroduction of its car-based pickup concept in the 1950s. Henry had made the first of these utilitarian workhorses during the 1930s Depression. Back then it was based on the Model A Roadster; now, it was plusher and based on the contemporary Ranch Wagon. The snazzy Fairlane-related Ranchero and new Retractible were stars of 1957, the latter being the world's first car with a fully automated, fold away, electro-mechanical hardtop. Both passenger cars were proof of Ford's innovative ways.

The Ranchero had a solid three-year run in full-size form, as a niche vehicle. It constantly posed the question as to whether it was a car, or a truck? It was also always cloudy concerning its market position, and buyer profile. It was all enough to lure rival Chevrolet into another commercial blunder, in the form of the 1959 Chevrolet El Camino. Seeing Ford garner fresh sales in a new territory with Ranchero, the Bowtie brigade came at Henry with their El Camino. The difference here was that while Ranchero saw Ford pony up relatively little in its creation, a mere $200 million, Chevrolet lacked a suitable base conversion vehicle. They had to go fully custom. Yes, it may have resembled a '59 Impala pickup, but the changes were many and the cost great.

Ford struck gold again with the 1957 Ranchero. It was the modern start of Dearborn's car-based pickup, utilizing the contemporary Ranch Wagon in full-size days. (Courtesy Bob Borum)

The 1959 Impala 'Martian flying saucer' styling, while popular now, didn't sit well in conservative late '50s America. More than that, by the time El Camino arrived, the economy was in recession. While the Ranchero did reasonable business for Ford, the El Camino failed to realize its hoped for sales. It all led to Ford taking the number one sales position in 1959, the first time this had happened since 1937. Compared to Ford's conservative look, Chevrolet had gone a step too far. Going beyond can be a good thing: Ford reasoned its Thunderbird would do even better business, as a larger, plusher four-seater personal, luxury sports job. This indeed proved to be the case. However, there was one rare lapse in judgment on Ford's part; it was all to do with the upscale Edsel.

Compared to the money Ford lost on Edsel, the Ranchero pickup was developed at half the cost ($200 million), and did well. (Courtesy Marc Cranswick)

Edsel and the late '50s recession

Edsel was a new brand to promote, intended as a medium price range, featuring convertibles, sedans and wagons. Medium price cars occupied the ground between normal family cars and the luxury segment occupied by Lincoln, Cadillac and Imperial. In this respect Edsel provided some in-house competition for Mercury. However, from September 4 1959, Ford dealers would have something more upscale to sell. Naturally, added value was the name of the game then and now. How else could Detroit pay for the UAW? So it was that FoMoCo marketing had Edsel's debut declared 'Edsel Day.' There was a mass advertising campaign for the best thing ... until the next best thing came along.

Edsel had many fancy touches. Engine torque rating was stated on the valve covers, preceded by an 'E' prefix. There was also push button 'Teletouch' steering wheel activated automatic transmission, and Bermuda trim level for the upscale wagon version. Only 779 of these nine passenger Bermudas were sold in 1958. The asking price of this family hold-all was a princely $3155: a tidy sum for the time. Although first year Edsel sales weren't bad, the estimated 200,000 unit sales projection wasn't met in 1957, and sales died away subsequently. Advertising, the art of making people do what they don't want to do, seemed powerless in the face of the economic recession.

Public relations declared 4000 advance Edsel orders were secure, but in the end the economic slowdown couldn't be overcome. The only real criticism that could be leveled against Edsel was the subjective issue of styling. Marketing declared "The

Edsel Look is here to stay," but most took exception to the car's horse collar grille. In '50s America, a car lived or died by its styling. Styling and marketing held as much sway as engineering, maybe even more so. This was a rare case when Ford got it wrong, but it wasn't the only one. Chevrolet shot itself in the foot with the '59 Impala, and Virgil Exner over-reached with the reverse tailfins on the '61 Dodge Dart.

In any case, the result was a near $400 million loss on Edsel, and the demise of the short-lived marque by November 1959. In the subsequent scapegoat hunt, high-ups in project Edsel were either demoted or fired, and Ford joined the rest of the industry in trying to please the thrifty buyer, which by now was pretty much everyone. Indeed, in contrast to the billboard high tailfins of the '59 Caddy, it was the budget Mobil Economy-run specials like Rambler American, Studebaker Lark and VW Beetle that were riding high. Said Lark even had a V8 engine option. As a matter of statistical fact, 77 per cent of 1959 Edsels were V8-powered and 92 per cent carried automatic transmission. So, it looked like domestic car buyers weren't looking for the wheel to be reinvented. A little less of what they liked would do fine, and Ford could oblige.

Ford's official 1959 press statement was "Common sense, not excess." Revised power team combinations and amended models brought practical effect to the slogan. Ford predicted 95 per cent of family car buyers would select the 292 base V8 in 1959, so compression ratio of this unit was

The Ford Fairlane, shown in 1957 form, could be optioned to a level that made the Edsel's role questionable. (Courtesy Todd Matthies)

dropped from 9.1 to 8.8:1, confirming regular fuel status. Two barrel carburetion was also standard on the size up 332 V8. Both could be combined with a newly simplified two-speed Ford-O-Matic and tall 2.91 rear end. Three-speed Cruise-O-Matic became a premium option. That said, there was some luxury around for Ford's Fairlane. The extravagant Skyliner Retractable and Air Suspension options continued into 1959, even though both were seldom purchased. The latter was mechanically simplified for '59 MY.

It seems Edsel's legacy was limited to the engine series named after it. The new FE (Ford Edsel) generation of medium block V8s set industry standards in the precision creation of thinwall cast iron blocks. Weight was saved by not wasting material when pouring the casting molds. The FE series displayed tighter tolerances, and culminated in the Le Mans winning side oiler 427 V8, which powered the Ford GT40. Some of its lessons were even applied to the 1990s Ford 4.6 and 5.4 Modular V8s. However, in Ford's 1961 V8 engine line-up, power ratings were decreased across the board by Robert McNamara.

McNamara and the Falcon

Robert Strange McNamara was a central figure in

Ford's transition from the extravagant '50s, through the 1958-61 recessionary years. He was Group Vice President of Ford Cars and Trucks, and was briefly president before leaving Ford to conduct the Vietnam War. McNamara was a big believer in statistical analysis. In World War II, he worked out bombing raids would be much more effective if planes flew lower. Naturally, although this was true, it didn't please flight crews due to the greater risk of being shot down.

During peacetime, he ordered an analysis of Ford vehicular fatalities to discern the cause of deaths. Upon learning a percentage of the fatalities were related to the car, and not driver error or road conditions, he initiated greater passive safety aids. These ran to padded dashboards, standard seatbelt mountings and optional seatbelt availability. Such systems were embodied in Ford's Lifeguard Design standard and optional features. Under McNamara's watch, the decision was taken to axe Edsel and reorganize the Ford model line, so that it was in keeping with value conscious times. As part of this, there would be the introduction of a new Ford, designed to take on the imports in the burgeoning small car market.

Although Detroit prided itself in being all things to all people, there was a growing segment in North

The Ford Falcon was America's first compact. Here, it's displayed in 1963½ Falcon Futura hardtop coupe guise. (Courtesy Jeff Thomas)

The first generation Falcon ran from 1960 to 1963. Dimensions were 181in/70.1in/54.4in for respective length, width and height. (Courtesy Jeff Thomas)

America seeking a smaller, easier to handle, thrifty machine that was cheaper to buy. Detroit hadn't been particularly interested in such cars, due to their low profit margin for automakers and their dealers. Such small imported cars in the '50s came from countries that were lower cost producers, with workers that earned less than their UAW counterparts. GM's response to anyone that felt they weren't being catered to was to say "A good used car is the only answer to America's need for cheap transportation." Some years later, a GM exec even opined that there must be something wrong with people that like small cars.

Contemporary industry thinking did ignore a couple of facts. Buying a used car wasn't that easy in the '50s. A winter or two in the snowbelt could introduce unwanted body ventilation. Plus, the average American annual mileage would add to wear and tear. Then there was the lack of a warranty, and the buyer still had a machine too big and possibly too thirsty for their personal use. Then, too, there was the reality that people were indeed buying small cars in appreciable numbers. The Morris Minor, Renault Dauphine and VW Beetle were all doing well in the 1950s.

The situation was highlighted in the 1959 fourth season episode of *The Phil Silvers Show*, titled *Bilko's Small Car*. Here, Fort Baxter's Colonel Hall had ordered a new Renault Dauphine for his wife, but was denied receiving the Renault, due to the expected chicanery of Master Sergeant Ernest Bilko. Bilko then schemes to use the motor pool

Initially, Falcon had three on the tree, or two-speed Ford-O-Matic. However, by 1962, buyers could enjoy four on the floor. (Courtesy Jeff Thomas)

as an assembly line, passing off Jeeps as imported European sportscars. He called them the Arrivederci, because they were a good buy in any language! The popular comedy explicitly mentioned America's need for a small car, and the virtue of good gas mileage.

Ford was wise to all of this, and its research found that many women considered their husband's full-size domestic cars to be too big. Ford research also found many buyers would prefer to buy American, if a smaller car existed at the right price. These facts would have a bearing on Ford's upcoming small car, and the one after that. It was sensible to buy a domestic car, because, to a large extent, at this stage mostly European imports weren't suited to US driving or conditions.

That there was practical convergence was often the product of happy coincidence, rather than intended design for the North American market. Volvo Amazons had good heaters and didn't rust out fast, because they came from cold Sweden. VWs could handle a highway sans strain, since they were 'bahn bred. The Beetle's air cooling made winter heating touch and go. However, having the motor over the driving wheels, was a boon in the snowbelt. High powered, nose heavy V8 sleds didn't exactly endear themselves when the going got slippery.

In addition, the lack of a good service network, with competent mechanics and ample supply of affordable spare parts, was frequently a minus point for small imports. The Renault Dauphine's one-time great American success quickly evaporated once buyers experienced the Renault's durability woes. There was also the subsequent need to resort to a shadetree mechanic to cover repair work that was usually out of warranty. VW had the reliability and service aspects down cold, which paved the way for that brand's success. Said Bug influenced Detroit greatly, in the development of what would become the new 1960 domestic compacts. Indeed, Chevrolet's Corvair would be rear-engined, air-cooled and possess four-wheel independent suspension, sound familiar?

Meanwhile, Robert McNamara was set on Ford's rival being a four-cylinder car, because the sales winning Beetle was. More than this, making the new Ford a four banger would save Henry $13.50 per car. For thrifty, statistics-driven McNamara, this was exciting! However, wise counsel at Ford advised him that an in-line six would be preferred by buyers. The car in question was the all-new 1960 Ford Falcon, America's first compact. Henry beat Chevrolet's Corvair and Plymouth's Valiant – also six-cylinder motorvated – to the economy car punch.

As for key dates, the Falcon program was approved on March 19 1958, with the car launched on September 2 1959. In development, measures were taken to keep weight and cost down. Base sticker in 1960 turned out to be $1974. For Falcon, a new smaller in-line 'Thriftpower Six' of 144 cubes was created. It was smaller externally than Ford's existing 223cu in I6, which was the base motor in full-size family Fords. However, the Falcon turned out larger than originally planned. Henry Ford II had prototypes substantially lengthened and widened, as

Robert McNamara was persuaded to let Falcon have six cylinders, rather than four like VW. The new 260 cube 'Challenger' V8 joined Falcon as a mid '63 MY option. (Courtesy Jeff Thomas)

he felt they were too narrow. Obviously, McNamara had been really honing in on the VW, given the planned in-line four and small dimensions.

As a basic economy car Falcon held no surprises, with SLA suspension and coils at the front, and four-wheel drums and a leaf sprung live axle out back. The irony was that the Ford Falcon idea originally hailed from 1935, when Edsel Ford had been behind the idea of an upscale new design. This eventually led to the new Mercury. The 1960 Falcon was half a hood shorter than other Fords. However, it didn't fall short on sales, even though critics reckoned the new car was too plain, ordinary and wouldn't amount to much. One comment even associated the new Falcon with Robert McNamara's nature: "He wears granny glasses and has put out a granny car."

Falcon got past a half million sales in year one, and was over a million units by the close of the second year. It still managed 396,129 sold in '62 MY. The public obviously approved of McNamara's frugal Falcon. Ads claimed "big-car performance and safety," plus comfort for six. Certainly, next to the dominant VW Beetle, the Falcon offered safer acceleration and greater interior space. Ford also assuredly got a sales lead on the Chevrolet Corvair and Plymouth Valiant, and with the respective outlandish layout and styling of such compacts, buyers were swayed towards Ford. Indeed, Falcon's success motivated the speedy creation of the Chevy II. Chevrolet quickly came to the realization it needed something more conventional to take on Ford.

Falcon also brought 30mpg economy, and for recession hit buyers this was very desirable. Now it

The only thing separating the 1963½ Falcon Sprint hardtop and 1964½ Mustang hardtop was styling. They were mechanical twins under the skin! (Courtesy Jeff Thomas)

seemed one could get the money-saving measures of small imports, allied to the greater durability, serviceability and conventionality associated with domestic brands. The winning ways of the Big Three's 1960 compacts, proved to be the death knell for most imported small cars. The only sales survivor seemed to be the VW Beetle. Ye olde Bug was the small economy car champ, and it seemed untroubled by Falcon, Corvair, Chevy II or Valiant. The Beetle marked a distinction between small domestics, and truly small cars. No one had mentioned the term subcompact by this stage, but they would.

After getting off to a flying start, Falcon went through a number of evolutionary improvements. 1961's Falcon Futura brought buckets and a console. For '62 MY Futura offered the passive safety of optional factory installed seatbelts. This combined with Falcon's unibody, made for greater crash safety than a full-size Impala on an X frame. In the middle of 1962 model year, came a Thunderbirdesque roofline and option of four on the floor. The latter a device popularized by imports. An expanded range even saw an eight-seater Falcon Club Wagon, to rival Chevrolet's Corvair based Greenbriar.

A couple for the enthusiast arrived in the exciting form of the 1963 Falcon Sprint and convertible

Ford added the versatility of Ranchero to the Falcon for '61 MY. This 1963 rig goes by the name of Rojo! (Courtesy Todd and Jill Reglin)

variants. The pinnacle for the first generation Falcon came in the form of the 1963 $\frac{1}{2}$ 260 Challenger V8 option. This was an upsized version of the all-new, lightweight Windsor V8, which made its debut in the all-new 1962 intermediate sized Ford Fairlane. A car and its ilk, also known as a 'King Size' compact. With this latest option, critics considered that Ford had commenced Falcon's 'great leap forward'. That is, from small, basic economy car to upscale, sensible family transportation. [4]

Indeed, the contrast to McNamara's VW Beetle fighter was tremendous. The 164bhp Challenger V8 could only be specified on Sprint hardtops and ragtops, numbered 10,479 and 4602 respectively. For features, the Sprint two-door hardtop had buckets, fastback and the possibility of smooth V8 power, plus four on the floor flexibility. It was all a curtain raiser to the much revised second generation Falcon of 1964-65, where the 260 cube V8 would be offered across the Falcon range. Such developments underlined that, while the Beetle was an economy import, Falcon was a domestic small car. As such, the Ford could be many things depending on what the buyer wanted. This last quality would be of major import, as an exciting new Ford that was just around the corner.

While VW Beetle had evolved, and was getting plusher and more powerful, Falcon evolved likewise, but in a distinctly American manner. For 1964, Beetle was getting a crank handle, sliding steel sunroof. However, 1964 Falcon featured new 'Razor-Edged' styling, with side paneling that afforded an optical stretched-out look. Falcon was still a compact 181.6in long, but appeared larger and more upscale than its predecessor. The Sprint package would incorporate the larger 289 Windsor V8. Glamour aside, critics felt American compacts were now reaching a happy medium as all-purpose family cars.

After WWII there was very little choice. Things went overboard by the late '50s, and the subsequent compacts were just too austere. In practical terms, the original 85 horse 144cu in Falcon with 3.10 axle and the four-cylinder Chevy II were too slow and cramped to serve as mainline family transport. You could still get that Mileage Maker 144cu in combination in the new '64 Falcon, but Ford and rivals offered many more choices now. It was bigger, but also better. In the wake of the late '50s recession, American Motors' boss George Romney predicted a new age of functionalism for the American driver. This was when car buyers were turning their backs on the likes of the Edsel, and switching to ones like the Rambler American, 1959 Studebaker Lark and McNamara's '60 Falcon.

If a new age of functionalism arose, it happened later for the European and Japanese imports and their patrons. However, for now, most American

Only the '63½ Sprint sported the 260cu in Windsor as an option. However, such V8s have often been swapped into 1st gen Falcons, like Rojo. (Courtesy Todd and Jill Reglin)

Falcon Ranchero was an early exponent of the plush small car. It was a vehicle type that would become more popular as time progressed. (Courtesy Todd and Jill Reglin)

buyers had money in their pockets, as George Romney departed to become Governor of Michigan. For 1964, Studebaker had a much revised Lark, and American Motors came at the market with an all new American. However, with good economic times afoot, buyers were showing more interest in intermediate sized offerings like Fairlane and Chevelle rather than the compacts, much improved though they were. It explained why Studebaker shut up shop in 1966, and why AMC's new boss Roy Abernethy took what some considered 'Puritan Motors' into the psychedelic era with two-seater AMX. And it was also why the latest Ford Falcon wasn't the austerity package of yore.

In spite of recent tough times, American buyers

hadn't lost their love of the extravagant. It's just that, for a while, buyers lacked the folding stuff, but don't worry, Dr Detroit could still provide. The third generation Thunderbird embodied aircraft design and fashionable 'missile overtones' in its styling. The interior designer on this T-Bird, Art Querfield, spent more time doing the interior than on any other car in his 40 years at Dearborn. Yes, the dare to dream Detroit was back! And just as AMC's new guy at the helm was wise to the swinging times, there was a rising star at Ford who seemed perfect for the post-McNamara jazzy era.

Lee Iacocca and the Mustang

Lee Iacocca had a sixth sense for emerging trends, and when they had run their course. He was an early believer in the youth market, and using sporty cars to improve sales numbers. Back in 1962, in his third year as a general manager, Iacocca got behind the Galaxie 500XL Sunliner. With fresh styling, buckets and a simulated engine turned metal instrument panel, along with the availability of a Holley triple deuce fed 406 V8 and four-speed, it seemed like the start of Ford's 'Total Performance' era. This proved a big departure in selling cars. Formerly, styling and gadgets were where it was at; not sports-related hardware. Plus, of course, the AMA (American Manufacturers Association) involved automakers signing an anti-racing pact in 1961.

Even by 1964, the full-size family car accounted for 40 per cent of sales. It was the core segment, into which major money was directed for innovations in drivetrain, suspension, convenience features, and such. In 1964, you could option a two-door, four-speed Galaxie hardtop with a 425 horse 427 V8. However, sporty didn't sell cars, and advertising didn't suggest you option Galaxie like you could ... or should! This was all about to change, with the coming of one of the most famous nameplates the world has ever seen.

It happened the moment Lee Iacocca peered over the shoulder of Don Frey, at the sketch of that week's automotive dream on wheels, and suggested a rear seat should be added. Add a rear seat; it didn't matter if it was only big enough for little Fido or your favorite hat, but it had to have a rear seat! One piece of inspired marketing led to another, and before you knew it, North America had fallen in love with the new 1964 1/2 Ford Mustang.

Mustang's first year production total of 121,538, compared to just 53,277 two-seater Thunderbirds sold during 1955-57, showed the value of having that rear seat. Unbeknownst to most of the public, the 1963 1/2 Falcon Sprint and 1964 1/2 Mustang were virtually mechanical twins. However, that all-new, fresh styling worked its magic in showrooms. As the Mustang's spiritual father, Ford Vice President Iacocca enjoyed the halo glow of the new coupe.

Ranchero showed Ford's wisdom. Keep a nameplate's sales going, by moving it into a smaller size class when conditions required. (Courtesy Todd and Jill Reglin)

It was a sports car for the masses, and must have started the decline of the British sports car.

Hear the slogan: "The Mustang is designed to be designed by you." The starting price was $2368, and the long options list spelt value-added all the way. Early cars had Falcon instruments within a padded dash. It showed Mustang made financial sense to Ford and the public. Entering the 'Total Performance' era, win on Sunday sell on Monday, Ford approached Texan racer Carroll Shelby with a view to creating a special Mustang. Shelby's initial response wasn't positive, saying you couldn't make a race horse out of a mule.

Carroll Shelby was an engineering realist, knowing production car limitations in racing. Porsche found that out with its 356, which led to the specialized 550 series. Shelby had wanted to win Le Mans by combining the AC Ace with the Ford 427 V8. With the Cobra lacking chassis sophistication, he created the Daytona Coupe. Concerning an homologation special for SCCA limited production model racing, Shelby said his guys at Shelby American did a real job creating the 1965 Shelby Mustang GT350.

Naming the new car had proved a headache, so Carroll Shelby asked a Ford guy to pace the distance over to a building yonder. It turned out to be 350 feet, hence the GT350's moniker. Then came the need to build and sell at least 100 examples. Shelby was skeptical that this could be done. He handed the task to a motivated fellow at Shelby American, and the job was completed. Hertz Rental Cars turned out to be a good patron. Soon tales abounded of Shelby Mustangs returning with tires changed and the special 306 horse – better than a K code, 289 V8 – replaced by a plebian two-barrel 289 grocery getter motor! It was all done by Shelby American, and that included 1967's big block edition, which paved the way for Ford's own factory 390 V8 option.

By 1966 the Falcon was in its third incarnation, and getting larger all the time. However, sales never recovered from the Ford Mustang's introduction. (Courtesy Ford Motor Co)

Mustang started the pony car race! By utilizing its extensive and growing options list, buyers could select a version tailor-made to their tastes. (Courtesy Ford Motor Co)

Room for a new small Ford

The success of the Ford Mustang came at the expense of Falcon sales. It started the problem in Detroit of sales cannibalization, when a new model steals the thunder from a brand's existing nameplates, rather than achieving conquest sales. Even so, Ford kept on improving its Falcon. The refinement of three-speed Cruise-O-Matic automatic arrived in 1965, along with standard front seatbelts.

Unfortunately, Mustang's coming brought the demise of the Falcon Sprint and convertible versions by the close of 1965 model year. Up to 1965, Ford Falcon TV ads and sales brochures had featured Charles M Schulz's popular *Peanuts* characters. Indeed, it was the first time anyone had seen Charlie Brown, Snoopy and the gang in animated form! However, Falcon was now adopting a more mature, family car stance.

1966 to 1970 saw the third and final US Ford Falcon incarnation. It was larger now, based on a truncated Fairlane platform. In the absence of a standard two-door hardtop, or ragtop, the Futura Sports Coupe became Falcon's flagship. A heater and defroster were now standard Falcon fare, but like Snoopy's pal hard luck Chuck, Falcon just couldn't catch a trick. Previous versions were fast deserting the Falcon range. The Falcon wagon now resided on a Fairlane platform, and even Ranchero joined the Fairlane range for '67 MY. In 1966, Falcon took to SCCA Trans Am racing. The model always seemed to be paving the way for, or backing up Mustang.

During 1967 and 1969, it seemed Falcon alterations were mainly done to stay legal with the latest or pending federal safety regs. 1967 saw a collapsible steering column and dual circuit brakes. In 1968, it was the turn of sidemarker lights for visibility, and by January 1 1969 front outboard shoulder belts and head restraints: all mandatory, government-required items. Indeed, it was the 1970 need for a locking steering column that spelt the end for North America's Falcon. The straw that broke the proverbial camel's back, it was just one more change for a slower selling line, and Ford had something new lined up.

Falcon didn't miss out on the arrival of Ford's 289 replacing 302 V8, and the Falcon name did see out the 1970 model year ... in strange fashion. The new 1970 $^1/_2$ Ford Falcon was, in reality, a decontented version of the new 1970 Fairlane/Torino range. Ford tooled up for this subline of two-

want more

F.P.M.?*

try a Shelby GT

*That's Fun-Per-Mile – yours aplenty in these two great new GT cars from Shelby American.

There's more F.P.M. when you have reserve performance. The GT 350 carries a 306 horsepower 289 cubic inch V-8. The GT 500 is powered by the 428 cubic inch V-8, descended from the 1966 LeMans winning Ford GT.

The F.P.M. is higher when steering is competition-quick, suspension is firm. Driving's *fun* with the safety of an integral roll bar, shoulder harnesses, disc front and drum rear brakes, wide-path 4-ply nylon tires.

Driving's *fun* with the Shelby brand of comfort and style. For more F.P.M., see your Shelby dealer P.D.Q.

SHELBY G.T. *350 and 500* The Road Cars *Powered by* Ford

Shelby American, Inc., 6501 W. Imperial Highway, Los Angeles 90009

Lee Iacocca supplied the idea; Carroll Shelby provided the image. The Shelby Mustang brought the big block V8 to Ford's little pony in 1967. (Courtesy Shelby American)

and four-door sedan, plus four-door wagon. In a way, it honored Falcon's economy car genesis. It also allowed prospects for the snazzy looking new Torino to save a few bucks. Luxury and comfort options were limited. Naturally one would go for higher trim levels to get that stuff. However, the full line of Fairlane/Torino motors were optional. Whether it was the base 250cu in in-line six or mighty 429 Cobra Jet V8, just tick the option box and it was in your car hold. If you wanted a stripper muscle car that featured a motor from the peak horsepower year, this Falcon coupe was it!

If things were rough for Falcon, the going wasn't exactly easy for Mustang either. If you build it, they will come. Unfortunately they did, in the form of Chevrolet's Camaro, Pontiac Firebird, AMC Javelin and Dodge Challenger, joining Plymouth Barracuda and Mustang. So, what had been a really big pie, was getting sliced up every which way. Worse than that, said pie was shrinking! According to the March

'70 issue of *Car and Driver*, pony cars accounted for a peak of 13 per cent market share in 1967, falling to 9 per cent in 1969. Indeed, 1967 calendar year sales for the segment hit 752,821 units.

Concerning annual sales figures, Mustang galloped to 540,802 sales in 1966, declining thereafter to 165,414 in 1970. Pony cars were getting pricier. By the time you optioned a big block V8, automatic and desirable comfort options like fast glass, a/c and eight-track player, you were into luxury personal car land. The general public were also getting weary of the speed option message. Insurance companies were treating monikers like Boss and Super Cobra Jet as an invitation to take your money.

The idea of Steve McQueen burning up the streets in his '67 Mustang GT 390 fastback was appealing. In reality, things were more like Mary Tyler Moore, looking somewhat lost on the highway in her '71 Mustang, moving interstate to a new job. Those formerly secretary specials were getting very pricey, and even the Shelby Mustang had become more boulevardier than bolide. It's commonly felt the 1967 Shelby Mustang was the pinnacle model, in blending looks with gentleman racer nature. Before that it was very raw, and afterward it became more

grand tourer. Indeed, between 1968 and 1970 it was renamed Shelby Cobra, as Ford brought the ultimate Mustang more in house.

In all, 13,765 Shelby-related Mustangs were built between 1965 and 1970. It was a number that paled in comparison with the rising wave of small car imports coming from across the sea. For a spell, American compacts had stopped 'em all but one. However, now the domestics were bigger, had gained plush accoutrements and acquired V8 options. It left the garage door open to a new wave of economy cars. They weren't all Beetles, not all European, and many were now hailing from Japan. Ford's line up had been getting bigger and bigger since 1965, but Henry and Big Lee weren't asleep at the wheel.

There would be a new small car, import fighter coming. Plus, Ford could see a middle ground between this segment, and existing domestic compacts. With two heads often being better than one, there would be two models. Following Mustang's lead, their nameplates would have a range or ranch connection, but first the larger car. It provided proof that between 1960 and 1980, the Falcon possessed one of the most versatile basic chassis designs in auto history!

Ford sold 490,252 Mustangs in 1969-70. However, 1970 would see the end of the Boss 302, as Parnelli Jones became SCCA Trans Am champ in the one they raced. (Courtesy Smokey Mountain Traders)

Car Craft magazine considered it tardy when its '70 Mustang Mach I 351 did a mere 15.23-second ¼ mile! However, slowing Mustang and pony car sector sales were truly worrying Detroit. (Courtesy Smokey Mountain Traders)

The search for economy continues

Observing the Ford Maverick in general terms, would produce the following description: 180in long two-door sedan with attractive fastback styling, chassis with front independent SLA (Short Long Arm) suspension, leaf sprung rear live axle, four-wheel drum brakes, FoMoCo Thriftpower sixes and pending Windsor 'Three Oh Two' V8. First impressions were of a mini Mustang, but all of the above gave zero indication of Maverick's purpose, nor the car or cars it was intended to, and did compete against.

Back in 1950 only around 21,000 imported cars were brought to America's shores. They were largely curiosity pieces bought by eccentrics, or dyed in the wool thrift seekers, looking for low price and running costs. However, by 1959 this tally had escalated to 600,000 cars! The need for economy in purchase price and operation had continued through the years. The faltering economy saw the trend amplified, with small car sales really kicked up from 1958. Size was also becoming more of an issue. Back in 1950, domestic cars were of reasonable dimensions. However, in the drive for more profit, and going with good '50s economic vibes, the girth of US cars had grown considerably.

American consumers were asking a question, one that was finally answered by Detroit's 1960 compacts. At this point, the Big Three thought they had the imports licked, and as for the Beetle? Well, they weren't really that bothered by VW's oddball, as they saw it. However, like a Timex, those imports took a licking and kept on ticking! It seemed like history was repeating itself. American compacts had grown in size, power and plushness through the '60s. In doing so, the imports had once again stepped into Detroit's complacency parking space. Robert McNamara had been away from Ford, busy dealing with the Vietnam War. However, the developing interim statistics would have interested him greatly. 1968 saw imported cars reach one million units, over 10 per cent of the new car market: or to Detroit management ... a helluva lot of oddballs!

In some parts of the country the percentage was even higher. In Southern California, imported car fever was running at 25 per cent, with market share in affluent Orange County 30 per cent! This latter figure was contributed to by rising sales of upscale, imported European brands. So, the traditional Buicks, Cadillacs, Mercs and Lincolns were being forsaken for Mercedes, Jaguar and soon BMW. It

The Falcon nameplate ended in North America affixed to an entry level Fairlane/Torino intermediate: the 1970½ Falcon Coupe. A stripper 429 Cobra Jet V8 muscle car wasn't a bad way to bow out! (Courtesy Bull Doser)

was the start of a luxury sector problem that the Big Three have been battling ever since. Outside the luxo realm, there was a persistent demand for something smaller and handier, cheaper and thriftier. It was a mission statement that domestic compacts no longer seemed able to meet. [5]

Even Europe had gone extra small in the wake of the 1956 Suez Crisis. However, the rise of the imported car in late '60s America seemed to cover more than just small or cheap cars. The size and permanence of Detroit's problem was shown by the East Coast dockworker's strike of 1969, industrial action that lasted for 57 days. Similar labor unrest transpired in 1965, and, mindful of this, many importers had accumulated five weeks' worth of stock, just to be on the safe side. However, in this case, safe wasn't safe enough.

So it was that the first quarter of 1969 saw the march of imported machines temporarily halted. On average imports were down 13 per cent, with their market share falling to 8.5 per cent in March 1969. In 1968 this figure had been consistently over 10 per cent, reaching a September record of over 13 per cent. The Big Four, including AMC, were ready to take advantage of the import respite. There were patriotic ad campaigns, discounts on domestics, and, just after the strike action, the introduction of America's first subcompact ... the Ford Maverick. In the words of *Car and Driver*, Maverick's April 1969 release happened thusly, "... along with an apple pie, hot dog and Sunday afternoon ball games advertising campaign." [6]

Compared to Ford Anglia, the 1960s Cortina had desirable features amenable to North Americans. (Courtesy Ford UK)

The Cortina put English Ford in the top 10 imported selling brands during the late '60s. However, Henry found captive imports would only take Ford just so far. (Courtesy Ford Motor Co)

Naturally Chevrolet and American Motors weren't going to miss such 'kick 'em while they're down' action. Both companies leaked information that their subcompacts were just over the horizon, too. In truth, the respective Vega and Gremlin were a ways off, but no matter: the seed of hope had been planted in the public's mind. To Henry's credit, Ford had something available in the here and now, and now was pretty important. In spite of strike action, not all the imports were taking things lying down. Fiat, God bless their heart, Opel and Toyota still got sales gains during the strike affected first quarter. Yes, Opel was up 8 per cent, Toyota 67 per cent, but Fix It Again Tony slayed all with an 88 per cent gain! Heavens to Betsy, they must have really wanted their small cars.

In all the upheavals, VW was still No. 1 imported brand, but its sales had fallen 20 per cent. Big mover and shaker Datsun was also down to the tune of 51

per cent. Buyers wanted their 510s, but just couldn't get them. English Ford (Cortina MkII) was the 7th best selling import in the first quarter of 1968, but in the same period of 1969 it had fallen to 9th. However, English Ford was still ahead of British Leyland North America (BLNA). BLNA had placed 10th in both years. Post strike, the imports flooded back, or to quote *Car and Driver*, they "came back like the Celtics … "

In May 1969 a new record was set, with over 105,000 imports sold. There were records posted by Toyota, Opel, Fiat, BMW and Porsche. Indeed, Toyota overtook Opel as the No. 2 imported brand, behind VW. Opel was GM's captive import, selling out of Buick dealerships. For GM, that Vega couldn't come a day too soon. Showing import diversity, compared to 1959, BMW and Porsche weren't economy brands. The former just launched upscale six-cylinder sedans and coupes, and Porsche was

There have been great Birds before
But none like this Bird

This Bird flies higher. Sweeps longer
Rides lower. Stands wider.
Takes you where others don't go.
With standards others charge extra
for. Power steering. Power ventilation.
Power front disc brakes. Radial-
ply tires. 429 CID V-8 and
Cruise-O-Matic transmission.

No Bird before has been so
dependable. Its systems are backed
by space-age technology. Its
smooth ride was designed by computer.

And no Bird before has given you so
much choice. Bench seats or
buckets. 2 doors or 4. Sunroof or no.
The luxury list goes on and on.
See your Ford dealer and
this rarest of all Birds, today.

SOARING
TO NEW
HEIGHTS:

1970
THUNDERBIRD.

THUNDERBIRD Ford

See your Ford dealer for a free Thunderbird catalogue. Or write: Dept. T16A, P.O. Box 1503, Dearborn, Mich. 48121

It seemed like Thunderbird, and all other FoMoCo lines, had been getting bigger since the mid '60s. That said, Ford had a couple of major small car releases for the '70s. (Courtesy Ford Motor Co)

only selling its 911s and 912s at this hour. While domestic rivals were talking small, Ford was actually delivering with Maverick.

Maverick meets world

It happened during a San Diego winter, at Ranch La Costa. There, under the resort's pavilion, Ford general managers, engineers and cars lay by the pool. Ford stated the purpose behind the Maverick: "It is a matter of raw economics." To boil it down, 10 per cent of Americans bought small cars, so Ford would build a small car. Who bought these small cars? Ford market research said two main groups.

The first group comprised the young, educated and affluent. They wanted a sensible car with some panache. The second group was older, less well off and with a lower level of education. Basically, the

usual old guy Pop Grundig types, who wanted basic A to B transportation, and weren't averse to buying a stripper. [7] Ron Wakefield made a kind of cynical observation, concerning who Ford's smooth and quiet Maverick appealed to: "... secretaries and to older people who want a little style with their slow driving." [8] Well, you would have expected that from import-centric *Road & Track*!

In the years leading up to Detroit's small car conundrum, the Falcon had been satisfying Pop Grundig, but the swingers were left cold by this growing compact. And those swingers were fast out numbering the Pop Grundigs of this world, according to demographic studies. Indeed, to cater to the growing youth market, Dodge had released its Dart Swinger for '69 MY. This was a low priced, hardtop stripper. It was in the vein of Plymouth's Road Runner, which could be optioned up as desired, and Plymouth hoped you would. Going with the youth angle, Swinger had a luminous body decal. It made an impact, and was cheaper than a badge. Maverick would use budget tricks, and lean towards the youngsters as well.

Ford openly stated that it felt Maverick would appeal to both buyer groups, the groovy and the grown ups. On this subject, the arrival of Semon E Knudsen, aka Bunkie, as Ford's President for the past year was considered influential. Although the Maverick project predated his coming, it was felt his presence would have a bearing on Maverick. As with his great impact on Pontiac, that would imply a youthful, sporty approach. At La Costa, various hued Mavericks were on show for the press to try. They showed that, for starters, Maverick provided limited choices for the buyer.

There were two sixes, the familiar Falcon 170 and 200 cube in-line motors. The gear selector, at this stage, was always on the tree, and always worked three ratios. Base Maverick was the 170cu in three-speed column manual, with full synchronization standard. There was also the well-known, and desirable, three-speed Cruise-O-Matic slushbox and a semi-automatic option. The latter was just Cruise-O-Matic minus the valve body, permitting full manual selection. It was a gloomy day at the press launch, but Maverick had bright appeal, and, as journalist Eric Dahlquist discovered, commendable pep. Trying the Maverick with 200cu in six and Cruise-O-Matic, the little Ford spun its rear wheels on take off, and grabbed rubber on the one to two shift!

On the face of it, and an attractive one at that, Maverick was Ford's new import fighter. However, time saw its list of rivals grow longer. (Courtesy *Motor Trend*)

At introduction time, 2.83:1 was stated as standard, with an optional 3.08 and even a 3.20 rear axle mentioned. Rims were 4.5in wide, and tires commenced with a 6.00-13-incher, and 6.45-14s and C78-14s as options. There was no power brake option for the Maverick's four-wheel drums, the car's only choice. Indeed, at first there was no mention of power steering. More than this, Maverick came as a swoopy looking two-door sedan, and that was it. No other bodystyles were apparent. *Car and Driver*'s Leon Mandel felt the interior was antiquated, like a 1930 automat. However, he judged the exterior to be as racy as a McLaren M12. And his conclusion? " ... Straightforward, somewhat austere confection and they will love it in Nebraska." [9]

Sink the Bismarck ... er Beetle!

When it came to openers, Ford underlined Maverick's apparent mission statement. Basically, that entailed getting the public to think Beetle. To this end, Ford had a conversation with itself, and in so doing let potential customers know what its new coupe brought to the table. This exchange took the form of a Q & A printed in the July 1969 issue of the *Ford Times*. Unsurprisingly, it was titled, "Ford's Amazing New Maverick." Ford and other automakers wishing to topple economy car champ Beetle, seldom mentioned the small VW by name in advertising or comparison pieces. The Beetle was always referred to as a "leading import," or some other indirect reference.

In Ford's dialog, it declared the new April '69 Maverick sought a middle-size ground between current imports and domestics. In doing so the 170 cube Maverick with three on the tree, delivered 22.5 mpg overall at Ford's test facilities. This was a mere 4.5 mpg lower than the noticeably slower VW 1500. 1969's Falcon 144 econoincher managed 25 mpg, but was also tardier. For figures, 0-60mph for the respective trio were 17.5, 20 and 21 seconds. The 200 cube Maverick dropped that stat to 14.5 seconds, or about the same as a full-size family car with a base V8. Such figures were all stated in the May 1970 issue of *Motor Trend*. Ford then claimed the Maverick was one of the most completely equipped economy cars of all time, at $1995 including full carpeting, a rear view mirror, heater and defroster, plus 13in wheels.

Indirect VW references continued, with Maverick

A 1970 Maverick two-door is displayed. Critics took exception to the Ford newcomer's limited optionability on debut. (Courtesy Wallerdog)

statements of a 'front'-mounted engine, plus how Henry's new ride had "wonderful styling," in contrast to the funny kind you found on an import. Similarly, the optional 200 cube six would deliver one in fine style, "... with pick up that will press you against the seatback." Wow, that never happened in a stock VW! Then there was that semi-auto option for Maverick 170, and nimble handling allied to a big car ride. And, of course, the 35.6ft turning circle happened to undercut the 36ft of the leading import.

Ease of service and repair were alluded to, and Maverick's bolt-on fenders, printed electrical circuits, 6000-mile oil changes, and 36/36 chassis lube schedule would keep Pop Grundig on the road while Herbie was in the shop! In those oh so thrifty times, a 6000-mile service interval was a real kicker when it came to Beetle-bashing. America's leading import lacked an oil filter, so needed oil changes every 3000 miles. Plus, the Bug relied on oil for heat transfer, whereas Maverick made out like a bandit, thanks to a conventional radiator.

Then there was Ford's modified Cruise-O-Matic semi-auto three-speed, which got one pondering VW's semi-auto dubbed Stick Shift, introduced in 1968. To show how each car company was eyeballing the other, mighty Chevrolet got in on the semi-auto game with a version of its Powerglide, available on Chevy IIs and Camaros: a response to VW, it would seem, trying to offer the lowest cost automatic going. However, the domestics would never admit to the impetus.

By the late '60s, the three biggest automakers in the world were GM, Ford and VW, in that order. Little wonder *Car Life*'s David Bean titled Maverick's introductory report as "The Exterminator – Ford's Maverick," and said the new Ford was a pretty, two grand bug bomb for Beetles, and a $100 million gamble for Ford. Even so, Ford had spent half the amount developing Maverick than it had the Ranchero. Indeed, the Maverick was done inexpensively and speedily. It allowed FoMoCo to get up and at 'em in the small car game, post haste!

Ford said that unlike the usual import, the Maverick had "wonderful styling that you can't put a date on." For once, it was truth in advertising! (Courtesy Doug Davidsen)

This very early Maverick coupe has the optional 200cu in I6 and Cruise-O-Matic power team.
(Courtesy Doug Davidsen)

Engineering Maverick

Many of Maverick's mechanical elements already existed. Ford drew upon Falcon, Fairlane and Mustang. The short, long-arm independent front suspension with drag struts was what one would expect. And, as per Ford practice, the spring and shock units were mounted on top of the upper arm, not in between the two arms, as per GM. Many of the front suspension parts were shared with Falcon, Fairlane and Mustang. The rear live axle, with multileafs, possessed the classic Ford Hotchkiss rear design. Even though it looked like Mustang back there, the hardware wasn't interchangeable. The four-wheel drums, Maverick's only choice, were the same as per six-cylinder Mustangs. However, Maverick employed a four-bolt pattern.

The official opening line from Ford was that it was only running power brakes with front disk applications. In their opinion, Maverick was small and light enough to get by sans power brakes. The brakes in question were 9 x 2.25in drums up front, and 9 x 1.5in drums out back. It all granted a brake swept area of 212in². According to Ford engineers, a Maverick with stock 6.00-13 tires could generate 0.87 to 0.9g deceleration. Aiding roadability, unlike contemporary Falcon, Ford's new coupe had a front swaybar standard. The go angle, came from tried and tested Falcon sixes. The base 170cu in I6 made 105bhp at 4200rpm and 156lb-ft at a tractable 2200rpm. Maverick's optional 200 cube straight six shooter brought 120 horse at 4 grand and 190lb-ft

at the same 2200rpm as the smaller 170cu in unit. Sounds like wheelspin just struck economy town!

That 200 cube six had the smoothness of seven main bearings, and both 170 and 200 I6s had new large port heads, and 191 CFM carbs. It's true that base Maverick packed more power than the Beetle 1500's 57bhp, but the Ford weighed more. It was 1807lb versus 2501lb. In actuality, the performance of a base Maverick with three-speed manual versus a base four-speed Beetle wasn't that different over the next few years.

In 1971, the Bug picked up a 1600 motor, and was within a second for 0-60mph. The two base

According to the July 1969 issue of *Ford Times*, a 6ft 2in fella could drive a Maverick comfortably. Ford also claimed the same sized guy would find the rear compartment accommodating.
(Courtesy Doug Davidsen)

For North American conditions, the Maverick was a sensible small car choice. Especially so if you wanted automatic transmission and some pep. (Courtesy Doug Davidsen)

models were practically equal by their last encounter in 1977. However, press and public alike had long ceased making comparisons between the two former foes by then. Standard steering was a major difference between the two. Maverick's slow, non-power steering ratio of 22.5:1 implied 5.2 turns lock to lock. The Beetle was on 2.8 turns and light with it, given the rearward weight bias. The solution? As with most domestic cars, just option power steering, and many did.

Small imports usually promised quick, light steering, and Maverick was a physically larger, heavier steed. Maverick was nimble next to a Torino, but less so against a MG Midget. However, sometimes it pays to be a Gulliver in Lilliput. As an auto giant, Ford had some sophisticated tricks up its corporate sleeve, to tilt things Maverick's way. Computer-aided design made Ford a leader in bringing a refined vehicle from drawing board to showroom, quickly. Refinement, or the 'Big Car Feel,' was an area small imports lacked. Ford engineers were proud of their use of computers, and their resources were impressive. There's more than one way to skin a cat. VW evolved a basic design over the years, Ford applied technology to a Falcon basis, to get Maverick where it needed to be, fast!

For starters, even the Maverick's very uneconomic styling was aided by computer. Computer graphics helped with body profiles. Numerical control was a system of computer technology that speeded the

transfer from blueprints and clay models to actual production dies. Computer design was used to create Maverick's rigid unibody structure. The Ford mechanical hardware was seen before, but what they were attached to was new.

Computers were instrumental in allowing engineers to minimize NVH. So, the optimal synthetic rubber compounds for suspension bushings and motor mounts, were selected for Maverick's purpose. Similarly, GM was using such an approach for optimal suspension tuning of its F body. Ford and GM made much use of the recently created, lightweight sound deadening material Amberlite. Such new textile products and sound deadening sprays in the engine bay kept heat and noise out of the passenger compartment.

Ford engineering's attention to detail allowed the drivetrain to be computer tested, so axle noise could be tuned out. American car buyers wanted a small car, but also one with sufficient interior width and quiet. As a result, and consistent with computer selection on most size classes of domestic car for the '70s, super soft rubber bushings for suspension and engine mounts were chosen. It was good for NVH, not so good for handling, but the result was the smaller, lighter Maverick tested out as quiet as a 1965 six-cylinder Mustang. This was in spite of the fact the 1970 Maverick was 100lb lighter than the original 1960 Falcon. It was also 325lb under a like-engined 1969 Falcon!

It was all Thriftpower straight talkin' sixes on debut. However, FoMoCo gave sports fans hope by saying the Windsor 'Three Oh Two' would fit! (Courtesy Doug Davidsen)

Maverick achieved all of this while being designed to a stricter crash safety standard. Ford had been pursuing crumple zone design since the late '60s, even though it was still a controversial area. Some still thought body on a frame was safer. Indeed, the oft-compared VW Beetle's body was kind of separate, in that it was connected to a platform via securing bolts. Concerning their unibodies, the 1970 Ford Torino and Maverick both had computer-designed crumple zones. Computer design had also been utilized for suspension geometry, spring rates, hood hinges and even windshield wiper movement pattern.

The end result of such optimal design technology, was that the new 1970 six-cylinder Maverick was cheaper, in real terms, than the 1964 ½ six-cylinder Mustang. However, the new car possessed even swoopier styling, and was more refined in key quantifiable areas. Maverick offered factory designed and fitted air-conditioning as an option from the start. In Ford parlance, it was Select Aire. This was something European Fords wouldn't get until the 1978 Ford Granada MkII. This was Europe's biggest, and most luxurious Ford. Indeed, it was a feature that Maverick's North American rivals – the Beetle and Datsun 510 – couldn't exactly match either. Both imports had dealer supplied a/c. The Bug's system was fitted at the dockside when it landed, if so optioned.

Road & Track mentioned the effectiveness of

Ford felt a Maverick starting price of $1995 would help it see the back of the imports, just like Falcon managed in 1960. (Courtesy Doug Davidsen)

Maverick's HVAC. It was a time when this area was one of the few things the import-directed journal praised on domestic cars. Ford's Maverick was somewhat of an automotive conundrum: a curious mix of high-tech in some places, but yesteryear simplicity in others. On the one hand, design and production techniques were cutting edge, as befitted a giant automaker. Renault, Simca or even VW wouldn't have had the computer power of Ford or GM. Then, too, sub-system modules behind Maverick's dashboard made assembly and repair faster and easier. In contrast, Maverick displayed economy typical of Detroit's approach to economy cars.

The most obvious example of decontenting, to use industry jargon, was the absence of a glovebox. It seemed like a very basic approach, until realizing the new 1982 GM F body lacked said item also! The Maverick coupe didn't have wind down rear windows, or standard power ones like an upscale BMW 2800CS. The Ford came with swing out rear panes, and a catch. Once again, this seemed consistent with being a simple machine, but the BMW 2002 and e21 3 series had the same arrangement. So did the contemporary Volvo 142S. All three Euro imports were pricey two-door sedans. What's more, in the December 1968 issue of *Road & Track*, Henry N Manney judged the pane catch on the 3 grand plus Swede to still be rattly.

The Volvo didn't get factory a/c until 1973. Still, it was odd for an American car to omit a glovebox, but Maverick's dashboard was consistent with domestic economy cars. Apart from a 120mph speedo and gas gauge, the coolant, oil pressure, alternator and brake fluid were all covered by warning lights – or idiot lights, as some critics called them. It was hardly full instrumentation, but, then again, Ford didn't mean it to be. All that stuff was on the GT40! Like Maverick, the Ford Model T and Model A were also simple cars designed and built with sophistication.

In 1970, Ford was using its strengths to answer the question: could a small, no frills car be profitably built in America, using UAW labor? Ford answered in the affirmative, making Maverick's economisms necessary evils. Indeed, Ford hoped its production high tech and efficiencies would largely overcome the two to four buck per hour labor advantage enjoyed by then low-cost producers Japan and West Germany. And Henry would be first with the so called 'interim' car, before the rest of Detroit's true small cars could leap off the drawing boards and into Mr and Mrs Average's garages across the nation. Many have asked, if a small, economical Ford was needed, then why not get one or two from Ford Germany, or Ford UK?

It was a question Ford always considered. From 1948, small numbers of the UK-built and designed Ford Anglia had been imported. Compared to the contemporary VW Beetle, the English Fords weren't really suited to American driving conditions. They couldn't exactly handle highway use. Too many

revs, and too few gears at only three. That said, importation of the Anglia continued through the '50s and '60s. Both the pre-1954 and subsequent 100E versions ... wound up drag racing! Rules led to racers shoehorning the biggest engines into the smallest cars, and they didn't get much smaller than the Anglia!

The Kohler brothers achieved notable success with their 'King Kong' blown, semi-hemi Chevy BB-powered E494A Anglia. It set a 1966 AA/GS world record, with a 9.23 ET. Such Anglias were certainly worthy adversaries during the Gasser Wars, and brought excitement aplenty in the realm of unsanctioned match racing. However, while Anglia won on Sunday, it didn't really sell on Monday. By 1967 the Anglia was joined by the Ford Cortina MkII. The latter was another 'captive import', sourced from the UK. With dimensions of 168in length and 65in width, a zippy Kent 1600 I4 and US-inspired styling, the Cortina GT two-door was much more like it, and sold reasonably.

Rival GM had done well with the Opel brand, importing the Kadett, Manta and GT sports car from its West German subsidiary. And you could see and buy them at your friendly local Buick dealer. Ford did likewise, and very successfully with the European Capri, sold through Lincoln-Mercury. For a spell, the Mercury Capri was the second best selling import, only behind the VW Beetle. All these cars, including the Italian Pantera, did well in their supplemental capacities.

They were niche players if you will. However,

The UK Ford Anglia was a winner in the 'Gasser Wars,' like Tom Langdon's Hole Shot 6, but not a major player in America's small car sales. (Courtesy www.langdonsstovebolt.com)

they were also always subject to currency fluctuations. Indeed, with the breakdown of the Bretton Woods Agreement system of fixing a basket of currencies against the US dollar, a new need for flexibility arose. The Deutschmark had to be allowed to rise in value to correct the trade imbalance between America and West Germany. So, both Capri and Beetle lost their price competitiveness.

Then there were the issues of model market suitability, and economically constructing a vehicle in America. Often, an appropriately sized European Ford or Opel would be too upscale, and possess too sophisticated engineering while lacking suitable power teams and features expected by mainstream American buyers at the price. Ford do Brazil would encounter some of these dilemmas, when deciding between local production of the Maverick or German Ford Taunus.

Then too, captive imports weren't always available at all dealers. Not all dealers had the parts supply, or servicing knowledge, to deal with such cars. Once the Anglia was done at the end of 1967, Ford decided not to import the new European Escort. Instead, by the start of 1968, it was planned for 650 Ford dealers to handle the Cortina MkII. This in itself was greater US coverage than any imported US Ford had enjoyed to date. [10] For America, the Cortina MkII was reaching the end of its life. Thoughts were entertained of the upcoming bigger, even more American looking, Coke bottle shape Cortina MkIII being imported.

The Cortina MkIII, although a medium/large European family car, was smaller in length and width compared to the Maverick coupe. This Cortina's front wishbone and four-coil suspension, would be pricey for an economy car. Power teams involved smog control-free Kent and Pinto in-line fours, four-speed manuals and C3 automatics. Only Ford Australia built such Cortinas with the Thriftpower 200/250cu in I6 mills. When it did, a very nose-heavy, understeering sedan was created in the process. The 302 V8 certainly wasn't in this model's wheelhouse, nor factory a/c. Then there was federalization to consider, in terms of the unholy trinity of smog, bumper and lighting laws.

So, it seemed the US Maverick would be a better idea to put on wheels. Ford considered the Maverick and Pinto more suited to US manufacture and sale than the European Cortina and Escort. Similarly, GM hoped Chevrolet Vega and Monza would take care of the small vehicle business that Opel used to do.

Ford was first to market with an interim sized car, before the wave of truly small domestics arrived. (Courtesy Bruce)

Using efficient production and design techniques, Ford hoped to close the 3 buck per hour labor gap on Datsun, Toyota and VW. Like the Ford Model T and A, Maverick was the simple car done the high tech way! (Courtesy Bruce)

As would be the way of the future, if you wished to sell in volume in America, a manufacturing presence within the country was needed. Ford Mavericks built before September 1969, even though they are regarded as '70 model year cars, lacked a locking steering column. However, newer Mavericks would have this, plus evaporative emission control.

In addition to closed crankcase ventilation, Maverick would be the first car in the world with a fuel evaporation control system. That is, gasoline vapors from the gas tank and carburetor would travel to a canister of activated charcoal, and be absorbed rather than go straight into the atmosphere. We were now in the emissions era of carbs with closed float bowls. Evaporative control continues to the present, but was first seen on California-bound 1970 Mavericks. It kept the smog Nazis of CARB (California Air Resources Board) happy. The feature made its way onto 49-state Mavericks for '71 MY. As part of Ford innovation, the 1971 Pinto was the first domestic with rack and pinion steering.

No direct rivals

With the uniquely sized Maverick, Ford hoped it had combined the best qualities of the imports and domestics into one vehicle. FoMoCo claimed better performance with the smaller, lighter Maverick, than base-engined domestic compacts. Projected gas mileage was midway between imported subcompacts, and heavier US compacts. Ford and domestic rivals often benchmarked the VW Beetle, but as Ron Wakefield mentioned in the May 1969 issue of *Road & Track*, the Datsun 510 was the real market mover and shaker. [11] Datsun and Toyota were putting the heat on VW, picking up conquest sales and expanding their dealer networks in the process.

The Datsun 510 was like a budget version of the New Class BMW 1600 two-door, and a very effective one. While Maverick coupe rolled into '71 MY with its 100bhp 170cu in six (2.8 liters), VW had a 60 horse 1600 and four-speed, and Datsun came with a 96bhp 1600 and four-speed. Curb weights for the three were a respective 2501lb, 1970lb and 2140lb. Front and rear track for the trio of two-door sedans measured out respectively as: 55.5/55.5in, 50.4/50.4in and 54.3/53.3in.

Lengths for Maverick, Bug and 510 were 179in, 161.8in and 162.2in respectively. Utilizing a three-speed manual, Maverick's 22.5mpg mileage went up against VW's 25mpg and Datsun's 25.5mpg. Indeed, Beetle TV ads mentioned an honest 25mpg, as the Age of Aquarius turned into the Era of Economy. Sprinting, a relative term with economy sedans, saw Ford, Datsun and VW on 417/465/330ft respectively, after the first 10 seconds. Driving ranges for the trio were a respective 360/302/270 miles. [12]

Although Maverick resembled a pony car, it was analyzed in strictly economy car fashion.

You couldn't imagine a Renault 10 pulling off alloy slot rims, but Maverick did! (Courtesy Bruce)

Such objective number inspection would never have occurred when judging the latest Mustang, Camaro and Barracuda trio. For example, the interior volumes of Maverick, Datsun and VW were 81.2/85.3/77.3cu ft. Does anyone know or care what those stats are for any regular pony car?!

However, in practical, econocar land, Maverick took up more space on the increasingly congested cityscape in relation to its internal space, compared to the small car imports. That said, the imports didn't have to accommodate an in-line six that delivered the torque most Americans expected. More than that, the trade-off for Maverick's less than stellar internal packaging was avoiding a resemblance to the proverbial 'box on wheels.' Or, as AMC styling boss Dick Teague observed concerning VW ... the Hindenburg!

Sadly, one had to be Consumer Union-like in this car class. So for Maverick, 510 and VW, front headroom brought a respective 37.6/39/42in. Front shoulder room broke down to 55/50.2/49.2in. Finally, rear seat headroom saw 36.1/37/35in respectively. Stats don't lie, Maverick's low build styling meant you had to leave that ol' fedora at home. However, Ford's wider, American-style dimensions implied less chance of elbow banging, as front occupants entered. [13]

Back in the day, trunk capacity was a big talking point concerning all categories of car. This was particularly pertinent to small cars. After all, that leading import of the time wasn't too hot in this

This 1971 two-door Maverick promised 22.5mpg overall, in manual 170cu in I6 form, according to FoMoCo test track data. (Courtesy Bruce)

department. That is, one couldn't insert a very great deal in a 1970 VW Beetle 1500. Ford designers were very proud of the job they did concerning the style-conscious Maverick. In spite of ponyesque fastbackness, Maverick, 510 and VW lined up with respective trunks of 11.3/11.4/7.1cu ft. Knowing they were behind the eight ball on this score, the upscale '71 Super Beetle adopted Ford style MacPherson strut front suspension, which boosted its 'frunk' by 3cu ft, and reduced turning circle to 31.5ft. So Dr Porsche had Henry Ford to thank for such upgrades! And don't forget, Maverick alone offered bench-style seating for three up front.

Indeed, pragmatic, penny pinching aspects of car ownership were under the microscope in Maverick comparisons, to the extent that six-cylinder Mavericks would require more sparkplugs and oil when a service was due. What's more, or perhaps less, Maverick's 13in tires wore out faster than Beetle's 15in tires. More rotation for a given amount of highway cruising, you understand? My oh my, now you know how VW Beetle overtook the Model T!

All these facts worried Pop Grundig very little. He had enough army surplus stock, squared away in his bunker to tide over Maverick into the 21st century! However, *Consumer Reports* would remind one of Beetle's better resale value, quality construction and materials. Then again, as Eric Dahlquist observed in the May 1970 issue of *Motor Trend*, Maverick and Beetle were not directly comparable.

On the record, VWoA's (Volkswagen of America) Stuart Perkins noted "It's not a Volkswagen, but then it wasn't intended to be. It's not revolutionary, but it's basic and will sell." Indeed, even observing price, Maverick wasn't really on a par with Beetle. The 1970 VW 1500 started from $1731, and the 1971

Would they still buy Mustangs aplenty, now that the smaller, cheaper Maverick had moseyed on into Ford's corral? Heck no! (Courtesy Bruce)

Super Beetle was $1934. Add even modest options and Maverick was over two grand, but no sweat, because it was more car.

By 1971, the most basic Datsun 510 two-door was $2040 and if anything could be learnt from the rise of Datsun and Toyota in America, it was that economical didn't automatically mean cheap. For the record, Ford expected Maverick to sell. Dearborn's projection ran to 225,000-400,000 first year sales, with a 117,500 unit rollout by the end of July 1969. A small Falcon, rather than a big VW perhaps, but a hoped-for best seller in any case, and it did come to pass. Maverick's 1970 model year total was a stellar 451,081 units!

In spite of logic dissuading direct comparisons, *Car and Driver* did just that in September 1969. In an introductory piece on the new AMC Hornet, which observed the small car game at the time, the journal lambasted poor Maverick. In *C/D's* mind there was no daylight between Maverick and Beetle. Both vehicles, in its opinion, were plain Jane economy cars, not small cars.

Just one bodystyle and engine format, with exterior color choice being the sole point of distinction between one Bug or Maverick and another. The same could be said about the Ferrari Daytona. In contrast, *C/D* judged the AMC Hornet to be a true small car. That is, Hornet could be an economy car, a diminutive land yacht, or even an insurance fighting junior supercar. It all depended upon the car buyer's fancy, when greeted by the extensive options list at the friendly, local dealership.

To *Car and Driver's* thinking, Maverick could be none of those things. Heck, you couldn't even get one with four doors! Now that's limited, almost back to the Model T's basic black. Was Henry Ford's spirit trying to exorcise the Edsel demon, or failing that, the Dodge Demon?! At this time, *C/D* couldn't foresee the rosewood appliqués of La Grande Bug, nor the plushness of LDO (Luxury Décor Option) Maverick four-door. Yes Bunkie, economy cars need not remain economy cars forever. Indeed, *Car and Driver* even took exception to Maverick's subcompact size claim. Giving statistical evidence, they proved Maverick was closer to Hornet and US compacts, than those real charming small cars. [14]

Most damning, *C/D* said Beetle and Maverick could only be one thing ... cheap! Plus, both ignored buyers that wanted convenience features in a small car. Getting down to the nitty gritty, Maverick was on a 103in wheelbase, versus Hornet with 108in,

Ford designers were very proud of Maverick's trunk, trumping that of VW 1500's cargo capacity: 11.3cu ft to 7.1cu ft. (Courtesy Bruce)

and Bug on only 94.5in. Comparing base to base, Maverick was 300lb under Hornet, which would make Ford's 105 horse, 170cu in six a sound match for Hornet's 128bhp, 199cu in in-line equivalent in those Econosix Wars. For length, width and height Ford versus AMC saw 179.3/70.6/52.3in play 179.3/71.1/52.6in. 1969 Plymouth Valiant with 108in wheelbase, brought 188.4/69.6/54in, 111in wheelbased Chevy II two-door sauntered forth with 189.4/72.4/52.4in. It was just as well for Henry that prospects didn't bring tape measures to showrooms!

From all of this, it did seem like Maverick and Hornet were quasi subcompacts. Not the mini intermediates that some, like *Car and Track's* Bud Lindemann, called 'em. The eternal Ford versus Chevy rivalry dictated an examination of interior space offered by Maverick two-door and Chevy II two-door. Front head/leg/hip room for the Blue Oval and Bowtie coupes were a respective 37.6/41.3/53.7in and 37.6/41.6/56.2in. In the rear it was Maverick's 36.1/31.9/46.1in playing Chebby's 36.6/32.6/56.1. In the crucial trunk battle Maverick had 10.4cu ft against Chevy II's 13.8cu ft, according to this particular info set. [15]

Based on the facts, while Maverick was a bigger car than Beetle – and easily 600lb heavier – it was also trimmer of line and more snug than domestic compacts or kingsize compact rivals. Other realities included how imports in general had progressed since 1960, in terms of reliability, dealer network coverage and vehicle performance. The Renault Dauphine was gone, but a low spec Volvo 142 may have floated someone's boat. There was market evidence of some buyers looking for a one or two year old Volvo 142 or Saab 96 V4, as an alternative to a new $1995 base sticker Maverick. Economy is in the checkbook of the beholder.

Maverick and Capri – a shared heritage

It seemed that in combining an 'in between size' with US mechanicals, plus a healthy dose of style, Henry had a unique and simple machine on Dearborn's books. Driving Maverick brought no surprises, and Mr and Mrs Median were probably happy with that. No incorrectly set tire pressure-induced oversteer to send them off terra firma! How did Maverick drive? In Ron Wakefield's words, as "American as apple pie." Ford engineers were enthusiastic about the job they did on Maverick's trunk space and handling. However, in objective terms, one discovered the slow but predictable responses of Falcon, and, not so surprisingly, a plain Mustang. [16]

Compared to the '69 Falcon, Wakefield found less body-roll and plow understeer. However, this baby was never going to bite poor ol' unsuspecting Maury Q Public, Corvair style. Maverick's manual steering was slow, and with only a quarter of a degree of caster, didn't self return well post turn. Perhaps interestingly, a similar experience, with the exception of sharper rack and pinion steering, transpired across the pond when *CAR* magazine sampled Ford Europe's Capri in its February 1969 issue. Its conclusion was that the Capri drove very similarly to the UK Ford Cortina MkII. Indeed, there was very little reason it shouldn't. On an engineering basis, the Capri represented a new unibody to which Cortina hardware was attached.

The new Capri drove slower than a similarly-engined Cortina, as it was heavier. However, being lighter than Falcon, the Maverick was quicker! Beyond this, Capri and Maverick had marked similarities. For one, the Capri was Cortina-based, and in America the Maverick effectively replaced the Cortina MkII captive import for '70 MY. The Capri and Maverick started around the same time, in terms of debut and dealership dates. In America they would share showroom space, albeit concerning Maverick's upscale Mercury cousin, the Comet. Both Capri and Maverick represented the Ford approach, at a time when Ford's overseas subsidiaries were very close in engineering layout, styling, design and marketing.

Both Capri and Maverick had much engineering attention directed at reducing interior noise levels,

Ford Maverick turned out to be a better production and consumer fit than the Coke bottle shape UK Ford Cortina MkIII. (Courtesy *CAR*)

and generally making things more refined in the area of noise, vibration and harshness. So, Capri drove quieter than the equivalent Cortina, and Maverick showed an edge over the heftier Falcon. As speculated by *CAR* magazine, it seemed with both newcomers that their fastback shape helped refinement. Better aerodynamics than a brick-like sedan, plus lowered wind noise. Ford engineers had selectively beefed up the unibodies of both to reduce NVH. It was typical of Ford's detailed effort to please mainstream buyers, so they could better enjoy the optional radio.

Pleasing the public was diametrically opposed to VW's economy car angle. Its bag was to inform the public that VW engineering and quality were first class, and to accept the finished result. However, even Wolfsburg had to yield to competitive pressure from Europe, Japan and America. The 1971 Super Beetle offered consumer concessions that were

Confounding *Car and Driver*'s September 1969 assessment, Maverick would go beyond mere economy car status, gaining a four-door and more for '71 MY. (Courtesy Ford Motor Co)

In development and design, the Capri and Maverick had similarities: stylish coupes using humble sedan mechanicals. The former was inspired by the Mustang the latter ate into Mustang sales! (Courtesy Shell)

new to VW. At Ford, Capri and Maverick were plain business as usual. The British press, concerning Capri, echoed the American press on Maverick: that is, neither coupe brought anything new to the table engineering wise, but did bring a great deal of marketing.

Observing July 1969's *Ford Times*, there was a pretty brunette sitting in Maverick, and another coupe shown with a mini folding trailer attached. The Rally Camp unit, made by Concord Products of Ohio, would be more easily pulled by the six-cylinder Maverick than a flat-four Bug or even the in-line four Datsun. In short, Ford let buyers see what interested them, and *CAR* concluded the success of Ford's time honored wisdom: "This is an approach which has paid Ford great dividends in the past ..."

And it turned out, sizable returns in the present. "The car you always promised yourself" in Britain, "The Sexy European" in America, or 1,172,900 first

generation Capris built between 1969 and 1974. This coupe went on to be the second-best selling import in America, for a time. It was the same deal with Maverick. Although industry experts wondered whether the new Ford would really achieve import conquest sales, they never doubted that Maverick would sell, and sell well.

Indeed, commentators were universally much more bullish concerning Maverick's prospects than they had been with the homely Falcon a decade earlier. Ron Wakefield delivered *Road & Track*'s take: "... it will succeed, but that it won't hurt the economy imports enough to matter." [17] The figures confirmed the faith, using the technical description: in 1969 model year terms, Maverick managed 127,833 sales, and 299,824 in its inaugural calendar year of 1969. Production was at the Kansas City and St Thomas assembly plants. It seemed that little ol' Maverick had hit the ground running!

In 1969 you might have caught the Leaf Habs ice hockey game on TV, when your viewing was interrupted by an ad for the new Ford Maverick. "1970's best buy, by far is Ford Maverick," said the ad. Then, in a folk tune rendition reminiscent of early Bob Dylan, Maverick was "Easy to buy, easy to run, easy to drive and real good fun. Plenty of room for long legs inside. Holds lots of luggage, got a clear, smooth ride, that's Maverick." And of course, you be sure to see your Ford or Mercury man, just as soon as you possibly can. Maverick, it's a great small car!

Maverick's main slogan, was its billing as 'The Simple Machine,' and Ford proved it with the help of five stewardesses. On TV, a bronze 1970 Maverick coupe lay disassembled, and Ford said: "We asked five stewardesses to put it back together again. The little ladies then proceeded to do what the UAW at this time preferred not to, and hey presto! They proved it. Maverick, the simple machine still just $1995, when everything else is going up!" The lovely ladies drove off in the completed coupe, which sported whitewall tires. In the fine print, those whitewalls would set you back another 32 bucks.

Even though the fuel crisis was a way off, the economy was a mite shaky. In the slowdown, inflation was still rearing its ugly head. Such costs were topical in Maverick's 'Slot Machine' TV ad, which aired in 1970. A need to cut costs and boost gas mileage was explicitly stated. Ford said, "Why gamble? We've got three sure things for you." Each pull of a casino's one-armed bandit produced a solution. First, plain two-door Maverick sedan. Second, the new Grabber Coupe. Finally, the just released economy family car … Maverick four-door sedan. FoMoCo said it saved you money, and remember Maverick: "The simple machine that always pays off."

The opposition also had its angles for print and TV ads. Indeed, it is rumored that in all the shenanigans, Henry Ford II stopped quite a few cornball ideas that were going to be used by Ford marketing. In the spirit of *Looney Tunes*, one was allegedly going to be: "Th-th-that's all, Volks." [18] Either way, VW wouldn't have been worried. Its Doyle Dane and Bernbach ads were famous. How does the man who drives a snowplow for a living, get to work? Obviously he drives a Bug, and the TV ad showed and spoke of good winter traction and avoiding a liquid-filled radiator that could freeze up on you … if you didn't use any antifreeze, that is!

In spite of its early '60s fall from grace, Renault hadn't left America, and still harbored dreams of hitting the big time. The infamous Dauphine was still on sale in the mid '60s, joined by the more modern, but equally quirky Renault 8. By the time Maverick came to pass, the updated Renault 10 was the latest in Le Regie's family of rear-engined, water-cooled rear drivers. What's more, Renault had adopted 'apology ads' in America. These basically involved admitting how unreliable their cars were, acknowledging their poor service network, and hoping for a second chance.

The 1967 Renault 10 ad was titled: "I won't buy a Renault no matter how good it is." This was the public perception created by many a past faux pas, or in a word, Dauphine. Said Dauphine wasn't mentioned by name, but Renault admitted some of its cars and dealers were "… a trifle short of perfection" a few years ago. According to the French automaker that was all in the past. Renault sales rose by 72 per cent between 1966 and 1967 in America. This was most likely due to an increasing desire for all small cars, rather than a specific improvement on Renault's part. Even so, the ads were instructive concerning perceptions of small economy cars.

Renault's 1967 R10 ad said some hated all little foreign cars. This was an indirect Beetle attack. That is, sub two grand small cars, namely VW, are noisy and hard riding. In addition to this perception, which was shared by more than a few people, the Renault R10 ad said: "Find another car under $2000 that has all that the Renault 10 has, and we'll buy it for you." Two grand was a psychological econocar ceiling, acknowledged by industry observers to still be alive and kicking in 1970. Naturally, Renault claimed its R10 avoided the pitfalls of small foreign cars, and had the quiet and good heater you only get from water-cooled engines. Then too, automatic transmission was optional. It was another small car prerequisite for North America.

History shows that Renault held onto the American dream, until Chrysler bought out its interest in AMC. In addition, the original Renault 5 was sold Stateside as the Le Car. This machine didn't exactly cover itself with glory concerning tales of practicality and reliability, by the time it bowed out in 1983. Japanese company ads didn't attack Beetle, or any opposition, they just plainly described what the cars had. The Toyota Corona, with shovel nose

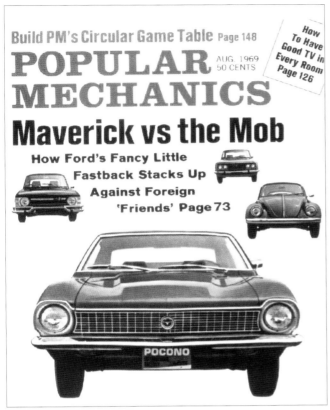

It happened at Pocono International Raceway.
A baptism of fire at the hands of *Popular Mechanics*,
and the import crowd. However, Maverick upheld
Ford honor. (Courtesy *Popular Mechanics*)

and optional two-speed Toyoglide automatic, was the first Toyota export model many people around the world experienced. A most conventional car in appearance, layout and controls, it made no special demands on the driver, and you could get factory a/c – although, as *Consumer Reports* discovered, the triple blower outlets took up the passenger-side glovebox and its door.

Renault reminded future victims that it was the seventh biggest automaker in the world. Toyota's ad said it was the number one car maker in Japan. VW and Ford were three and two, so they felt no need to state the obvious. Toyota's 1967 Corona ad spoke of its 90 horse 1.9-liter engine, stating "Get your hands on a Toyota. You'll never let go!" and "You get so much for so little." In April 1967, *Motor Trend's* Robert Schilling said solid products like the Corona went a long way toward removing the doubts about quality that consumers once held, regarding Japanese goods.

A day at the races – Economy Quartet visit Pocono

With the ad spiel out of the way, how did the various cars perform in objective testing? *Popular Mechanics* auto editor Bill Kilpatrick answered that question in the August 1969 issue, by way of a four-car group test. This *Road Test* roll call featured Maverick 170 six two-door at $1995, 179.4in long, 2501lb; VW Beetle 1500 at $1799, 158.6in long, 1808lb; Renault 10 four-door $1775, 167.5in long, 1825lb, and Toyota Corona two-door $2135, 162.4in long, 2260lb. All cars had manual transmission, and the Renault was the only four-door. The Toyota was the only car available with two and four doors at this stage. All cars had a 12/12 warranty, except VW, which offered 24/24. Cars were tested with no optional extras.

The magazine had tried out all four on the drive from New York to Pocono International Raceway. Immediate observations were the Maverick's sweeping dashboard, wide accommodative front bench, and, in *Popular Mechanics*' words, cornball upholstery. VW was austere, functional and had impressive workmanship. Renault brought a comfy interior and creature features missing in the others. However, there was the annoying quality of having the ignition on the left of the steering column. The Toyota had the most stylish interior, and the biggest imported mill, a 90-horse 1.9-liter I4. The Renault came with the smallest motor, a 48bhp 1.1-liter four pot. That said, the French sedan claimed an 85mph top speed.

Pocono International Raceway in Eastern Pennsylvania was under construction at the time. On the track, VW did 0-60mph in 24.5 seconds, Toyota was on 18 seconds, Renault recorded 22.5 seconds, and Maverick aced 'em all with 15 seconds flat. As an overtaking maneuver test of engine flexibility, the 40-60mph move in top gear saw VW and Renault tied on 22 seconds. Maverick took a mere 14.2 seconds, but was beaten by Toyota. The mpg range of Maverick was 22-26. VW did 24-28, with Toyota's response being 27-31. Renault won the frugality feature, with a most miserly 30-34mpg.

Panic and controlled braking saw the Renault's standard four-wheel disk brakes win out, with short and straight stops. VW got close, with Toyota pulling up kind of short, but *Popular Mechanics* noted how the Corona sashayed a lot in doing so. Maverick was controlled, but with long stopping distances. Rear brake axle tramp, tripped up the car's rear end.

Surprise.

A machine famous for not breaking down.

Seems like most machines you buy today end up costing you more money just to keep them running. That's what makes Ford Maverick so exceptional. Maverick is a simple, uncomplicated machine— so there's less chance of *anything* going wrong. What's more, a good-looking, family-sized Maverick can be yours for surprisingly little money. Standard 6 or optional V-8. 2-door, 4-door or sporty Grabber.

1972 Maverick 2-door Sedan shown with optional Accent and Protection Groups, white sidewall tires and tinted glass.

FORD MAVERICK
FORD DIVISION *Ford*

If reliability is important to you.

Ford had independent reliability survey data showing Maverick to be a domestic car leader in minimizing frequency of repair. (Courtesy Ford Motor Company)

Objectively, all agreed that Maverick was a winner on interior space, Renault for seat comfort and VW for workmanship. Beyond this, it came down to personal preference, and so too with buyers.

VW's warranty, resale value, and, from 1971, four free computer diagnostic check ups were hard to pass up. Toyota was increasingly the sensible, middle ground choice, with an expanding dealer network. Automakers like Renault and Fiat had some nice design touches, but their unreliability, limited service coverage and quirkiness were still impediments to car ownership.

The test also shed light on Maverick. Apart from good scat, a lack of four on the floor in an economy car and axle tramp joined another Detroitizm, namely a need to slam doors to shut them properly.

Assembly line Al, we are looking at you! Then there was the issue of size: at 70.6in wide, Ford's coupe was a much bigger car. *Popular Mechanics* said Plymouth Valiant and Rambler American, were Maverick's real foes. However, beyond the Thanks Vermillion and Freudian Gilt trick paint, the journal also noted that Maverick possessed real substance.

Of course, the public likes the concept of the good guys versus the bad guys. After all, Starsky and Hutch were in a Gran Torino. So it followed that in advertising, VW was public enemy number one, and Beetle was Maverick's raison d'etre. On that score, *Popular Mechanics'* editor Bill Kilpatrick said no dice concerning Maverick knocking on the imported car's collective door: "we doubt if they'll drop dead." [19] Then again, perhaps they should have been worried? After all, when the second biggest automaker in the world puts out a no nonsense, stylish looking sedan that isn't greatly bigger in size or price than your car, and has a much bigger service network, maybe you should care?

The other factor was compromise. In these kinds of group tests, it seemed like it would be wonderful if you could take the best qualities of each car, and put them together in one machine! Even when *MotorWeek* lined up the VW Rabbit, Nissan Sentra, Dodge Colt and Renault Le Car in a 1982 face-off, the same held true. But no, you couldn't do that. In the past, the trade-off in speed, space and safety, for just a little more economy, was great indeed. Many drivers with a preference for Detroit conventionality may have felt Maverick's compromises to be closer to their ideal.

Maverick in the marketplace – selling the simple machine

The figures were hard to ignore. In 1968, VW sold a total of 563,522 vehicles, and Datsun plus Toyota sales accounted for 109,000. Ford research calculated the import market to be 985,767 that year, or plenty of room for America's first subcompact: the 1970 Ford Maverick. Bunkie Knudsen wasn't in on the Maverick caper from day one, but Lee Iacocca was. Big Lee had never warmed to the plain ways of the utilitarian Falcon. So, he dressed up that compact and created the hugely successful Mustang. Iacocca could see the market was moving towards smaller vehicles, and didn't approve of Bunkie Knudsen's subsequent corporate oversight of Mustang. That is, successively larger, plusher, more powerful and expensive coupes.

Annual sales were in decline, as prospects became reluctant to add their John Hancock to bigger monthly payments and insurance premiums.

The result was applying the 1964 ¹/₂ Mustang formula, once again. On the very same April 17 launch date, a new sporty two-door Ford coupe rode into town. Maverick was ready for a high noon battle with the imports, plus Dart, Nova and whatever else was going. Concerning the Beetle et al, FoMoCo announced in ads that it was "The End of Foreign Intrigue," and it probably was! The statistics also suggest that Maverick's appearance hastened the demise of the original Mustang. Records were indeed broken at Ford, as Maverick arrived with both guns blazing, and soon, a Blazer Stripe seat trim option. As a 1969 effort, Maverick's April to December tally of 127,833 units was superior to 1964 Mustang's 126,538 showing.

Even though the economy was in a post-MacNamara Vietnam funk, Maverick's 1970 total of 578,914 wasn't far off 1964 Mustang's near 620,000 figure. However, by 1970, 1964 was three and a half lifetimes ago in car years. Mustang in decline had fallen to a 1969 model year total of 299,824. It was increasingly not a good match for mainstream tastes and pocketbooks. The secretaries were now signing up for Maverick! With Mustang versus Maverick '70 MY total, it was 190,727 playing 451,081. The reason was simple. In tight times, a buyer visits their local Ford showroom and sees two fastbacks. One has fresh new styling, is slightly smaller and cheaper to buy. So it was that Maverick, using just a couple of in-line sixes, out accelerated Mustang where it counted: in sales.

The handsome stranger in town went by the name of Maverick. Maverick is defined as an unbranded range animal. As a secondary meaning, it can be an unconventional entity of radical thinking. Certainly, Maverick was a unique size in spring 1969. Plus, the idea of taking on the Beetle with a mini pony car was an audacious one. Ford wanted Maverick to seem far out, and to appeal to the kids of the 'Now Generation.' So, even Maverick's enamel paint wasn't just paint. Ford announced in ads "Goodbye old paint," and say hello to hues like Anti-Establish Mint, Hulla Blue, Original Cinnamon, Freudian Gilt, Thanks Vermillion, Black Jade, Champagne Gold, Gulfstream Aqua, Meadow Lark Yellow, Brittany Blue, Lime Gold, Dresden Blue, Raven Black, Wimbledon White and Candy Apple Red.

Yes, in the psychedelic era, even paint wasn't

With its 1972 Maverick LDO (Luxury Décor Option), Ford was first in taking on small luxury imports like the Audi 100LS, BMW 2002 and Saab 99. (Courtesy Sidney Canhedo)

paint anymore. Just some hallucinogenic marketing trip! Ford, AMC and Mopar were using jazzed up colors like Big Bad shades and High Impact hues at the time. GM were using misleading color names, Pontiac GTO's Orbit Orange looked more like yellow. Maybe John Z was smoking the funny stuff, before he did his DeLorean? But this was all on hot coupes, not humble economy cars. Was Maverick the new Mustang? Some were asking that question. Pop Grundig would never have said Hulla Blue, and the salesman wouldn't have dared mention it. No, he would have asked for the blue sedan, and hold the 200cu in six and deluxe interior. In fact, 50 per cent of 1970 Mavericks had the optional 200 cube six. Maverick's styling – longhorn cow head logo, placed mid-grille – was decoration enough.

At the start of production, American buyers were getting supply from FoMoCo's Kansas City Plant and St Thomas assembly factories. Dearborn was added in 1972. Canadian buyers were catered for by Ontario plants in Talbotville and Oakville. What they got up to the end of '69 MY, was a 170cu in or 200cu in I6 powered coupe, with two spoke tiller, and Ford style partial horn ring. At this time, the ignition switch was still on the dashboard. True

The big 250 cube in-line six became a Maverick option from mid '70 MY. It could only be had with the Cruise-O-Matic. (Courtesy Sidney Canhedo)

'70 MY 1970 Mavericks had the ignition switch on the soon-to-be federally mandated (January 1970) locking steering column. The steering wheel was now free of the horn ring, too.

The car dealer experience

According to the 1975 *Ford Annual Report,* annual sales figures saw 288,342 1969 Mavericks, with 340,214 units following in 1970. The task of selling naturally fell to the dealers. They were, and certainly had to be, enterprising concerns. To understand just how enterprising, the American automotive market into which Maverick made its debut has to be considered. While it is true that imported cars were taking a worryingly large slice of the domestic market (8.9 per cent West Germany, 3.7 per cent Japan, 2.6 per cent other), in 1970, 84.8 per cent of cars sold in America came from domestic automakers. [20]

In 1970, Ford had over 6000 dealerships

The Maverick represented a small car refuge from escalating domestic vehicle size, post-1965. (Courtesy Sidney Canhedo)

nationwide, but it would only be 1977 before Toyota had 1000 US outlets. Then, too, one would have to wait until 1978 before a foreign automaker built cars on American soil. This was VW's Rabbit plant in Westmoreland, Pennsylvania. However, that was all in the future. If you were a car dealer in the here and now, you would have more pressing problems. Apart from Chevy, Plymouth and AMC dealers, your number one concern would be outselling Ford dealers in your locale. After all, they had similar stock to get shed of. Well, it seemed Ralph Williams had an angle on that.

Ralph Williams wanted to sell you a Ford, and would try to do so through Ralph Williams' Ford, located in California's San Fernando Valley. It was apparently the world's largest Ford dealership. Allegedly, by 1969 Williams was worth $60 million, and sold $60 million worth of Fords annually. He did so with a great deal of direct and indirect TV advertising. Ralph Williams bought up most of the air time going, and built on that with TV appearances on shows of comedians Johnny Carson, Joey Bishop and Jonathan Winters, as well as ... you bet your belly button ... *Laugh-In. Car and Driver's* Kyle Given described Williams as the, " ... last and the best of the great midway spielers." [21]

In spite of all of this, Williams didn't have a winning personality, nor the matinee idol looks of a Tab Hunter, for that matter. He used TV to deliver factual information concerning his dealership and stock. Indeed, he was also moving into Chrysler and Plymouth products in Houston, Seattle and San Francisco, plus a national car rental chain. Fords were also sold at the aforementioned dealerships. He met Bunkie Knudsen, and was impressed with him, although he didn't personally know the new Ford president beyond this one single encounter in an elevator. Williams had some thoughts on the new Maverick, and how Detroit operated.

"They'll do to it what they did to the Falcon … Load it up with options. Pretty soon the dealers will be getting $4000 Mavericks and we've already got a lot full of $4000 Falcons. That's the thing that gets me down." He mentioned zero consultation between the dealer and automaker, and they should be consulted, because ultimately they have to sell the cars. There was more pessimism from Williams, "The Detroit mentality. Those guys are geared to think in certain ways and it'll never change." [22] There certainly was the fear of price bracket creep, with Maverick. Industry critics thought Maverick might indeed follow Falcon, with the simple machine becoming a larger and more expensive one.

This would leave space for another new entry level car, like Pinto. In 1969, Lee Iacocca – himself something of a maverick – had some thoughts about traditional Detroit, and said the following to *Time* magazine, "You dumb foot draggers – you in Detroit – what took you so long to know imports were going to hit a million? Now the market is damn well defined, and you know what the market says? 'Give me a hell of a good buy for two grand, will you?'"

In any case, there was a recognized three-step process for selling cars: start with a product, then use advertising to bring prospects to the showroom, followed by the Hull-Dobbs system of sale. This last step was the agreed standard method of selling cars in America, named after a Ford dealership in Knoxville. Like a casino, it was set up so the house always comes out a winner. Of course, never underestimate the value of a pitch man to bring prospects through the door in the first place. Ralph Williams was one, and there were contemporaries and predecessors in Los Angeles and other parts of the country. Insomniacs heard their message on local TV ad breaks before, during and after the *Late, Late, Late Show*. No doubt while watching something like a black and white 1940s Sherlock Holmes movie starring Basil Rathbone.

Cal Worthington was a contemporary, and competitor, of Ralph Williams. He made the claim

"I can outsell that guy in the Valley." To help him achieve that, he used his dog, Spot. The thing was, Spot wasn't actually a dog, although Worthington played along in the ads to the effect that he was. Spot was obtained from a nice Okie, as Worthington described him, and was chained – Spot, not the Okie – to a car bumper during the TV ads. Spot was actually a gorilla, and smelled something awful too! Cal Worthington was immortalized in the 1984 movie *Cannonball Run II*. In this film, the Uncle Cal character was a dealership owner with a chimpanzee limo chauffeur, and the ad slogan: "If a monkey can drive, so can you!" It certainly showed Worthington's style.

A predecessor of Ralph Williams, who ended up working for him, was Chick Lambert. Lambert had a dog called Storm, and this time Storm was indeed an honest to goodness canine creature. Well, a dog may be man's best friend, but you have to be careful

Maverick LDO's color-matched hubcaps were like those on the Daimler-Benz W114 Compact. It was the start of Ford's upscale Mercedes style era. A 1973 Maverick LDO is shown. (Courtesy Ford Motor Co)

of pitch men sometimes. Some film has come to light recently of Chick Lambert doing mid '60s TV ads for Ralph Williams' Ford, where he makes defamatory comments concerning his employer's appearance and character. Due to the colorful language Lambert used concerning his employer's casino gambling, and the ladies of the evening that Williams allegedly encountered it's highly unlikely these ads ever went to air. Lambert's motivation? Whether a joke, or disgruntled employee, it remains a mystery.

Some facts that are beyond doubt concern Ralph Williams' admission that he never thought Mustang would sell all that well. Williams and GM brass were both proved wrong on that score. Similarly, Williams couldn't see the distinction between a four grand Maverick and a four grand Falcon, but Lee Iacocca could. The difference was size, and as the '70s progressed folks did indeed want smaller cars.

There was a postscript to the Ralph Williams story. By 1972, he and his dealership were the subject of a court case concerning misleading and deceptive conduct. By 1989, a now 59-year-old Williams was working as a pitch man for dealership Friendly Ford. This Ford outlet was also the subject of a court case concerning misleading and deceptive conduct.

So, the buyer had to exercise some caution regarding what specification they were getting, and the price paid, for a Falcon, Maverick, Tempo, or any Ford, Chevrolet or Plymouth. It was caveat emptor all the way, and unsettling when Ralph Williams referred to a potential customer visiting his dealership, as "the mark". This was one reason car buyers were heading towards VW, Datsun and Toyota. The product was more of a set meal deal, with fewer options and wiggle room for tomfoolery.

Car servicing and honoring warranty work also seemed an increasing problem with domestic brands. *Road Test* magazine's 1st gen Chevy Camaro survey bore this out, in the journal's August 1970 issue. The magazine also remarked that such problems used to be associated with imported cars, and their infamous shade tree mechanics. It's what swayed consumers back to the Big Three during the early '60s. Entering the '70s, it seemed buyers liked their Fords, and Chebbies, but increasingly had to resort to trusted specialist shops to get a square deal.

It was certainly a competitive market, if the dealer training films and TV comparison ads were anything to go by. In trying to match up Maverick with domestic compacts, it wasn't apples versus apples, but each claimed they had the best recipe for Mom's apple pie. If anything, it showed Maverick had stolen the march on domestic rivals. Indeed, Chevrolet and Plymouth seemed spooked by Henry's 'Simple Machine.' Dodge's dealer promotional film for

Another 1973 Maverick LDO four-door. As buyers eschewed performance, they increasingly wanted luxurious small cars. Maverick met that desire. (Courtesy Bull-Doser)

the 1972 Demon was proof of this. This kind of film gave dealers a 'know your enemy' heads-up concerning facts on the product, as well as angles to use against the opposition. Dodge's film was titled: *Dodge presents ... An unfair comparison.*

The film stated the known fact that small sedans and coupes of the Demon's and Maverick's ilk were popular with the mid-20s crowd. Dodge also had some fun with FoMoCo's Simple Machine slogan, "Simple machine? Maybe austere would be a better word." The odd thing was that between the cream-colored Demon and bronze Maverick coupe displayed, it was Henry's two-door that seemed the more upscale of the two.

Yes, Maverick had a lower sticker price, but also had the lean, not lowball, look of Ford's contemporary European models, Escort and Capri. The gist of Dodge's gambit was that the Demon came with more features, in a larger car, to compensate buyers paying more than a Maverick. Dodge rested its case specifically on: standard rubber cargo mat, pillarless hardtop styling, and naturally, more car. Then again, weight ain't the econocar's friend.

Demon to Maverick it was 192.5in/2885lb /108in, versus 179.4in/2653lb/103in for respective vehicular length/curb weight/wheelbase. Maverick was up on front headroom, so too with rear legroom, but all other dimensions went Demon's way. As they should – it was a bigger two-door sedan. Therefore, Demon's larger stock 198cu in I6 would prove no livelier than the Maverick, due to weight. Indeed, such comparisons only served to show that Demon and Maverick were in different size classes. And, as you would expect, Dodge lost no time mentioning that Demon came with a standard glovebox, and Maverick did not. The statement that Demon had an optional glovebox lock served to show how much emphasis had been placed on feature to feature comparison in the past. However, consumers were already moving away from this basic viewpoint. A car no longer had to fit them, in Detroit's literal sense. Based on MSRP data, as of November 25 1971, Dodge suggested Maverick required the $39 optional Thriftpower six to match Demon 198.

The Demon and Maverick would then be $2526 versus $2397. Dodge tried to explain that

"Put a little Sprint in your life." That's what the print ad said concerning Ford's special edition 1972 Sprint trio of Pinto, Maverick and Mustang. (Courtesy Doug Bauer)

The Sprint package implied a Classic White exterior, dual racing side mirrors, and a patriotic color-coordinated red, white and blue interior! (Courtesy Doug Bauer)

The Ford Sprint special edition trio, commemorated the pending 1972 summer Olympic games in Munich, West Germany. (Courtesy Doug Bauer)

the difference was compensated for by stronger residuals. Emphasis was also placed on Maverick's limited engine choices, and absence of four on the floor. Not to mention a standard tire disadvantage, and lack of power brake option. But, of course, if people wanted all that stuff, there was still Mustang.

Sales figures bore out Ford thinking in this respect. What's more, who wanted a hi-po 340 V8 in an economy car? It seemed that buyers were largely satisfied with the way Maverick came, and the options it possessed. Of course, pure logic never won the hand of marketing's fairlady, Datsun or otherwise, and Dodge had a real Duesie when it came to talking up Demon. For starters, strangely it called Maverick's coupe styling unattractive, referring to the chopped-off tail as lacking in style. Obviously, the Mopar men had never seen the Alfa Spider's Kamm tail. Then, proceeding into blue sky thinking on acid, they suggested the following: Demon had a style "… more akin to a Jordan playboy in Somewhere West of Laramie, and a girl with the wind in her hair." My oh my, even with a rubber cargo mat as standard, that was stretching it, kid!

Dodge picked up on one truth concerning Ford power teams. The 250cu in I6 could only be had with the three-speed Select Shift Cruise-O-Matic. With this engine, that automatic was a mandatory option. In theory this implied that unless you

specified the automatic transmission, the 250cu in Maverick would be delivered sans gearbox!

It's a practice Ford applied to its other lines, too, into 1973 model year. Some industry commentators were saying Ford was sailing too close to the wind with trade practices law. The bottom line was that business practice made a model look cheaper than it actually was. However, in real terms Maverick did undercut domestic rivals, and they noticed.

Ford was still playing on Maverick's dependability, thrift and good value in ads, like the 1972 TV commercial with a guy wandering all over the road on a bicycle. Ford said, "Next time your car reduces you to two wheels, please don't thumb yourself a ride. Thumb yourself a Ford!" Mention was made that the '72 Maverick was one of seven great Fords, and we then saw Mr Bicycle going the other way, now happily driving a bronze Maverick coupe! The comparison ads didn't stop coming either. Apples to oranges or no, Ford and its rivals were still facing off Maverick against the usual suspects.

A 1973 Maverick TV commercial was presented by actor Gil Gerard. It showed a $2394 Duster, $2355 Nova, $2346 Dart and $2240 Maverick arranged vertically. Then, one by one, the Plymouth, Chevy and Dodge drove off. That left the value leader, a green Maverick coupe. It was the cheapest, and the ad claimed all cars were comparably

The Maverick was never officially sold in Australia ... but this '73 Coupe made it Down Under! (Courtesy Warren Cox)

reserved for Maverick coupes. Of key commercial interest was Maverick's new option of four doors for 1971. No, Maverick never offered a wagon, but the new four-door could claim to be a true family car. Plus, a large car for the '80s, in post-downsizing times.

New Mavericks and market analysis

With the very final vestiges of Falcon bid adieu, it was high time for a larger Maverick in North America. The four-door brought a wheelbase stretch to a former Falcon, matching 109.9in. Length for the 1971 Maverick four-door was 188.6in, with width remaining the Maverick's business as usual 70.7in. Maverick four-door afforded a great deal more rear compartment space. However, vehicle trunk and height remained equal to the coupe's at 53.4in and 11.3cu ft respectively. If you wanted more four-door, take a trip to Torino.

Sporting an Edelbrock air cleaner, this 302 Windsor was another stranger to Aussie shores. For the local Ford Falcon, the Geelong foundry focused on 302 and 351 versions of the Cleveland V8. (Courtesy Warren Cox)

equipped. Of course, the ad was only 30 seconds long, and there was fine print, but, once again, Maverick's attractive styling was extolled.

More importantly, there was a consumer awareness flavor to the ad. Detroit had a rough time with quality control, especially at the start of the '70s. For fit, finish and reliability, the 1971 cars had seen some snafus, to say the least. Cars that should have come with gloveboxes, like *Consumer Reports'* Gremlin, did not. Apart from the activity, or inactivity, of the UAW, dealership selling practices had been more opaque than transparent. So, consumers wanted a fair deal, and tried AMC's Buyer Protection Plan, or an import.

The aforementioned 1973 TV commercial, showed an animation of hands shaking, with the reassuring Ford voiceover saying "Come see Maverick at your Ford dealer. We want to make you happy." Spiel or no spiel, Maverick as a range had evolved by 1973. There were more choices of all kinds for potential buyers. In mid '70 MY came an appearance package called Grabber. This was

For '73 MY, federal 5mph impact bumper law increased Maverick coupe's length to 185.4in. (Courtesy Warren Cox)

Back to the Maverick coupe; the special edition Sprint package of 1972 was hard to miss. There was even a Sprint trio, Pinto Sprint, Maverick and Mustang Sprint. On your mark, get set, go! The Sprint package was instead to commemorate the upcoming 1972 summer Olympics in Munich. The event was virtually held in BMW's parking lot, and infamous for a terrorist act that grabbed world attention. FoMoCo could have known nothing of the latter, nor that in a post fuel crisis world it would be buying turbocharged in-line six diesel engines from BMW. This was for its 1980s Lincoln LSC Continental Mark VII.[23] The buy in was to satisfy CAFE: yet another automotive joy for the future.

Fortunately, all of these incidents had yet to transpire when Maverick Sprint and its similarly liveried cousins came out. The package was only for coupes, and featured white and blue two-tone paint, red pinstripes, and a similarly patriotic color-coded interior. On the rear fender panel lay a stylized USA flagshield.

Yes, if Roger Ramjet owned a car, this would be it! The Sprint package cars are rare and collectible. Of the three, the Pinto Sprint is the rarest find in top quality condition, compared to Maverick and Mustang. This lower survival rate reflects the Pinto's entry level new car price. It was regarded by the public, like rivals Gremlin and Vega, to be an inexpensive disposable car. In fact, this carries to even non-Sprint versions. More Mavericks and first gen Mustangs survive in sound condition because they were more expensive cars to begin with.

In total, 15,425 Maverick Sprints were built. Highlighting the cosmetic nature of the package,

and the buying tastes of the time, all Sprints came with a bench front seat. The most popular power team on said Sprint was the 200cu in six- and three-speed manual gearbox. However, base 170, second option 250 I6 and 302 V8 were all possible for the Maverick Sprint. It seemed that safety and sporty didn't sell at Dearborn by 1972. In reality, this was probably the careful Machiavellian plans of Ford marketing coming to fruition. Those seeking greater economy could choose Pinto Sprint, while performance/plush swayed prospects to Mustang. With buyers choosing a 200 cube Maverick Sprint manual, FoMoCo was maintaining the Maverick's position as its Simple Machine.

If the Grabber package was representative of the past when the pony car was riding high, and Maverick Sprint was of the present, then the LDO pack was a sign of things to come. In 1967-70, a wave of upscale European imports had arrived that were very popular: cars like the Volvo 140/160, BMW 2002, Saab 99, Audi 100 and Peugeot 504. At the highest price point, there were the BMW 2500/2800 and Mercedes W114 Compact. These sedans were sized how US compacts used to be, and were luxurious in a non-Caddy, Lincoln or Imperial way. Not spartan, but not luxurious in the traditional American sense either. However, they were a handy size, well made, and refined in handling and braking, as well as being adequately powered.

Detroit didn't have a response to this kind of sedan, and the first step towards this new age, small luxury car from a domestic brand was the late '72 MY Ford Maverick LDO (Luxury Décor Option) and its Mercury Comet counterpart. The LDO package spelt out Ford's intention that it wanted in on the small luxo game. In doing so, Maverick LDO predated subsequent domestic responses. These involved the 1974 $^1/_2$ Dodge Dart SE, 1975 Chevrolet Nova LN and 1978 AMC Concord. Such sedans couldn't bring an advanced chassis to the table. However, they did bring more attention to refinement in the small car class.

Once again, the Dart and Nova were physically larger cars. Then, too, the formula with Dart SE and Concord was very much traditional US luxury, just scaled down. All mini luxo domestic entries were rewarded with strong sales, and American buyers took to the mini land yachts like ducks to water. After all, solid lifter Boss 302s and Camaro Z28s were all so passé by now. In FoMoCo's case, the LDO package was available on both Maverick two- and four-door iterations. As an ensemble, LDO brought reclining bucket seats with glove-soft vinyl, deep pile carpeting, faux woodgrain dashboard panel trim, radial tires, deluxe body-colored wheel covers and the obligatory vinyl roof.

In keeping with domestic rivals, Ford had put much lab work into the amount and placement of sound deadening material and suspension isolating bushings. It was all to deliver more of the quiet and plushness that domestic car buyers favored. And, as per Maverick versus Bug, it's debatable whether Maverick LDO and its ilk really did garner conquest sales from European imports. It seems more likely that such small, luxurious American cars simply stole sales from large luxury domestic models. That is, satiating the luxury buyer's desire to downsize.

Even prior to the fuel crisis, many were finding even intermediate cars like Torino Brougham to be too big and expensive. For these buyers, Maverick LDO was just right, and the six-cylinder Thriftpower motor provided the aforementioned adequate power. Indeed, next to the Mercedes 240D, the six-cylinder Maverick with 200cu in I6 base engine from '73 MY was the proverbial greased lightning incarnate! So, the Maverick LDO ad line seemed correct: "Luxury and comfort that cost thousands more on other cars."

Points to note were Maverick LDO's reclining buckets, sourced from the new European 1972

One concession to economy was the absence of a glovebox. This feature would arrive on 1974 Mavericks. (Courtesy Warren Cox)

In the subcompact class of 1969, only Maverick and Toyota Corona offered a bench front seat. However, buckets were increasingly the norm. (Courtesy Warren Cox)

Ford Granada. They were something the new '73 Chevy Camaro Type LT could not offer, not even as an extra cost option. Certainly the Maverick LDO, Camaro Type LT and comparable coupes were of this new, 'luxury in a smaller size' vein. The Maverick's trimmer dimensions were appreciated, and its color-matched wheels were significant. Many buyers were favoring the Mercedes-Benz brand of restrained luxury.

The cars of the three-pointed star were known for their color-keyed wheel covers. This Ford-painted decoration facsimile was the start of Dearborn's 'Mercedes Era,' which would stretch into the 1980s. Here, various design and styling elements were adopted by Ford and domestic rivals. Certainly the AMC Concord and Pacer took the Mercedes front grille route, by the late '70s. Compared to GM and Chrysler, Ford was an early adopter of new tire technology. Radials on Maverick LDO today, and Michelin TRX metric footwear on Fox platform Mustangs tomorrow.

On the subject of radial tires, Lee Iacocca subsequently wrote that Henry Ford II looked upon them with much disdain. This was purely because of the French Michelin connection, and, according to Iacocca, he didn't want them on any of his family's cars. However, radials were on the Ford option list as early as 1968. It was also the standard tire on high-end FoMoCo models like Lincoln and Thunderbird by the start of the '70s.

As an option, LDO made a summer 1972 debut at $421, according to a dealer invoice. At the time, Select-Aire factory a/c was $362.73 and tinted glass $35.94, so as mentioned, LDO wasn't cheap. However, it was popular and effective. Over 20 per cent of Mavericks were LDO-equipped, which said something about America's increasing desire for small luxury cars. *Popular Science* magazine said LDO did more for Maverick than anything Ford had tried out on the little car to that point in time.

In June 1973, *Popular Science* conducted a four-car group test concerning domestic V8 compacts. With the subcompact Pinto around since '71 MY, it was now easier to speak of Maverick in compact terms. In came the usual suspects of Nova, Hornet and Valiant, but Maverick LDO won out for quietness, luxury, handling and maneuverability. In a point recognized by buyers and industry critics alike, for many years a domestic car's character, was greatly affected by how it was optioned. With Maverick, LDO was the option to get!

It was in rear accommodation that the Maverick coupe was a trifle snug, compared to domestic compacts Nova and Valiant. (Courtesy Warren Cox)

A couple more elements LDO brought inside were European-style door card armrests. These items would figure greatly on the new Mustang II, a car Lee Iacocca wished to be a "Little Jewel." In real world living, Maverick LDO seemed to steer a sensible path between the Euro imports it sought to emulate, and the domestic gaggle it mostly fought with for sales.

Maverick LDO didn't have front-wheel drive or inboard disk brakes like an Audi 100LS. However, it didn't subject its owner to the legion of problems, that North American Audi owners had to endure during the '70s and '80s. That was most certainly a time of keeping up appearances, paving the way for the yuppies to be. The Audi 100LS seemed a Mercedes Compact wannabe. In this role the Maverick LDO was more than a match, and a thriftier one at that.

The luxury focused Plymouth Valiant Brougham and Mercury Comet with 'Custom Option' were Maverick LDO contemporaries. Limitations of the LDO package, apart from the lack of European chassis design sophistication, was its tan-only

1973 was a bumper sales year for the industry. Maverick was on 291,675, against only 134,867 Mustangs. (Courtesy Warren Cox)

This 1973 Maverick coupe, features the top 302 2bbl V8 option. (Courtesy Richard Zapach)

interior color scheme up to '74 MY. Then too, if you ordered Select-Aire a/c, the evaporator/blower box took up an inordinate amount of Maverick's parcel shelf. Yes, it's true, even Maverick LDO lacked a glovebox until '74 MY. However, it did have bumper guards and whitewall radials. The latter item was a big factor in Maverick LDO's roadability advantage over domestic rivals in the aforementioned *Popular Science* group test.

In meeting or exceeding expectations, the attractively styled Maverick's 302 V8 delivered performance commensurate with an engine of that nature. However, in the *Popular Science* test, the square-set looking Nova's 350 V8 underperformed, given its displacement, and Chevy small block reputation. In creating a small luxury car, from a domestic base, Maverick LDO even predated Cadillac's Nova related 1975 Seville. It was also eminently more successful in convincing buyers, they were really getting something for their money, unlike the underdone GM J car based Cadillac Cimarron.

Along the way, Maverick's small annual changes saw a chrome grille adopted for 1973, that used to be optional. The same went for the new base 200cu in I6 of 1973. The 170 six was history, as tighter smog law saw a switch to bigger powerplants industry wide. Indeed, Maverick's now first option 250 1bbl six was rated at a mere 98 net SAE horses.

In 1970 it was Grabber's top motor! All the while Ford needed sales, and Maverick provided them. The same couldn't be said of the Mustang. However, there was the exception of 1972. That model year, both Maverick and Mustang were on a 254,964 total. In 1973, it was Maverick all the way, to the tune of 291,675 versus 134,867.

Annual calendar Maverick sales, according to the 1975 *Ford Annual Report*, saw respective totals of 251,047, 230,322 and 282,818 for 1971, 1972 and 1973. Dearborn was added to Kansas City and St Thomas assembly plants in 1972, concerning Maverick production. In Lee Iacocca's view, Bunkie Knudsen's old-style pony car approach of more of everything, bar the EPA-induced performance drop, was turning his Mustang into a commercial irrelevance. Meanwhile Maverick, which was originally only intended as an interim car, was holding steady.

1972 had seen a resurgence in Mustang and pony car sales in general, with the sector picking up during March and April. Of course, Mustang profited from the sales windfall resulting from GM's April 1972 174-day strike at its Norwood, Ohio plant. With no new supply of Camaros or Firebirds, Henry was in luck! Pony car fanciers, historically never the most loyal of repeat buyers, switched to Mustang, as well as Barracuda, Challenger and Javelin. Possible general reasons why the once-flagging ponies had revived, were myriad: Corvette insurance premiums,

The tried and true 302 V8 performed better in Maverick than in the heavier Mustang. You could really dodge the insurance Allstate guy with a subcompact V8. (Courtesy Richard Zapach)

1973 Maverick, and the Ford range itself, carried the TV dealer slogan: "We Want To Make You Happy." There was a rising awareness of consumer protection being necessary in the early '70s. (Courtesy Richard Zapach)

the long waiting list on the Datsun 240Z, a need for 2+2 accommodation, and even returning Vietnam veterans, with combat pay burning a hole in their pockets.

Maverick, as well as the hot-selling Pinto and Torino ranges, got Ford out of trouble in 1973. It was in late May 1972 that Ford engineers got caught fudging the 50,000 mile EPA emissions certification process. They had swapped out sparkplugs during certification, to pass the stricter 1973 test. After the feds found out, the emissions test had to start over. This delayed the release of the 1973 Fords. Of course, it should be noted that Chevrolet missed out on the introduction of a new Chevelle in 1972, leaving Ford with all the gravy thanks to the new '72 Gran Torino. The 1973 emissions test woes were part of the reason for Mustang's sales collapse that year.

Beyond any one reason, buyers were giving pony cars another gander because, in the early '70s, such coupes were increasingly the answer to their automotive prayers. The public wanted smaller, lighter, easier to handle and park vehicles with style, that were also cheaper to buy and feed. Next to the

full-size, and even mid-size, domestic cars, pony cars made dollars and good sense. By the same token of 'best fit for the garage,' so did Ford Maverick. In the Grabber and its Mercury cousin Comet GT, Henry had some small pony cars, too. That said, Maverick sales had fallen noticeably since 1970. This was because it was no longer alone as an interim subcompac.

America needs more small cars

Maverick emulated Mustang in its market start. Both had the whole enchilada to themselves. In Mustang's case it surprised everyone, and it had more than a two-year lead before the Camaro came calling. This wasn't the case with Maverick. A year after its debut, there was another small domestic car vying for sales. Soon, there would be more homegrown subcompacts on the prowl. It was always understood that a new wave of American small cars were on the horizon. As stated in the September 1969 issue of *Car and Driver*: "It's no secret that American Motors, Ford and GM all have something smaller in the works." [24]

Indeed, earlier in 1969 all the major players had announced their intentions, or at least as much as they could publicly disclose, concerning the small car game. By late 1968/early 1969, there was major interest in this sales segment. The Big Four, as Leon Mandel called them, were all watching each other carefully. Mighty GM had originally thought of a scaled down Chevy II as sufficient. However, upon learning of leaked Ford Maverick plans, plus its own market research, GM reasoned something more specialized was required.

So it was that XP887, what became known as the

Rear fender well intrusion and limited space for occupants in the back, but Maverick was plenty roomy up front. The 37.6in of front headroom matched the Chevy II two-door exactly. (Courtesy Richard Zapach)

Maverick's dashboard readouts were domestic economy car basic. However, many imports like the Volvo 140 series and VW Dasher had unreliable instrumentation, according to *Road & Track* owner surveys. (Courtesy Richard Zapach)

Chevy Vega, saw the whole nine yards undertaken during its development. So important were small cars that GM used the Fiat 124 and stretched Opel Kadetts as test mules. The target was a four-cylinder car 172in long, with rumors of an aluminum block. This all did come to pass. GM chairman James Roche claimed there had been breakthroughs in technology and various investigations with component suppliers, so that the new Chevy would be class competitive. In the works were possible 12in wheels, and expansion of the Ohio, Lordstown facility to a capability of 400,000 unit per annum.

American Motors, the King of Thrift since Rambler times, were in the small car game. New chairman Roy Chapin confirmed a crash program for a real subcompact, coming in 1971. AMC's new direction was to do niches, but in small car matters the economy experts were taking on GM and Ford directly. AMC Hornet seemed an intermediate step to smallness, like Maverick. Plus, AMC's early small car plan involved a truncated Hornet, not unlike GM's mini Chevy II. However, once again something more market specific was recognized as needed. Indeed, the head of AMC styling, Dick Teague, said a distinctive looker was necessary once all those small Chevrolets and Fords were on the highway.

Chrysler President Virgil E Boyd said that if their studies showed a small car was viable, they could build one of their Chrysler Europe cars in America. He said it would either be a Simca, which were

being sold as captive imports at the time, or a UK Rootes Group car. They eventually just sold the UK-sourced Plymouth Cricket captive import. Some saw the small car bonanza as a fad on the surface, and Chrysler liked to say that's how it saw it. In reality, it abandoned a planned US design that was going to be made in America. The reason for limited Chrysler Corp participation was lack of funds.

In early 1969, Ford's new president, Bunkie Knudsen said, "We'll see how it sells." That is, the success of Maverick in the marketplace would determine the future of a smaller Ford of US design and manufacture. Known fact shows that plans for the Ford Pinto's production were already well advanced, having begun in the summer of 1967, with formal project work from August 1968. Ford's Product Planning Committee approved the Ford Pinto in December 1968, with the Ford Board of Directors signing off on the subcompact in January 1969. In spite of the secretive Knudsen, Pinto would follow Vega as a 1971 model year car. AMC Gremlin beat out all by entering the scene on April 1 1970. In any case, Lee Iacocca's small car foresight showed he was no April Fool.

Iacocca foresaw the rising interest in small cars. When the mighty GTO was wowing them, the Mustang created a smaller class of high-performance American cars. Now, from Mustang to Pinto, it was an equine of a different color. Green for economy, rather than red for redline fever! Internally, the Pinto was known as 'Lee's car,' and with it Iacocca exerted much influence. From Pinto's speedy deadline, to limits of $2000 and 2000lb, Ford went Beetle hunting ... again! Now the ads compared Pinto with Beetle, and Maverick could become its own kind of not so small car.

In January 1971, *Road & Track* lined up Ford Pinto with Super Beetle, Toyota Corona, Datsun 510 and Chevy Vega. Pinto, Super Beetle and Vega were new for '71 MY. Pinto and Beetle both had 1600cc fours, four-wheel drums, four on the floor, and identical 21.1-second $1/4$-mile times. Once again, Ford doubled the oil change interval, but VW doubled the warranty. Pinto was $1939 and Super Beetle was $1934, a better match than with Maverick indeed.

Pinto's Kent in-line I4 and four-speed brought 22.6mpg on test. It was a stat similar to Ford's overall figure for the 170 cube, three-speed Maverick. In real world driving and ownership, the six-cylinder Maverick two-door looked like providing more value for relaxed performance. It spoke to the times: that to get a saving in price, road space and better handling, all of which Pinto offered over Maverick, the trade-off was disproportionate.

Car and Driver ran a 15,000 mile comparison test of Pinto and Vega. Highlighting the compromises of vehicle choice, it concluded Pinto was better suited to town work, Vega for highway. [25] Going against advertising and buyer behavior,

'73 MY was the final hour of mostly small bumpers. Many post-1973 Mavericks have been backdated to the delicate, pre-federal impact, chrome bumper look. (Courtesy Richard Zapach)

C/D advised not to choose on price, but suitability: "... you're buying a car, not a price tag." [26] So, Ford provided the consumer with choice. More than a few decided Maverick was as small as they wished to go, but of course, new being new, and advertising being what it was, Pinto's 352,402 '71 MY sales outpaced Maverick. When buyers visited Ford showrooms, they were now greeted by an even cheaper small car.

Price and size being eternal car buying factors, sales cannibalization transpired within Family Ford. However, Vega and Gremlin were in the mix, too, and certainly with pony car wars, the domestic small car market pie was getting sliced finer. As with Maverick, the question was whether Ford's Pinto had achieved conquest sales from the Beetle, or from Japanese competition? It's suspected Pinto sold mostly to the domestic car faithful, and to Ford fans foremost, with the realities of an existing trade-in – like grandma's hand-me-down '60 Falcon or dealer proximity – being dominant factors.

Then there were the wildcards of Toyota, Datsun and soon Honda. The '71 Toyota Corona Deluxe looked like a car American buyers already knew. No more shovel nose, very plush, quiet, and, with zero to sixty in under 14 seconds, zippy as well. The cost was $2200. Datsun would also move onto the bigger, fancier 610/180B: not as sporty as the previous 510, but it was right up Mainstream Marty's alley. Honda sold some cute, motorcycle two-stroke powered microcars, called the 'Z.' However, the front-wheel drive Civic of 1973 was a real small car, below even Pinto in size, but with a lively and miserly 1.2-liter transverse four, sub 15-second 0-60mph and under 20-second $1/4$-mile. This four-speed economouse made many friends, especially outside the snowbelt. In wintery locations, Japanese cars showed a propensity to rust, shared only by Chevy Vega and Italian cars.

By the time the dust had settled, import no longer meant just Beetle. The hopes of conquest sales also seemed to be fading. Domestic car fanciers bought domestic, and import buyers bought imports. With the latter, Japanese automakers seemed to have wrestled the econocar market from VW by 1975. They had also grabbed the sporty car sector from the British. However, Maverick got into a solid sales position. Contrary to *Car and Driver*'s prediction, it was now an economy car, a luxurious small sedan, or even a latter day Mach I, if that grabbed you?

Maverick and the aftermarket

There used to be an oft-seen, butterfly transformation of a secretary in movies. A plain-looking soul with high collar, put-up hair and large glasses would encounter a gentleman who would suggest removing said glasses, and cue the transformation. With a toss of the hair, and one undone button, plain Jane was suddenly Raquel Welch! Well, it would seem that by May 1969, *Car Life* magazine had seen that movie, too, and said, "Take off those glasses, Miss Falcon. Why, you're beautiful!" It added that it appeared plain Miss Falcon had a sleek new shape, and that it too saw the 'Pocket Mustang' potential in Ford Maverick. [27]

The automotive transformation wasn't new, either. In May 1965, sister publication *Motor Trend* had run the tale of "Two Comets: Hot & Cool," and in October 1969 *Car Life* followed up with "Hot And Cold Running Mavericks." The sub headings "Some Like It Cold" and "We Like It Hot" were references to the 1959 movie *Some Like It Hot*, directed by Billy Wilder and starring Marilyn Monroe. Naturally for an enthusiast publication, as they all were in those days, except *Consumer Reports*, the magazine liked it hot! But, how to achieve this outcome? In 1965 it was simple: just factory order two different 289 V8-powered machines. The sensible 2bbl Caliente with automatic and a/c, or the four-barrel Cyclone with 4 on da floor.

Ticking option boxes with 1970 Maverick wasn't an option, they simply didn't exist. *Car Life*'s factory-ordered desirable '70 Maverick, was shown in their October '69 issue. It cost $2427, and included good stuff like 26 buck 200cu in six, $174 Select-Shift autobox, $39 Accent Group, which afforded the 6.45-14 mid tire option, and $61 AM radio. With this ensemble, a genuine 99mph was recorded at 3900rpm, 0-60mph in 13 seconds flat, and a 19.4-second pass at 73.8mph. Not forgetting 20mpg overall, and *Car Life* did attain Henry's gas mileage claim. Such figures came courtesy of a highway-compliant 2.83 rear axle.

Outstanding figures for an economy car of the day, allied to slow response, but the predictable steering and handling expected from a domestic coupe. Two problems here were, first, Ford's billing of Maverick as an import fighter – imports were agile, great handling small cars – and second, where to get the upgrades? Answers were supplied from the FoMoCo parts shelf and aftermarket, along with help from selected dealer speed shops. Timing was important, too, because after Maverick's debut, more items were at hand.

For starters, much of the Maverick's handling limitations could be fixed with parts that were already available. Standard steering had a 22.9:1 ratio, and 5.5 turns lock to lock. That said, the faster power steering hardware from Fairlane or Mustang could be swapped in. Using the Fairlane's steering sector and shaft cut the number of turns between locks to 3.7. The common fear when attempting this mod was that it would make Maverick's manual steering too heavy. However, this proved not to be the case, with effort generally unaffected.

With suspension, Maverick's standard front 0.69in swaybar could be replaced by a 0.85in unit from a Mustang GT, or even the 1in swaybar from

A modified '72 Maverick coupe was backed by *Fast & Furious* movie franchise star Sung Kang, in the guise of Project Underdog, aka UDog. (Courtesy *Autoweek*)

Project Underdog made its debut at the 2016 SEMA Show. It was subsequently auctioned off to fund future youth auto shop outreach programs. (Courtesy *Autoweek*)

the hallowed Shelby Mustang GT350. However, some found the latter's veritable baseball bat to be overkill. It would make Maverick's handling too stiff. Maverick had no rear swaybar, optional or otherwise. Neither did the 1st gen Camaro Z28, for that matter. Manufacturer consensus of the day was to run stiff springs and a fat front swaybar. That said, ADDCO made a 0.50in rear swaybar for Falcon and Mustang. By the start of 1970, the company had one for Maverick, too.

Trans-Dapt also offered a 1in front swaybar for Maverick from the start of 1970. It also had a rear lift kit (part no. SP-971), and planned a rear swaybar for Maverick. For new shocks, Gabriel Adjustomatic units were around, plus Gabriel's Silver E Mustang shocks could be machined to fit the Maverick. Mustang front springs could be adapted, and custom rear leafs were possible. For wheels and tires, Maverick's optional 14 x 4.5in rims, came with Goodyear Polyester Power Cushion 6.45-14 tires. However, even the top option C78-14s were really enough for serious action.

On the stock 14in rim, Goodyear Polyglas D70-14s would fit and bring a welcome improvement in roadholding, stopping distances and traction. The optional 200cu in six with three-speed automatic amplifying torque had more go than many realized. In January 1970, *Hot Rod* reported an 18.5-second pass at 72mph, achieved fair and square at Orange County International Raceway. This was warp speed compared to an economy import. The D70-14s were useful here, and with the power increases

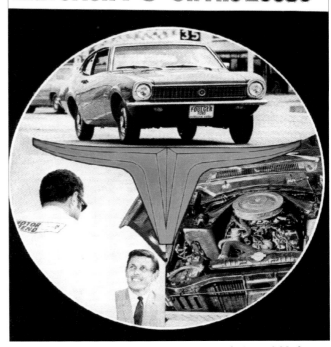

Early on, Ford built a test Maverick Boss 302 for internal evaluation ... but speed shop Foulger Ford offered one to the public! (Courtesy *Motor Trend*)

possible with the Thriftpower six, it was commonly agreed that the Polyglas D70-14s were the biggest tires possible on Maverick. This took into account standard wheelarches and possible use of wider aftermarket rims.

There were several possibilities concerning larger wheels. Trans-Dapt did five-bolt wheel adapters, which allowed the use of Ford Torino GT rims. With these rims, big Goodyear F60-14s were usable on the Maverick with some fenderwell work. It also depended on whether you spent much time in parking lots, turning lock to lock, or whether snowchains were on the cards? By the late '60s, plated chrome reverse steel rims were a popular aftermarket item on a wide range of cars. Keystone even had a plated rim for VWs.

Fenton Co's chrome reverse 14 x 5.5in rim carried Ford's four-bolt 4.5in circle mounting pattern, to suit Maverick. Well-known concern American Racing Equipment's magnesium alloy rims could be drilled to fit Maverick's bolt pattern. This applied to

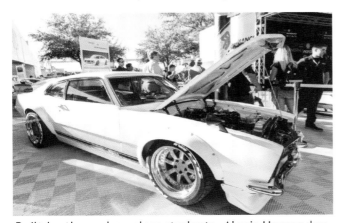

Built by three shop class students, Alexis Hernandez, Christian Quiroz and Tony Chen, Project Underdog featured a near 400-horse 2.3-litre Ford Eco Boost in-line four, with custom GReddy turbo. (Courtesy *Autoweek*)

the company's four-spoke 13in Libre 6in wide rims. Its new 200-S was very wide at 14 x 6.75in. Once again, it could be drilled to accommodate Maverick's bolt pattern. That said, it was an awfully big rim for Maverick's wheelwell.

American tire companies were mighty tardy in introducing radials. However, in 1965 Firestone was the first to selectively market its F-100 in some parts of the country during spring. Its 6.50-13s and 6.50-14s fitted both Falcon and Mustang, and would fit Maverick's original 13in and 14in factory rims, too. Although smaller in width than many bias-belted tires of the day, testers found the radials held on better, permitting higher cornering speeds. For too long, bias-belted tires were the base tire that domestic automakers designed their suspension systems around. On performance cars, firm suspension settings took advantage of softer bias-belted tires. Such suspensions became too stiff once radials were fitted. The whole suspension had to be retuned to take advantage of the constructional properties of radials.

With a much improved chassis in terms of handling and control, thoughts turned to hot rodding the Ford Thriftpower six. No problem; the aftermarket had parts for Falcon and Mustangs, with six-cylinder motorvation. There were also existing Ford parts and ideas for extracting more power. Plus, there had been six-cylinder Gasser classes in drag racing for years. A revised Thriftpower cylinder head, with square intake manifold and flat top, along with 30 per cent more flow, had arrived with Maverick. Basic theory for raising power was to combine the 170cu in head with the 200cu in block.

Normally, the 170 six had an 8.3:1 CR, and the 200 cube six possessed 8.7:1 CR. Both supped regular grade gas. However, combining the small chamber with the big cylinder, plus shaving or milling the head, raised the compression ratio. 0.040in of milling increased the CR to 9.6:1. 0.050in of milling, plus a steel shim head gasket from Autolite (part no. C9DZ6051-C) produced 9.7:1 CR. It should be noted that the raised compression ratio necessitated a diet of premium gas. This wasn't really a problem while high octane leaded gas was still available. The next big change for the Thriftpower six was carburetion. This mod was slightly different than usual, given the Thriftpower's constructional nature.

Showing the economy, non-performance orientation of Ford's six, the intake manifold and

The answer to low cost transportation is simplicity itself.

Maverick is simple to buy. You can do most repair jobs yourself. Maverick gives you great gas mileage. And that's with a standard peppy 100-hp engine. Maverick is designed to need one-sixth as many lube jobs and half as many oil changes as the leading import. And an independent survey says that Maverick has the lowest frequency-of-repair record of any American car. 2-door, 4-door, or sporty Grabber. Three economical Sixes or low-cost V-8. See your Ford Dealer soon.

MAVERICK
The Simple Machine

MAVERICK Ford

With the coming of Maverick Grabber Coupe, the simple car got sexy. Even so, tighter smog law meant a 5bhp drop to 100 horses, for base '71 Maverick's I6. (Courtesy Ford Motor Co)

cylinder head were one unit. That said, it could be made hi-po by removing the head/intake and applying an Offenhauser/Autolite triple carb adapter kit. A 1in diameter hole was cut into the head/intake at each end for the additional carbs and mountings. The kit included hole-cutting instructions, mounting adapters and a progressive linkage assembly. It was the kind of thing you saw on a T-bucket ... or Jag XKE!

The two additional carbs to go with the stock 200cu in motor's 156 CFM Carter 1bbl unit were early Ford Falcon 144 cube-sourced 146 CFM (part no. C2DZ9510-A) units. Additional fuel lines for the outer carbs and three small dome air cleaners were required, too. Of course, the central carb could be the Fairlane 250cu in one-barrel 210 CFM unit (part no. DOZZ9510-E). During 1969, Holley was already working on a big 1bbl bolt on carb swap

Ford initially released Maverick Grabber Coupe with a 250 cube I6 option. This proved attractive to the junior supercar crowd. (Courtesy *Car and Driver*)

The 1970 Ford Torino Cobra Jet 429, with Drag Pack, represented the zenith of the muscle car era. (Courtesy Robert Cuillerier)

kit. Man-A-Fre had a kit for under 50 bucks in 1970, with adapter mount, to replace the stock 200cu in Carter carb with a Rochester 2bbl unit. The 170 and 200 cube sixes used the 250cu in edition's big

valve and port head, and it was possible to just swap in the whole Fairlane 250 six. This version of the Thriftpower unit was slightly taller and wider, plus 30lb heavier, than the 170/200 sixes, but would indeed fit. A machined head with Jahns high dome pistons would yield more horses as a standalone mod.

With more air and fuel now ingested, a sports camshaft could be used to make more power. Iskenderian 321 CY camshaft and springs would help. This unit's 260 degree duration was much more radical than the stock 120bhp 200cu in I6 unit's cam. To aid high rpm operation of the overhead valve Ford six, Windsor 289 V8 valve springs (part no. B6A6513-A) and early 260 V8 retainers (part no. C3426514-B) were apt FoMoCo parts. With an hydraulic cam, stock standard 1.50:1 200cu in I6 rocker arms would suffice. However, with a solid lifter job, early adjustable Falcon rocker arms were needed. To make everything fit, shims or Ford sourced shorter pushrods could be utilized.

On the exhaust side of the equation there were various headers for Ford's Thriftpower I6. Man-A-Fre had tube headers costing under $70 in 1970; then there were the Doug Thorley Tri-Y $1^5/_8$in headers that would fit into Maverick's single pipe exhaust system. Six-cylinder specialist Jack Clifford also offered headers for the Thriftpower six. From here on, it was into a regular 1.75in Maverick 170/200 six single exhaust system, but the Mustang 250 six 2in setup would bring gains, including the Mustang's muffler.

Any coupe that resembles a bona fide pony car should have the option of four on the floor, and Maverick did not. At first everything was on the tree, then came the subsequent option of 'three by the knee.' Once again, parts shelf raiding and modification could make it look like a factory job. Ford's light duty four-speed would bolt onto the Thriftpower six, but Maverick's stock driveshaft needed shortening, and the 200cu in motor engine bell housing, clutch and flywheel were also required. This would all fit, but the chief hurdle was Maverick's floorpan. To clear said floorpan required a bulged transmission tunnel. This probably explained why the hot-rodded Maverick 200s created by *Car Life* and industry performance expert AK Miller kept the stock three-speed manual.

It was easier to bring a change in rear axle ratio. This was needed to overcome the Maverick's standard economy car gearing, and to improve

Sasha Kangleas with the 1970 Mustang Mach I 351, in Chris Doyle and Richard Middleton's *SXdrv* magazine. (Courtesy SXdrv.com)

*Car Craf*t's May 1970 Econo Racer group test, included a loaded $4101.20 Mustang Mach I 351. Holy option overload Batman! And then there was insurance … (Courtesy SXdrv.com)

acceleration. The Maverick rear axle was the same as the Falcon and Mustang unit. Between Maverick's press unveiling and production, a 3.20 rear end was approved for the car. It was a ratio in common with Falcon, too.

On the Falcon a limited-slip differential was also available, something that was never listed for North American Mavericks. This highlighted the Ford policy of keeping Maverick economy-oriented. Falcon and Fairlane intermediate pre-dated the Mustang, so both enjoyed some performance hardware and versions. Falcon could have a lsd, and Fairlane received the 271 horse K code 289 V8, before Mustang. However, Maverick came after Mustang, so all the sports stuff was for the latter coupe.

This didn't deter enterprising souls from substituting Mustang's 3.50:1 rear axle ratio, an lsd or even 4.00 rear gears! With the last item, the popular Hone-O-Drive aftermarket overdrive unit practically created a four-speed. It resulted in

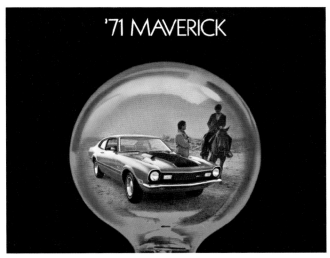

'71 MAVERICK

To combat insurance and inflation, Ford had a 'light bulb' moment. The 1971 Maverick Grabber was the better idea that Henry put on wheels. (Courtesy Ford Motor Co)

Maverick Grabber had the glamour of a dual dome hood during 1971-72. (Courtesy Ford Motor Co)

an effective final drive ratio of 2.78:1, while also improving scat thanks to the 4.00 rear axle. So what were the concrete results? Well, first industry observations set the scene. In October 1969, *Car Life*'s Jim Hamilton said that initially everyone thought Ford Capri and Maverick would be one and the same car. In the end, one stone couldn't kill two GM F bodies.

Hamilton said Ford undertook internal model comparative analysis. To suit its respective markets, an equivalent Capri was one grand pricier. For this you got a smaller coupe with better internal packaging, handling and quality. Hamilton said he tried one of the first Capri 2000 GTs built. In trips out of London, England, the smog control-free Ford V4 proved strong. The Ford Escort-bred suspension really worked, too. He kept up with an Aston Martin; ironic, given Ford's future ownership of the same. Hamilton mentioned how in Europe, corner to corner times outweighed the $^{1}/_{4}$-mile sprint. [28]

Ford targeted imports with its Maverick advertising. In a *Road & Track* March 1969 Volvo owner survey, the journal said import buyers expected their acquisition to handle well. With the modifications outlined, Maverick did now handle very well. *Car Life*'s October 1969 report on its modified Maverick said the changes imbued the Ford coupe with the agility of an import. Improved handling response was also matched by greater acceleration than stock.

Using a three-speed manual car with worked 200cu in six-cylinder mill, 0-60mph was 8.3 seconds, backed up by a $^{1}/_{4}$-mile showing of 16.9 seconds at 89mph. All modifications were carried out for under 500 bucks. Engine mods were reputed to lift power output, from 120bhp to 180 wild horses. The revised 1970 Maverick coupe was now truly living up to its Mini Mustang image, with great value. In fact, *Car and Driver* tested a $5500 BMW Alpina 2002 in 1967, producing equivalent times of 8.3 seconds, and a 15.9-second pass at 87mph. At around 3 grand, the modified Maverick certainly showed the small Ford's potential.

There were well-known entities in the performance scene that were looking at the potential of smaller six-cylinder domestic cars in 1969/70. Ford had initiated a long press preview for the Maverick over the winter of 1968/69. Fred and Carl Offenhauser did the triple carb kit, applying to six-cylinder Fords. AK Miller, who would later do the turbo four package for the Pinto based Pangra, was investigating increasing the power of Ford's 250 six. Miller created a '70 Maverick coupe called the Boss 200. In a similar vein to *Car Life*'s modded Maverick, the Boss 200 featured a worked 200 six and three on the tree manual gearbox.

On the way to the El Mirage dry lake for

This Maverick Grabber 302 is one of the 38,963 1971 model year Grabbers built. (Courtesy Ray Parrish)

performance testing, Miller's blue coupe recorded 26mpg. When it reached El Mirage, a 17.1-second ¹/₄-mile at 80.10mph was forthcoming. It also managed a 111mph top end. Better performance and economy than the stock six, and only 10mph slower than the very expensive BMW/Alpina. Observations were that the three-speed was very awkward to use. A four-speed would fix this, and by closing up the ratios bolster gas mileage and performance.

There were great hopes at this time for a new wave of small performance cars. Appealing domestic cars that were also affordable. "Small dimension cars are enjoying their second phase, and this time the taste is going to last longer." There were also hopes that such thinking would flow to Hornet, Duster et al. [29]

There was a cautionary addendum: "They might also get huge V8s, which could easily put us all back in another predicament ten years from now." Back in 1960 the same hopes prevailed, and Mustang was initially a lithe little thing with a lively 289 V8. However, by 1970 it was 429 V8-powered, thirsty and as expensive as the Dickens. Then, too, by 1971 AMC created the Hornet SC/360. This V8-powered coupe was an insurance fighter, but still showed Detroit's 'more is better' V8-focused nature. In 1970, *Hot Rod* had extolled the benefits of good performing, easily maintained, small displacement cars.

One area that wasn't modified on Maverick was

Fords are known for their rugged longevity. This '71 Grabber has been with the same owner since 1974. (Courtesy Coast Collision & Car Care, Mississippi (228) 762-7781)

its braking system. *Car Life*'s stock 200 cube 1970 automatic, stopped in 370ft from 80mph, but that figure increased to nearly 500ft by stop number eight! As the drums heated up, they got erratic. Front brake locking was accompanied by boiling brake fluid. Most magazines agreed that Maverick needed a front disk brake option.

Utilizing the FoMoCo parts shelf, Mustang drum brakes were larger, and the aftermarket could supply better quality linings. Then, too, wider rims and bigger tires would put a larger footprint on the road, to help reduce stopping distances. Oftentimes the standard tires on imports and domestics, were too skinny, and could be overwhelmed by the brakes. However, that was if lock up was still possible.

If a Maverick Boss 200 was ahead of its time, then the idea of working on your car for modification, service and repair harked back to earlier times. As would happen with Pinto, Ford put out a DIY (Do It Yourself) service manual. *Car Life* judged this book as informative, and reminiscent of Ford Model T and A times. In the 1970s age of high price, poor service, when it could easily cost $100 to do points, sparkplugs and ignition timing at a dealer, *Car Life* regarded DIY Maverick service to be necessary. *Car and Driver* reached the same conclusion in its 15,000 mile Pinto and Vega evaluation report of November 1971. Better service at lower prices was swaying buyers first towards the VW Beetle, then Datsuns and Toyotas.

Ford's high-performance preview

Howard Freers was chief engineer for Ford Small Car System Design, and in the lead up to Maverick's April 1969 release, shared some upcoming attractions and information concerning Ford's new subcompact. Freers had been Fairlane executive engineer in the mid '60s. Back in 1964, Fairlane handed sporty car duty to the Mustang. So, for 1965 Ford's intermediate was put purely in family car mode, and became a real square. However, a burgeoning intermediate muscle car sector sparked by the Pontiac GTO made Ford reconsider Fairlane's role.

Howard Freers was in charge of livening up Fairlane, and the result was the 1966 Fairlane GT and GT/A, the latter possessing a sports shift console stick that encouraged driver usage. Now, in early 1969, Freers could say he and his team were working on a handling option for Maverick. He said it was ready for production, and came with 30 per

cent stiffer springing, revalved shocks with better seals and a bigger front swaybar. This last item was 0.75in, as opposed to the standard 0.69in unit. No mention of a rear swaybar, though.

At the start of 1969, Koni agent Kensington Products supplied shocks to Ford, for what was referred to as a "fun car." No doubt it went to Freers' team. A fast ratio steering kit for Maverick, to be available over the Ford parts counter, was also announced. In the same spirit, 6in wide 14in rims and Firestone Wide Oval D70 tires, were also to be optionable within a few months of Maverick's release. Indeed, Freers said the D70-14 tire was the largest size to meet snowchain, trunk load and wheel well clearance requirements. This was Maverick's factory recommendation. [30]

At this time, a 3.20 rear axle was also announced for Maverick. Freers also said the following, on the subject of four-speed availability: " ... relatively sure we'll see a four-speed before we're through, but not for months." It was an essential piece of equipment, on contemporary sporty cars. A year later, in mid 1970, it was already known that Ford had built and tested a Trans Am Maverick 302, for the purposes of internal evaluation.

The Mustang had triumphed in the 1970 SCCA Trans Am championship, driven by Parnelli Jones. It seems that, as a semi factory-backed entry, the Maverick was being groomed to take Mustang's racing place at some point. Ford even planned a

On this coupe, the 302 V8 became 308 cubes. And the Edelbrock Performer RPM Air-Gap intake, Lunati 51028 cam, Edelbrock Performer 1.90 heads, with fuel supply from a Holley 750 vacuum secondary 4bbl carb, make this Windsor small block anything but stock! (Courtesy Greg Holland)

A 1972 Maverick Grabber. That year, Ford sold 35,347 Grabber coupes. (Courtesy Greg Holland)

1971 Mustang Boss 302. There was also promising word that a Maverick in possession of Ford's new 300 horse 351 4bbl Cleveland V8 was on the tarot cards. Excitingly, such a Maverick coupe would undercut the already stripper Plymouth Road Runner by 400 bucks!

However, in a rapidly changing auto climate, not everything foretold by the crystal ball came to pass. Although the fuel crisis was yet to surface, other concerns had. Insurance premiums were sky-rocketing, which with the Muskie Smog Bill and a shaky economy made for a terrible trio, morphing Ford's Total Performance era into one of Total Economy. It looked like buyers would be increasingly into Maverick for its original economy car purpose, albeit an American economy car, not an imported one. For this, and mainstream tastes, Freers' team had selected soft suspension for the normal Maverick. It looked like all Fords would get softer from here on in.

Don't despair, though, because dealers are the last to know if the automaker has had a change of heart. All the hallowed dealership speed shops representing the Big Four were still going at full steam. You could in fact get a Maverick Boss 302 ... but only if you visited Chuck Foulger Ford. Yes sir, this patriotic speed shop had been planning a Maverick V8. You could have one, even before the actual '70 MY Fords had even arrived. Yay!

Foulger Ford had a plan, which mostly involved substituting Ford Mustang hardware. For starters, get one Boss 302 V8 (part no. C8ZZ6077Y), and a 1969 Mustang small V8 four-speed with 2.32 low (part no. C9ZZ7003A) or 2.78 low (part no. C9ZZ7003F). The rear of the transmission would mount on Maverick's crossmember. The correct height water pump would be $11^5/_8$in above the top of the front crossmember. Boss 302 insulators and mounting brackets were employed.

Front suspension mods saw some trimming and welding of spring towers, cut down '69 Mustang front springs, plus a 0.85in swaybar and HD shocks from the 1969 Mustang parts list. HD Mustang front drums, spindles and tie rods rounded-out that front end. Foulger Ford did a custom set of 3 leaf rear springs, with a 120lb-in spring rate. The Mustang and Maverick had the same rear spring centers, and a 1966 Mustang hi-po 289 axle housing was what your Maverick needed (part no. C4DDZ5705A), making use of the expected staggered rear HD shocks and spring plates from a 1966 Mustang.

As would occur when folks began improving their Mustang II V8s, you were seeking out pre-1967 Mustang hardware. That is, before the Mustang went to the FE series big block V8. It goes without saying that a bonafide mini supercar would need a four-speed with direct top gear. To achieve this, get a 1969 Mustang Shelby Cobra driveshaft, and cut off 1.5in. You would be using Maverick's upper clutch arm, plus a V8 Mustang's lower clutch arm. It seemed like Ford had set up Maverick with a four-speed in mind. Four on the floor required that the shifter come back, and it could, because the 1966 Mustang tube crossmember was narrowed on the right side, and would go under the V8's oil pan. Said crossmember carried part no. C522526A.

Other essentials were a Boss 302 radiator, 1968 Mustang rear braking assembly and big

A built-up C4 automatic, featuring a 2800rpm stall speed torque converter going into an 8in differential with 3.40 gears and a mini spool. (Courtesy Greg Holland)

This originally Californian Grabber coupe has black buckets and was ordered with a floor shifter. Small imports popularized floor shifts in the economy sector. (Courtesy Greg Holland)

As a '72 MY Grabber, this coupe still has most of its original Bright Lime paint. The green Grabber side and hood stripes are also original. (Courtesy Greg Holland)

Owner Greg Holland and his Grabber host an annual MCCI Mini Meet in Chatham VA. (Courtesy Greg Holland)

block Mustang 390 rear swaybar, narrowed by 3.3in. Using a 3.91 rear end, all the above got you to sixty in 6 seconds flat, and a 14.35-second pass at 100.11mph. All achieved by *Motor Trend* with two people aboard plus test recording equipment, as revealed in its August 1969 issue. So, before 1970 even started, Maverick was living up to Ford's initials: First On Race Day! What a thing to do to a $1995 econocoupe!

It still had four-wheel drums, since Maverick didn't have a power brake booster for years. Foulger Ford would have had to engineer one of those, so Maverick could utilize the Mustang's disk brake option. Given that Ford itself hadn't done so to that point, it was unfair to expect a dealership to. It would be pretty neat finding an early Foulger Ford-converted Maverick, because it would still have had the ignition switch on the dash. In keeping with the times, soon Baldwin-Motion Chevrolet would drop a LT1 350 V8, into a Vega. Then there was Randall American's Gremlin 401 XR. Small cars with mighty V8s, but Ford was first with its subcompact, and Foulger Ford was first with a Maverick Boss 302 that the public could buy.

However, not everyone had access to Foulger Ford. Then, too, most Ford buyers are interested in stuff available nationwide and factory direct. Factory Maverick power steering was announced just prior to Maverick's public unveiling. That would help with evasive maneuvers and mountain road driving. As for more Maverick V8 availability, aftermarket specialist Trans-Dapt offered engine swap adapters. Trans-Dapt's boss, Willie Garner, had a Maverick

with a Boss 302 and four-speed, which used the adapters. It also had a 1957 Ford wagon rear axle. More of that raiding of Henry's parts shelf! Trans-Dapt also had Maverick hood locks for that racer look, part no. SP-920. However, what of Ford's own Maverick V8?

Here comes da ... Grabber?!
When Ford let the public buy a Falcon V8 in 1963, it did engineering preparation work to make sure it was all safe. This ran to a beefed-up unibody, suspension and drivetrain. It allowed Falcon to accelerate from a 170cu in six, to the 260 cube Challenger Windsor V8. With Maverick, Ford built up to that point with the 1970 1/2 Grabber package. The Grabber pack was of a cosmetic nature, and Ford said as much in its ad: "… more of a jazzy firecracker, than a super bomb."

Insurance companies would put a 25 per cent loading on your premium if an automobile was classified as 'High-performance.' This was judged on a power to weight basis. With a 3000lb compact, more than around 285 horses gross got you into hot water. This resulted in junior supercars like the AMC Hornet SC/360, Chevy Nova SS 350, and Dodge Demon 340 V8s. These machines, plus the Maverick Grabber 302, were group tested by *Motor Trend* in January 1971.

Even so, inflational insurance saw buyers choose a size and price class under the compacts. By 1971 model year, it was the Chevy Vega GT, Ford Pinto Rallye, AMC Gremlin X and, once again, Maverick. That was Maverick's unique quality, it straddled

This modified 1972 Maverick Grabber is called Spooky. Front 11in Baer four-piston calipers, plus drilled and slotted disks, join a Wilwood master cylinder and stainless steel lines. Creature comforts include Classic Auto Air Street Rod Cooler III a/c, custom power windows, Auto Loc power door locks with key fob remote, and custom power trunk release. (Courtesy Nick Dominick)

2006 Hyundai Tiburon buckets on a custom track bracket and stock rear bench, trimmed in color and vinyl factory-correct material. A custom center console features coolant/volt/oil pressure readouts, dual cupholders, USB ports and storage area. Dynamat sound deadening aids refinement. (Courtesy Nick Dominick)

both size classifications, just as with economy cars. The Vega and Pinto were in-line four-powered. The Chevy's aluminum block proved troublesome and underpowered. Plus, rough and noisy, in an especially bad way. Pinto's 2-liter four was potent, but AMC aced such small cars with its big 232 and 258 cube I6s. The latter was optional on Gremlin X, and made for quite a performer. Indeed, many domestic subcompact buyers chose Gremlin over Vega and Pinto, because AMC offered a big six.

Then, there was Maverick Grabber with base 170cu in six, and for $26 a 200cu in six, plus coinciding with Grabber's introduction, an 84 buck formerly Mustang six. This motor made 155bhp at 4 grand, and a useful 240lb-ft at a limbo-low 1600rpm. This 250, and the commercial vehicle, truck-related 300cu in edition, were all about torque. Even so, Maverick's 250 six, had 5hp more than Gremlin's 258 I6. *Car and Driver*'s 1970 August issue outlined Maverick's jump from econocar status. From its test data, a 1970 Beetle 1500 semi-automatic did a 21.2-second $^1/_4$-mile. Ford's Capri 1600 improved this figure to 20.2 seconds, with Maverick 200 on 19 seconds. The new Grabber 250 achieved an 18-second flat pass at 76mph. It also stopped in 238ft from 70mph, compared to 236ft for *C/D*'s earlier Maverick 200.

Braking wise, Grabber brought the same 9in drums all around, as with earlier Mavericks. The

automatic, costing $201, was a mandatory option on all Maverick 250s. You could specify the 250 cube motor on any Maverick, and the Grabber pack was available with any Maverick coupe. So, all Thriftpower sixes were okay. Similarly, once the Grabber became a distinct model for '71 MY, any of Maverick's four engines – 170, 200, 250cu in sixes or 302 V8 – could be selected with Grabber. A vinyl roof retailed for $84. Yes, the same price as the 250 motor! On *C/D*'s early Grabber 250, B78-14 WSW tires were a 30 buck option. So, what exactly did a buyer get for $194?

The 1970 $^1/_2$ Grabber package implied 14in rims with chrome hubcaps and trim rings. There was exterior decoration in the form of black sidestripes, fender decals and blackout paint decoration for the hood, grille and lower back panel. Color-keyed dual racing mirrors came with left-hand remote control. Bright metal window frames and drip moldings, plus a black rear decklid spoiler joined the race, too.

When you consider the number of expensive cars, import and domestic, that came with only one side mirror, Maverick Grabber seemed worth it. Little wonder *Car and Driver* declared that Grabber could be "... a big hit with young ladies who like both a bargain and style." [31] It should be noted the '70 $^1/_2$ Grabber retained Maverick's mid grille logo, and lacked front grille driving lights. Plus it rode on 14 x 4.5in rims, with 6.45-14 tires as stock

This Ford Motorsport Boss 347 V8 has: four-bolt mains, AFR 1388 aluminum heads, 2.02in intake and 1.6in exhaust valves, Comp Cams camshaft with 0.220/0.220 duration, Comp Cams 1.6 ratio roller rockers and Edelbrock Pro-Flo 3 multi-port electronic fuel-injection. The result is 423bhp at 6200rpm and 418 lb-ft at 4600rpm. Gateway Performance Super Stock GT adjustable MacPherson strut front suspension joins Unisteer power rack and pinion steering, too. (Courtesy Nick Dominick)

A Performance Automatic Street Smart AOD four-speed overdrive unit, supported by a custom crossmember, connects to a Strange Engineering chromoly 3in driveshaft and a Currie 9in +Nod Sportsman differential. The True Trac axle has a 3.25:1 ratio. (Courtesy Nick Dominick)

standard. Weight distribution of this 2877lb coupe, was 53.5/46.5 per cent, front to rear. On the inside, a deluxe steering wheel and front buckets were upscale options.

Introductory colors for the Maverick Grabber were: Grabber Yellow, Grabber Green, Grabber Blue, Bright Yellow and Thanks Vermillion. For '71 MY Freudian Gilt, Anti-Establishmint, Original Cinnamon and Hulla Blue were added. Substance for the whole shebang could come from Ford's F code 302 V8, which arrived in Maverick for 1971. This was the single exhaust, 210bhp (gross), two-barrel 302. It could be teamed with a three-speed manual or three-speed Select Shift/Cruise-O-Matic. Either way, the shifter came on the tree, unless optioned otherwise.

Maverick's tight design packaging left little room for duals, or even a larger diameter single system, but not to worry. The 'Now Generation' really dug swinging Maverick Grabber, to the tune of 38,963 '71 MY sales. Ford's ad for the '71 Grabber rightly said " ... and a little more jazz." With the 302 V8, there most certainly was. A revised standard equipment list implied: faux dual dome hood, front grille driving lamps, and an off-center Maverick grille-located nameplate badge with red shadow effect. Maverick Grabber's '70 1/2 equipment

remained intact, plus deluxe steering wheel and buckets continued as options. Striping, decals and contrast paint stayed black. However, there were now some engineering upgrades. For one, the long promised D70-14 tires on 14 x 6in steel rims. This item was originally $98.90, and brought benefits for braking and visuals, plus handling naturally. Also of importance, Maverick's handling kit had arrived as a $12 option. With a Mustang GT sized 0.85in front swaybar, stiffer springs and revalved shocks, it was money well spent.

Wire diameter of the front coils was increased, with spring rate up from 255lb-in to 280lb-in. The asymmetrical rear leaf rate, went up from 77 to 120lb-in. At this time, handling kits, or HD suspension, were just about the best domestic car option going. Weight distribution with the 302 V8 became 56.8/43.2 per cent front to rear. The V8 saw Maverick brakes upgraded. The four-wheel drums were now 10in for all Maverick 302s, not just Grabber. Maverick 250s got these stoppers, too, when optioned with D70-14 tires.

In spite of the promises, Maverick's '71 MY axle ratio choices alternated between 2.79 and 3.00, depending on engine, transmission and whether Select-Aire factory a/c was present. The bottom line was, if you wanted your Maverick 302 with 3.00 rear gears, you had to specify a/c. Choosing a/c with any engine would bring the 3.00 rear axle. From 1972 to 1976, this was Maverick's sole axle choice.

Cal Tracstraction bars and four-leaf rear springs aid road bite. So do Magnum 500 rims, sized 15 x 7in front and 15 x 8in on the back, shod with Cooper Cobra tires, sized a respective 235/60 front and 255/60 rearwards. Easy Performance sequential LED tail-lights are hard to miss. (Courtesy Nick Dominick)

What kind of scat did a Maverick 302 produce? Zero to sixty in around 9 seconds, and mid-16s in the quarter. As expected, somewhere between AMC's Gremlin X 258 and Nova SS 350.

Grabber's progress

Maverick's size put it with the Gremlin, as much as anything. In 1971, Maverick Grabber 302 trumped Gremlin X 258. However, in 1972 the new Gremlin X 304 V8's 8.5-second 0-60mph time beat out the Grabber V8. Fewer people cared by this stage, but there were plenty of nervous MGBs and BMW 2002s around. Even Datsun 240Zs weren't invincible! With Maverick, the sky was the limit concerning the 302's build-up potential. Big cam,

This 1972 Maverick Grabber was originally bought new for $3008 from Treadwell Ford of Mobile, Alabama. (Courtesy Shawn Simpson)

porting and polishing milled heads, plus higher comp pistons, forced induction and even nitrous. Fuel-injection from an '80s Foxstang even. That said, in Maverick's era, smog law was getting pretty ornery.

1972 saw compression ratios drop industry wide, for no lead gas. For Maverick's 302 that implied a descent from 9.0 to 8.5:1, and a 143bhp net horsepower rating. Emissions tightened again for 1973. Compression ratio fell to 8.0:1, with a commensurate decline in the pony tally to 140bhp. By the automotive day of reckoning that was 1975, the 302's CR was still 8.0:1, but 302-powered Fords like Maverick and Mustang II were down to 129bhp. Well, at least the paint and tape got cheerier. By 1972, sidestripe, decal and decorative color choices had expanded to four. No longer just Model T black.

1972 also witnessed Maverick 250s and 302s receive a stronger five-lug rim. By '74 MY, all Mavericks got the five-lug design. It was something absent on Foxstangs for many a year. By 1973, the Grabber's Dual Dome hood was no longer. That said, the Maverick's handling kit became standard on Grabber. Radial tires and forged, not cast, aluminum *Starsky & Hutch* slot rims arrived as options. An also optional Sound Package carried sound deadening. It was standard with the LDO package, which also got Maverick's handling pack. A revised standard vinyl bench seat rounded out the changes.

In 1973 model year, testers were still impressed how well the Capri's 2600 V6 revved out, in spite of smog law. However, buyers were increasingly interested in Maverick LDO, but not Grabber. 1973 Mavericks had safety door beams standard, plus environmental and safety aspects were more and more on people's minds. So, Grabber sales fell to 35,347 in 1972 and 32,350 in 1973. For '73 MY, Grabber's hood tape decoration was revised to match the new flat hood pressing. Side stripes and valence trimming were changed, too.

On the subject of Grabber getting a standard handling kit in 1973, it may have been prompted by the heavier 1973 5mph front impact bumpers, necessitated by the feds. In 1974, even more substantial 5mph impact bumpers were fitted, front and rear by law. Then, too, it may also have been a final marketing gambit in the Maverick versus Beetle rivalry. In 1973, VW released the limited edition Sports Bug, with paint, tape, sports seats, firmer suspension and radials. The Sports Bug seemed to

By 1972, the stock Maverick 302 V8 was down to 8.5:1 CR and 143 net horses. However, this 5.0 V8 roller motor, with mild cam and performance helpers, makes more than double that! (Courtesy Shawn Simpson)

Some magazines subsequently observed that the Maverick's early parcel shelf was more useful than its later glovebox! (Courtesy Shawn Simpson)

fix the Bug's oversteering tendencies of yore. All that was missing was the 1835cc flat-four, so beloved by the aftermarket. Reminiscent of AK Miller's Maverick Boss 200, why didn't automakers build cars like this? The consensus was that Ford and VW already sold all the Mavericks and Bugs they wanted. Mr and Mrs Mainstream didn't need a hotrod.

As occurred with Maverick LDO, there was some decontenting of Grabber towards the end. 1974 saw the deletion of the rear spoiler, countered by the first-time availability of a front disk brake option for the Maverick. Like the glovebox that replaced the parcel tray in 1973, front disks had been a long time coming. Basically waiting for the original Mustang to bow out, meaning Maverick no longer had to be held back.

Note also that North American Beetles stayed with four-wheel drums to the end. This was another reason for Maverick remaining with four-wheel drums for so long. Ford engineers adapted the Mustang II's front brake calipers and master cylinder for Maverick's front disk application. In Grabber's final model year of 1975, a power front disk option was introduced for all Mavericks.

In 1974 and 1975, a respective 23,502 and 8473 Maverick Grabber coupes rolled off the line. The 1975s featured Mini Magnum 500 styled stamped steel 14in rims, shod with raised white letter radials and decorated with trim rings. Those tires were all the rage, as the Grabber's standard

hubcap, WSW tire and trim ring combo of 1970-74 faded out. As a cosmetic package, Maverick Grabber was replaced with the Maverick Stallion for '76 MY. Grabber's sales had been cannibalized in 1975 by the arrival of the Mustang II Mach I V8. The concept of a similar car that did the same job in a smaller size and price class appealed to stagflation enduring, post-fuel crisis buyers.

A genuine Maverick Grabber can be discerned by the third and fourth digits of the car's VIN. A regular coupe would have 91, but a Grabber would sign in with 93. Similarly, with so many V8 swaps afoot, an authentic Maverick V8 requires an 'F' as the VIN's fifth digit. In addition, all Maverick V8s of North American origin had an 8in differential. This unit proved sufficient for handling the F code 302 V8. [32]

Indeed, whether it was Falcon, Comet, Maverick or Mustang II, the conversion to V8 power was accomplished by a team of Ford engineers, considering space, body durability, suspension tuning, braking, etc, to a degree the individual or even dealership would struggle with. That's why the sage advice is always to start out with a V8-engined car, if that's your engine performance route of choice. It's easier to hotrod a Maverick 6, or Maverick V8, than to put a V8 into a six-cylinder car.

The Maverick Grabber V8 never got a four-speed. Once again, it was Ford trying to protect Mustang sales, openly stating early on that it suspected even a V8 option would interfere with Maverick's economy car mission. And although some FoMoCo dealerships tended to do 'specials,' for the most

Ford's familiar C4 three-speed automatic was beefed up to cope with this coupe's hi-po 5.0 V8. Four-wheel disks respond to the brake pedal. (Courtesy Shawn Simpson)

The factory interior has been complemented by a billet steering wheel, aftermarket auxiliary gauges, Grabber Green color-matched trim and custom seat covers. (Courtesy Shawn Simpson)

part it was Lincoln-Mercury outlets focusing on the Comet. However, there was one exception ... Hub Ford's Maverick 'El Toro!' Visit Hub Ford and say ole! For El Toro! was the real thing ... no bull.

With El Toro!, Hub Ford hoped to steer buyers its way, with a dark blue '71 Grabber coupe decorated with black stripes, interior logos and special wheels. In addition, the dealership even engineered authentic duals for its El Toro! As an historical legacy, the Maverick Grabber hailed from the time of the muscle car, pony car era when imaginative nameplates ruled. GTO Judge, Swinger, Boss, Mach I, AMX and Road Runner. Yes, Grabber was the sporty version that every volume-selling model range had to have. From a relaxed, care-free time when a performance machine had to be a coupe, that's Grabber!

Maverick's wide world of options

Maverick's interior never ventured far from its humble origins. Even Maverick Grabber lacked special instrumentation, or special anything beyond deluxe steering wheel and bucket seat options. Observing Ford's 1971 price guide, a second printing January 1971 edition confirms what buyers got, or didn't get, with their Maverick and/or Grabber.

When the press first saw Maverick, it judged it to be pricier than small imports, but with generally cheaper options. Now in '71 MY, Maverick prices and options were on the rise. Forget about that sub 2 grand bargain basement base price. The cheapest

Maverick, a two-door job, retailed for $2175 list, with the four-door $2235. The price guide rounded prices to the nearest dollar. Grabber was now a distinct model, costing $2354, suggesting Grabber content totaled $179.

This Grabber surcharge seemed equal to that creating Mercury's 1971 Comet GT cousin: $178.80 to be precise. The price guide seemed to suggest that the Grabber came with the 200cu in six standard. However, the Comet dealer album said Comet GT came with the 170cu in six. Even so, it seems both started with the 170 cube Thriftpower motor. Tighter emissions for 1971 meant said 170cu in six was down to 100 gross ponies, and the $39 optional 200cu in six was on 115bhp, with the $79 250 cube six making 145 horses. The 302 V8's Maverick debut price was $169. In common with domestic rivals, the popularity of the V8 option was because it felt so much livelier than the sixes. This was probably because Detroit set up its sixes as torque-biased work horses, purely for economy, truck and commercial applications.

A floor shifter now set one back 25 bucks, and the Cruise-O-Matic three-speed auto was $183, and worth it for flexibility, convenience, economy and performance. Just a swell choice all around, compared to the three-speed manual. The $26 Consolette could only be had sans floor shifter, and was necessary for the $15 electric clock option. Select-Aire factory a/c was the Maverick's single priciest option at $374. A Convenience Group

The factory Grabber Green exterior is matched by factory stripes and a rear spoiler. Ridler rims and 8in Positraction rear with 3.50 gears complete the picture. (Courtesy Shawn Simpson)

The Maverick and Comet would do good business, during the fuel crisis demand for thriftier, smaller rides. (Courtesy Shawn Simpson)

The Grabber Green exterior, Dual Dome hood and striping are all factory original. However, the front spoiler is a custom item. (Courtesy Shawn Simpson)

A 1973 Grabber coupe at the Sterling Ford Ottawa Car Show. By '73 MY, Grabber gained 5mph front bumpers and standard HD suspension, but lost the 1971-72 Dual Dome hood. (Courtesy Bull-Doser)

brought cigar lighter, left hand side remote control color-keyed racing mirror, and interior day/night mirror, all for $18. A rear window defogger was $28.

Full tint was $51 on normal Mavericks, but only $37 on Grabbers and those with the Accent Group. This ensemble brought bright window frames/ drip moldings, color-keyed carpeting and wheel covers, for $52. However, it couldn't be had on the Grabber. Essential power steering was $95 in '71 MY, and High-Back Buckets were $101. The latter was always a Grabber option. They weren't available on Maverick four-doors, or cars with plain vinyl trim. The fancy buckets came with deluxe door trim cards, and could be had with deluxe woven vinyl or Blazer Stripe Cloth/vinyl trim. The Tu-Tone Roof paint option was $28, and a Protection Group delivered front and rear bumper guards, plus vinyl insert bodyside moldings for $48.

The Protection Group wasn't optionable on a Grabber. 6.45-14 WSW and B78-14 BSW tires were both $29. The latter was mandatory on four-door sedans with factory a/c, and on any V8-powered car. B78-14 WSW tires cost 58 bucks, with the top D70-14 bias-belted Firestone Wide Ovals retailing for $88. Plain vinyl trim was an $18 option, and standard on the Grabber. The fancy Trim Option interior was $34 on Grabber, but $52 on other

Mavericks. Naturally some options clashed with Grabber, or were cheaper on the sporty coupe, since it already came with some items standard. The optional 3.00 rear axle was 12 bucks, and HD 55 amp battery cost $14. This last item was standard on 200 cube Mavericks with Select-Aire.

An oft-made comment concerning import and domestic cars of the era, was that you very rarely saw a base model. Dealers frequently ordered a car with some options, either because those were the popular items people wanted, or to increase the sale mark up. In addition, you didn't always get what you expected with a Grabber, Camaro Z28 and such. Some items believed standard, were actually options. One item that did come standard on Maverick V8s was the kind of scat commensurate with a late '70s Trans Am W72 400.

Although Maverick Grabber V8 appeared meek in 1971, its acceleration was equal to a non-ringer, disco era Trans Am and other coupes of the medallion malaise. Naturally, 1972 and later Maverick V8s got slower, as smog law and heavier bumpers reduced bang for buck. It was an industry wide problem. A 1971 Maverick V8, would eventually match the acceleration of a 1981 North American Porsche 928 V8 automatic. Now that's progress!

CHAPTER
Five
Mercury's Comet

A new small luxury car

In a 1959 print ad, Mercury's marketing manager, a Mr J. Emmet Judge, presented the many virtues of the '59 full-size Merc. Solid engineering, quality and economy ... Yes, Mr Judge, a most trustworthy fellow with his picture in the ad, made reference to Mercury's selective air intake system. Hot underhood air to get your engine warmed up faster, switching to a cool intake stream when off-choke. The result was superior gas mileage. In the late '50s recession, even a medium price brand like Mercury had to be frugal.

It didn't stop there, as Mercury, the winged messenger of the gods, had more. Apart from the economy claim, and reminder to watch *The Ed Sullivan Show* on a local TV station affiliate, a new small luxury car was in the works. Ford would soon be a leader in the domestic car game, along with the Falcon. However, according to *Road & Track*'s April 1960 issue, long before the new Falcon was in production, a deluxe version of this Ford compact was being tooled up. The car was Mercury's new Comet, released four months after Falcon, and closely related.

In basic engineering they were twins under the skin. The difference lay in wheelbase, sheetmetal, trim and standard equipment. Falcon sat on a 109.5in wheelbase, but Comet raised the stakes to 114.5in. At the time, 110in was regarded as

Mercury Marketing Manager J Emmet Judge outlined Mercury's engineering quality and selective heated air intake system in 1959. The latter was a gas mileage saver, directed at recessionary times. (Courtesy Ford Motor Co)

the compact limit. So, as Ford would later do with Maverick, it created an introductory car for the pending intermediate class, or 'kingsize compact' if you will. The coming machine was the slightly larger 1962 Ford Fairlane. The Comet came with fresh new front and rear styling, along with new quarter roof sections.

Critics recognized a badge engineering job when they saw one, akin to British concerns BMC and Rootes Group. However, there was solid value with Comet. For a mere $85 over the Falcon, Comet buyers received a veritable shopping list of useful and desired standard equipment. At the time, dual horns and sunvisors, four headlamps, front and rear armrests, deluxe steering wheel/hornring, cigar lighter, courtesy lights, automatic choke, vinyl headliner and more chrome got the public's vote. The strategy of lots of standard equipment, at a competitive price would be used by Japanese automakers a decade hence. Mercury's 24/24 warranty spelt quality, and that was also picked up by later imports.

Styling, a make or break subject in this era, worked to Comet's advantage. The distinctive, laying-down tailfins struck a positive chord, both with buyers and magazines. *Mechanix Illustrated*'s Uncle Tom McCahill was an admirer, especially of the Thunderbirdesque roofline. In pre-Mustang days – some would ask were there ever such times? – the T-Bird association added a touch of class. Generally, the 1960 Comet looked like more than the money it cost, and more car than Falcon. Or, FoMoCo had successfully differentiated the Falcon and Comet in the public's eyes.

Comet's wheelbase increase was kinda functional. Although it added length aft of the rear passenger area, so there was no extra interior space, Comet's ride comfort and luggage capacity were boosted over Falcon. That said, with an extra 93lb to haul, Comet was slower and thirstier than an equivalent-engined Falcon. This was in spite of 3.56 versus 3.10 rear gears.

For figures, *Motor Life* found that a two-speed automatic Comet 144 tested out 9 seconds slower to 60 than Falcon! But no matter, Comet sold around 28,500 units during the first six weeks alone, and nearly 183,000 in 1964. The public had spoken, and the customer is always right. This original Comet involved Ford innovations and elements, the kind seen on subsequent Maverick and its subcompact Comet counterpart. Ford had pioneered unibody construction in America with the 1935 Lincoln Zephyr. Falcon/Comet's Thriftpower six was designed with simplicity, low cost and weight in mind.

The six straight shooter weighed a mere 357lb, sans flywheel. This was even though only its pistons were aluminum. The cast crankshaft with cored holes saved weight. Compared to Ford's full-size 223cu in base six, the 144 motor had 122 fewer parts. When the stroker 170cu in Thriftpower arrived for Comet in '61 MY, it was only 2 per cent heavier than the 144 cube edition. Mercury was mighty glad of Comet's coming during the recessionary slowdown. It brought new buyers into Mercury showrooms, and allowed salesmen to upsell prospects to a large Mercury. In 1960 the Comet was sold by Mercury, but it wasn't branded as such until 1961. However, there was another new Mercury that wasn't doing so well.

After Ford introduced its kingsize compact, the Fairlane, a Mercury counterpart called Meteor tagged along for the ride. Like Falcon to Comet, Meteor was Fairlane in slightly upscale threads, and toted a longer wheelbase. Meteor lasted but two model years. By 1964 it was gone, and *Popular Mechanics*, for one, expressed its disappointment concerning Meteor's short life. The journal felt not enough had been done with the concept. There had been a limited sales effort, with no wagons, hardtops or convertibles. Then, too, Meteor sat in showrooms with what *Popular Mechanics* described as its "precocious little brother," Comet. [33]

Comet had hardtops, wagons and convertibles.

The 1963½ Mercury Comet S-22 V8 was a balanced sporty sedan. It marked the early days of the high-performance car game. (Courtesy Marc Cranswick)

It looked a lot like Meteor, and was almost as much car, but for hundreds less. More than that, while Comet was doing the showroom shuffle, it didn't have a V8. Comet didn't receive a V8, until Meteor was practically out the door! If a potential customer arrived at a Mercury dealership and was a little snug in the pocket, it was the easiest thing in the world for Sammy Salesman to move him towards Comet. A more affluent prospect would be ushered towards the full-size Mercury. That left poor Meteor as piggy in the middle, and that was a shame. Meteor possessed a V8 option, the new Windsor small block no less. *Popular Mechanics* felt that the Meteor was the ideal, all-purpose, refined family car of moderate size and great value.

The press thought it had a handle on Comet. *Popular Mechanics* said, "When Comet first hit the market back in 1960 it was a stretchout, slightly styled up version of Falcon." [34] *Road & Track* added its view in January 1961, "... the Comet offers that extra something that many people seem to want and are willing to pay for." That something didn't seem to be acceleration or gas mileage. In both respects Falcon trumped the heavier Comet. Indeed, when *Motor Trend* tried three Mercs in May 1962, the gas mileage penalty of an overworked small engine became apparent.

Motor Trend's Comet was a sporty S-22 number, with 170 motor and two-speed Ford-O-Matic, and ... a/c! The underdash a/c system on 1962-64 Comets resembled the Comfy Kit type made by the Texan company of the same name. In any case, this Comet S-22 had poorer cruising speed economy, than the large Mercury Monterey, with a 390 4bbl V8 and three-speed Cruise-O-Matic that the journal was simultaneously testing.

The Meteor 221 V8 on test also happened to have the two-speed Ford-O-Matic. In spite of the standard three-speed manual offering superior acceleration and economy, buyers seemed to gravitate to the Ford-O-Matic. So, that's what magazines often tested. And, as many critics of the day noted, Detroit seemed to put the gearboxes with the most gears, only in powerful, large-engined cars, that could have gotten by on less.

So, six-cylinder Comets were mostly stuck with a two-speed slushbox, and buyers didn't seem to mind. They did seem to care about smaller size and price, though, which was probably why they sided with Comet and not Meteor. Quality also counted, a known Mercury trait. The Comet carried a 24,000-

mile/two-year warranty. It was the kind of assurance that VW offered on the Beetle, but few others did. And handling mattered. On a rough road course, *Motor Trend*'s three Mercs steadfastly refused to bottom out, and displayed minimal roll. Mercury suspension was judged firmer in 1962 than the Detroit norm.

Aside from carrying a lower price than larger size lines, the Comet brought style and sporty feel with its S-22 version. This bucket seat coupe equivalent to Falcon Sprint came with a $2282 sticker for '62 MY. Once again, it seemed to be just what the market ordered, or in the words of Ford Vice President and GM of Lincoln-Mercury Division Ben D Mills, "The Comet should attract even greater acceptance among sporty minded buyers while continuing to improve on low cost, dependable transportation." Things got sportier for '63 MY, by utilizing the Ford UK-sourced four-speed for the Thriftpower six. Then too, there was the Rotunda made tachometer kit. The sporty S-22 version was referred to by Ford as a luxury model. That aside, a Raytel two-way CB radio was optional.

Regardless of whether the public really wanted it, as far as Comet went, domestic compacts were muscling up with V8 power. For '63 MY the 144 was gone, and as a '63 half iteration, say hello to the Comet S-22 V8! In parallel with Ford's Falcon Sprint, small Fords could now enjoy the performance and refinement of the Windsor V8 that arrived with Fairlane for '62 MY. The version in question was the expected 260 cube, 164 horse 'Challenger' V8. It was no drop in job, Ford made sure such compacts could handle a V8.

Changes for performance and safety saw more metal being selectively added to the unibody, bigger 10in drum brakes, plus a truck-like rear axle. The Warner Gear four-speed cost $188, as opposed to the light duty 90 buck job used on sixes. The result was a stiffer, safer structure, where the additional power could be utilized. *Motor Trend*'s May '62 issue Comet S-22 automatic did 0-60mph in 22.2 seconds. The same journal tried the 63 ¹/₂ Comet S-22 V8 four-speed, shown in its August 1963 issue. This hardtop coupe slashed the 0-60mph sprint to 11.5 seconds! It was the start of the '60s performance era, but more importantly, Comet now had much safer overtaking capabilities.

Motor Trend's V8 Comet hauled down from 60mph in just 146ft. Stops were straight and true, quality brake linings kept fade at bay, and quality

from Ford's Pico Rivera, Californian factory was excellent. Comet S-22 V8 was a complete package. *Motor Trend* pronounced it a real man's car, and an enjoyable one at that. For 1964 the improvements kept coming. When Ford released a V8 edition, related improvements in body, chassis etc were given to non-V8 versions the next year, or soon. This happened with Maverick and Mustang II in the '70s. 1964 Comets carried a mini Continental look, and genuine, ever so solid, big car feel.

With the demise of the Mercury Meteor, Comet got an upscale variant called Caliente. Appropriately, a hot four-barrel 289 Windsor V8 could now be optioned. To complement this motor, try Mercury's new three-speed Merc-O-Matic. It was the automatic choice for flexibility and performance. However, for all the changes since 1960, Comet was no bigger. It was still a 195in long family car, sitting on a 114.5in wheelbase. That is, it got better, without getting bigger. The market seemed to reward this move. What's more, Comet proved its worth in racing. The '63 Comet did a 100,000 mile endurance race at Daytona. In the process, Comet broke over 100 world endurance records. 1964 Comets even ventured into the East African Rally.

Comet – the muscle car

At this point, circumstances overtook the successful Comet. Ford's intermediates were having some trouble. The Meteor hadn't been a sales hit, and Fairlane was under pressure from the competitive corporate might of GM's four divisions. Falcon had a new, sort of companion model, called Mustang. This removed the need for Comet to help Falcon, and the Mercury was reassigned to complement Ford's Fairlane. It was a move that would take the nameplate into bigger circles. This included the muscle car wars.

Mercury had reached number six in the 1961 sales race. It was also observed that the 1960-65 Comet was sized equally to what had been called 'The Right Size Ford.' That is, Ford's 1949 family sedan. Industry experts felt that if Ford and others had refined that kind of moderate machine, there would have been no need to head off the imports at the pass with the 1960 compacts. Comet retained its restrained 195in length and 114.5in wheelbase dimensions for one more year, 1965. That year, the new Comet Cyclone went for the sporty side of the street, with standard buckets, tach, console and 289 V8.

For 1965, Ford switched from Warner Gear to its own Ford-built box. The Cyclone could have the K code 289 V8 and a scooped aluminum hood, which was an industry first. Come 1966, and Comet sized up to the true intermediate class as Fairlane's partner in crime. The newest sedan was 203in long, with the new Comet Cyclone GT as the latest member of the shoehorn supercar set. Underhood lay a FE series 390 cube four-barrel 335 horse hi-po V8. As a cousin of the Fairlane GT/GTA, it was sub 15-second $^1/_4$-miles all the way.

It seemed the economy sector, for domestics at any rate, was dead. Now the Mercury buyer wanted luxury and performance. It was a new world, in which only AMC and Cadillac weren't in the supercar game. Yes, it seemed like Pop Grundig had swapped Mobil Economy Runs for the Chrondek Christmas tree! Then, too, in this latest performance scene, buyers craved hardware and looks. Back in the Flathead V8 days, ol' Mercury was a real mover and shaker. Plus, the early muscle car years saw street racers seeking an out-of-the-box $^1/_4$-mile showroom job. Now, you had to have scoops, stripes, vanity mirror and deluxe interior, which weren't cheap.

The new 1966 Comet Cyclone, manual or automatic, made one eligible for *C/D* stock drag racing under NHRA and AHRA rules. For this task you might have wanted, an "off the menu" rear end. Participating dealers could supply same, up to a mountain master '5.67' ratio. Even American Motors moved from Rambler to Scrambler, and a 1970 Rebel Machine. With these winds of change, quality seemed to suffer. The '65s were Fort Knox solid, but *Car Life* found the '66 Comet and other contemporary makes and models displayed poor panel fit.

Even the Comet name was getting de-emphasized, to use industry jargon. In Mercury's 1967 range, only the 202 series entry level sedan and Voyager wagon held onto the Comet prefix. Comet was associated with economy overtones, and marketing wanted buyers to think upscale and racy when handing over the foldin' stuff – individuals like Lincoln-Mercury's Ralph Peters, who was in charge of the product planning staff. The performance market was where the action was at. Mercury would now sell a ride to let all those cool cats scat!

In this Total Performance era, even the rubber you were burning got better. In 1968 Goodyear

By 1966, Comet had sized up to a full intermediate. The 335 horse Comet Cyclone GT was Mercury's first foray into the supercar ranks. (Courtesy *Motor Trend*)

MERCURY COUGAR

American. (Cougars to be raced will be powered by a specially prepared 289-cubic-inch V8 engine.) Following are specifications of the Cougar Group 2 from which the special version derives. Body style: two-door hardtop. Engine: Mercury overhead valve V8. Bore & stroke: 4.00" x 2.87". Displacement: 289 cu. in. Compression ratio: 10.5 to 1. Brake horsepower: 341 @ 5800 rpm. Torque: 300 lbs.-ft. @ 4000 rpm. Carburetors: two 4-barrel. Transmission: 4-speed synchromesh. Suspension: independent coil, front; leaf, rear. Brakes: double-caliper, vented disc, front; drum, rear. Wheelbase: 111". Overall length: 190.3". Curb weight: 3223 lbs.

The sporty Mercury Cougar at Daytona in 1967. Mercury often name-dropped Cougar in ads, to lend a youthful element to the brand. (Courtesy Ford Motor Co)

brought out its Polyglas tires, seen on so many pony and muscle cars of the day. These were bias-belted jobs with a fiberglass belt under the tread, and were supposed to give the best of bias-belted and radial tire properties. For '68, Caliente's place had been supplanted by the new Montego name. That year, buyers were getting acquainted with fastback styling,

the new 302 Windsor and wild 427 V8. The 427 proved more elusive than the Scarlett Pimpernel. For 1969, the more budget friendly Cyclone Cobra Jet 428 lived up to Mercury's latest slogan: "Mercury's Got It!" And boy, did it ever.

Comet could have it, too. It was possible to option the 428 Cobra Jet V8 in the sole remaining Comet – namely, a basic two-door hardtop. That same fate would befall Falcon in 1970, with such nameplates finishing as stripper muscle cars should the buyer have desired. Not a bad way to go. This was the final curtain call for Comet as Mercury's intermediate, but the start of Ford's new Thriftpower 250 cube in-line six. It had seven main bearings and could be built up for lower classes of drag racing: a cost effective way to emulate heroes Dyno Don Nicholson and Fast Eddie Schartman. 1969 also witnessed a new Ram Air hoodscoop.

In August 1968's issue of *Motor Trend*, Eric Dahlquist had the following to say of Cyclone Cobra Jet 428: "It's a club Mercury is going to use to beat into oblivion the idea that their cars were ever considered 'stones.'" There had indeed been a disconnect between FoMoCo's successful race cars, and the humble machines sold in showrooms. Ford fans wanting more would have said too humble. No longer, for now if one could meet the payments and insurance premiums, then there was no need to settle for a paper tiger. The Cyclone Cobra Jet 428 was judged somewhat of a bargain, at a mere $3700.

The 1969 Mercury Cyclone 428 Cobra Jet was as serious as it got with contemporary musclecars. (Courtesy Roger Pirtle)

Where did that thrifty 1960 Comet 144 go? Probably the same place as good gas mileage. *Supercars* magazine said, "Indeed, the hot Cyclone only came with the hot 428 V8 motor, and a respective town and turnpike gas mileage rating of 7 and 11mpg!" Before the fuel crisis, this wasn't a big deal, but could be annoying. The tank would empty fast, and required mandatory premium gas *every* time it did. And things got even bigger for 1970.

Ford, as ever, had been watching the market closely, and figured intermediates were the future. A great intermediate would take conquest sales from full-size cars, which fewer and fewer buyers wanted anyway. So it was that the new 1970 Torino Brougham and Mercury Montego MX Brougham made a case that anything larger was superfluous. All the luxury trimmings and a 429 V8 option delivered a verdict in favor of intermediate or mid-size. Look past the meek 302 two-barrel or sensible 300-horse Cleveland 351 4bbl; it was the 429 or nothing. With this big block in performance applications, there was a choice of three: standard, Ram Air or Ram Air with solid lifter cam plus Drag Pak. The last carried a rear end so tight, highway usage was liable to turn you deaf!

Road Test sampled a "mild" Cyclone GT in March 1970, with Ram Air 429 and hydraulic lifters. It made an almost practical 375bhp. Leaving the Select Shift automatic to do its thing, a 14.61-second pass at 99.22mph was forthcoming, once wheelspin of biblical proportions was overcome. However, here was an attractive 4000lb, stiffly sprung, live-axled bolide. It had 60/40 per cent weight distribution, so *Road Test* discerned much understeer. The test staff also experienced tremendous heat soak through the firewall from the 429 V8 four-barrel. So much so, you almost needed to open all windows. Vent wings were gone by the end of 1967.

Cyclone GT was a hedonistic joy, but Mercury and Ford had other concerns. The Torino was outselling its Mercury counterpart three to one. *Car and Track*'s Bud Lindemann observed the '70 Cycone GT on TV, and said of the Mercury versions: "They're quieter, give a better ride and invariably offer more costly trim both inside and out, but the buying public hasn't caught on to the bargain yet." Indeed, *Car Life* in its July 1968 Cyclone 428 CJ report said '68 Fords were prone to rattles, but not Mercs.

In addition, on the 1970 Cyclone that *Car and Track* tested, Mercury's special touches ran to extra sound deadening and rubber cushioned torque boxes. Ford couldn't include such items on its lower priced equivalent versions. In the same respect, such quality differences were apparent between Ford Maverick and its Comet cousin. Naturally, the Maverick handsomely outsold the upscale, subcompact Comet.

Other differences between the Fords and Mercs, involved Mercury not using contemporary 'play on name' descriptions, concerning exterior paint colors. They were too mature for that at Lincoln-Mercury. However, as *Car and Track* explained, Mercury did provide value for money. Lindemann introduced a base-engined Cyclone GT 351 two-barrel, with three-speed slushbox and standard suspension. This coupe cost $3646 as a base sticker price. Zero to sixty arrived in 9.2 seconds, and braking was none too good, given the optional front power disks fitted. *Car and Track* recommended Mercury's Cross Country Ride package of HD suspension as essential to curb understeer.

In the end, Bud Lindemann had this to say on Cyclone GT 351: "a little on the docile side, but a fair performer." He promised a report on the 429 edition, for those that liked things more violent. He was right, too. Mercury had the right stuff, for a price. In 1971, the final year for the hi-po big blocks, you could order a Cyclone Spoiler, with spoilers and NASCAR-oriented 429 with aluminum heads, plus shaker scoop. FoMoCo held onto high compression performance motors into 1971. GM got ready for the comp drop early.

And that was it. As quickly as the muscle cars had come, with attendant public interest, they were gone. A victim of inflation, federal smog and safety laws, a weary public that had always preferred comfort over speed. So, with all this and a tidal wave of small imports, too, it was high time Mercury brought back that small luxury car that used to sell so well. It was time to welcome back the Mercury Comet to dealerships. This time it was a subcompact relation of Ford's Maverick, and it happened for 1971 model year.

The new subcompact Comet

Lincoln-Mercury was a subdivision of the Ford Motor Company. As such, by 1970, it utilized the same engines, running gear and major components from Ford. Although in some cases, major items like the 460 V8 inserted into Continental Mark III were created for high-end L-M models to begin with. [35]

Mercury: better ideas make better cars.

Better Sports-Specialty cars . . .
Cougar

Better Intermediate cars . . .
Cyclone / Montego

Better Standard-size cars . . .
Marquis / Monterey

Better Small cars . . .
Comet

MERCURY
LINCOLN

With Cougar seemingly getting bigger by the minute, there was definitely space for Comet as Mercury's new small car for 1971. (Courtesy Ford Motor Co)

Moving into the '70s and '80s, specialized divisions of the Big Three had a harder time distinguishing their wares. The styling and engineering freedoms of yore were budget constrained, due to economies of scale and general cost minimization. However, even into the shared era, Lincoln-Mercury was still known for good quality and design. Certainly the Mercury Montego and Cyclones had displayed desirable refinements compared to their Ford brethren. And the new Comet would do more of this good stuff.

Mercury was known for copious chrome and quality. These elements would figure on the new Comet, and like that compact '60 MY iteration, L-M was pursuing the niche of the small, upscale cars, possessing moderation in all aspects. Obviously styling differences between Maverick and Comet, involved the latter's forward thrusting, power dome hood and horizontal bar grille. Rearwards the tail panel featured Montegoesque tail-lights with crosshair lenses. Due to the new Comet's narrow nature, there were four tail-lights, not the six of its larger intermediate cousin.

Apart from the Lincoln-like and Montego-matching styling elements, it was quickly noticeable that Comet was a tad classier than Maverick. More chrome on the outside, and even base trimmed versions had an interior that said Mercury, not Ford. For all this, the Comet was basically a Maverick in general styling and engineering. This implied two and four-door sedans, with a four-bearing, 100-pony, Thriftpower 170 cube I6 to get the coupe and four-door rolling. As a range it was a formal '71 MY release, but *Car and Driver* took an early gander in its 1970 October issue, and provided some pre-release info.

Car and Driver said Mercury got an exclusive on the 302 V8, as opposed to Ford with its Maverick. The earliness of this statement is shown by the journal quoting the '70 MY power outputs concerning the 170 I6 and 302 V8, as 105 and 220bhp gross respectively. In reality, the Maverick and Comet ranges gained V8s for '71 MY. However, Mercury did have an exclusive on that 302 until mid '71 MY. *Motor Trend*'s 1971 Buyer's Guide said 1971 prices were pending fall labor negotiations with the UAW.

Base seating for Comet involved the expected vinyl and cloth trimmed bench. It had a 5in range of adjustment on ball-bearing seat tracks. However, more lavish Comets were more befitting of the Mercury brand. More so than with Maverick, there was interest as to whether a Comet four-door sedan

Comet takes the best small car ideas: like easy handling. Great gas mileage. Easy maintenance. And the low price. Then adds big car styling without skimping on luxury. Like the bold powerdome hood. Colour-keyed carpeting. Cloth-and-vinyl upholstery. And lots of room, even in the 2-door Comet. The slightly longer 4-door Comet seats 5 in comfort with no difficulty at all. Gas mileage? Great; with either the potent 302 V-8 or any of the three thrifty Sixes. 3-speed

Comet
Mighty small, mighty nice.

Select-Shift automatic transmission is optional. There's even a Comet GT! Mercury Comet: a great small car with big ideas.
Prices from $2,508 F.O.B. Oakville.

Foreground: Comet 4-door sedan. Upper left: Comet 2-door sedan. Upper right: Comet GT Certain items shown on these two pages are optional.

From your Mercury dealer.

The 1971 Mercury Comet range on show. Compared to Maverick, it was all about being upscale, and an alternative to Toyota Corona, Audi 100LS, and Torino Brougham, even. (Courtesy Ford Motor Co)

could take on upscale European imports, as well as serve as an alternative to lure former full-size domestic sedan luxury buyers looking to downsize. Concerning those anticipated 1971 prices, a Comet coupe V8 was $2387, whereas a Maverick V8 coupe was $2373, including the necessary B78-14 BSWs.

Thoughts of a small, luxury sedan turned to the four-door Comet sized 188.6in/70.6in/53.1in for length, width and height. This kind of machine was tried by *Car and Driver*, and reported on in its July 1972 issue. It was a V8-powered, automatic sedan with a/c. The automatic and factory a/c cost $177.96 and $359.59 respectively. Power steering was included at $92.45, as well as the $11.55 handling pack. Staggered shocks had arrived on Mavericks and Comets for '71 MY, and if such small cars reached a certain weight when optioned, the larger 10in cast iron drums, 2.2in wide at the front and 1.8in rearward, would replace stock 9in units. These larger brakes were flared and finned at the front.

For control and driving pleasure, the handling pack was considered essential. Front coils were 19 per cent stiffer, there was an oversize 0.850in front swaybar, with firmer rear shocks and 34 per cent stiffer rear leafs, too. This mechanical package brought 14 x 6in rims. Indeed, creating the luxo Comet involved selecting the right options. The $151 Interior Group brought front reclining buckets. In common with so specified Mavericks, these involved 15 backrest positions, and 60 degrees of travel. They came from Ford Europe, and had dense foam in a broad cushion. Plush carpeting came along for the ride, as well as what Mercury called "Audi type" front armrest/door closing handles. It was an indication of Mercury's inspiration and aspirations for projected image.

Shagpile carpet graced the dashboard shelf, matching the carpet, and the $40.45 Consolette – a separate option – included electric clock. It was familiar to upscale Maverick owners. To achieve the refinement that luxury buyers expected, the Deluxe Sound Package consisted of more pads, absorbers and coatings than a stock Maverick or Comet could muster. Pads were double standard weight and size. There were more underhood pads, as well as in the trunk. Rubber isolators were employed under the front coils, complementing softer rear leaf bushings.

The result of all the additions was *Car and Driver* declaring its Comet to be the quietest car tested under full acceleration, up to 70mph. At 73 decibels

Down to 143bhp net on an 8.5:1 CR by '72 MY. It was still enough to light up the rear end of this Comet coupe V8! (Courtesy www.curbsideclassic.com)

it also cruised quieter at 70mph than the exalted Citroën SM. *C/D*'s test subject was also specified with the $240 Luxury Exterior Option, which was also considered essential. This brought Firestone DR78-14 steel belted radials, which came with a 40,000 mile guaranteed tread life. This really meant something, given the average American mileage was 20,000 miles. It seemed buyers were more enamored with the longer tire life, than the handling and road holding advantages that radials brought.

The Luxury Exterior Option also brought wide, full-length protective body side moldings, front and rear bumper guards, and color-keyed wheel covers. The last item was like that seen with the Maverick's LDO pack. With the aforementioned option groups, plus some additional piecemeal options, like $27.73 rear window defogger, *C/D*'s Comet V8 four-door cost $3689.70. The journal assembled some imported car comparison stats for the: 4.2 grand Audi 100LS, 12 grand Mercedes 280SEL 4.5 V8 and 4 grand Volvo 142E.

The Audi was the only front-wheel drive machine. The Comet and Mercedes were V8-powered automatics, with the Audi and Volvo as four-speed stick shift sedans. The Comet and Audi sported carburetors, whereas the Mercedes and Volvo were fuel injected. In the 1/4-mile the Comet tied with the Volvo on 17.2 seconds, the Mercedes was back on 17.9 seconds, and this left the Audi last with 18.6 seconds. Braking from 70mph saw the Volvo win with 188ft, next came Audi on 193ft and Comet with 196ft. Finally, the Mercedes halted after 210ft. Volvo and Mercedes came with four-wheel disk brakes, the Audi had disks front and drums rearwards.

Time to enter the 'Bronze Age' with 1973 Mercury Cougar and Comet coupes. This trim package majored on a bronze vinyl roof and Saddle Bronze paint ... or your choice of six other colors. (Courtesy Ford Motor Co)

Comet arrived with 10in drum brakes all around, as per Maverick V8. They were non-boosted, with no other option. As per Maverick, the standard Ford line was that there was no room underhood for a brake booster. Given Comet's four-wheel drums and weight, Ford concluded there was no need. Audi narrowly won the gas miser title, with a range of 20-24mpg. Next was Volvo on 21-23mpg. Mercedes supped 11-14mpg, leaving Comet looking thriftier with 11-18mpg. So, having a V8 automatic with some pep carried a gas mileage penalty. However, prior to the gas crunch, this was of smaller import than a car's reputation.

In North America, Audi had the worst name for owner problems. Mercedes was the most trouble-free, with Volvo not that far behind. Indeed, at this stage, Volvo's slogan was "The 11 year car." Ford possessed owner survey data proving Maverick and Comet were reliable cars. Of the models *C/D* tested, the Comet, Volvo and Mercedes V8 had excellent driveability, but not the Audi. Given stricter smog laws, it got more ornery by the second. Magazines did like to compare data on recently tested vehicles. However, in reality as *C/D* conceded, it's unlikely a Mercedes man back then would have visited an L-M dealership. Thus, Comet was best judged in absolute terms.

By contemporary standards, the 302 V8 imbued the Comet with a sense of urgency and refinement.

Car and Driver and Mercury product planners had sought the V8 option for Comet. Zero to sixty in 9.7 seconds, with the sedan hitting 42mph, 75mph and 103mph through the C4 automatic's gears. With 3.00:1 final drive, the Comet could reach peak power rpm in top gear. Brakes offered good modulation and fade resistance, but rear lock up and longer than ideal stopping distances were a concern. Ultimate handling brought understeer, but was generally secure. Ride on poor surfaces couldn't match the expensive imports, and those radials seemed to bring ride harshness. *Car and Driver* said L-M wasn't used to dealing with such a light, short wheelbase car, so further tuning may have yielded better results.

Like the 1949 Ford, the Comet seemed to be the right size car in contemporary luxury circles. The

This Comet ad was written by a woman.

Ford doesn't believe that you should talk to women any differently than you talk to men. But you know how it is when men write for women.

They tend to get cute.

And really, there are certain obvious things you should know about the Mercury Comet, and the many valid reasons why it's such a good buy in an economy car.

Without a decent engine, a compact has no soul. Comet lets you choose the kind of performance you want by giving you a multiple choice of engines and transmissions.

The Comet is easy to handle. I'm five foot two, and I find it no strain to maneuver.

It's built from the same kind of steel as the biggest Mercurys, so you feel secure about strength and durability.

And let's be honest. I care about my surroundings, and the Comet interior is super, with colour-keyed carpeting and great striped seats.

Those are bench seats, incidentally, so you can easily install an infant perch. (The carefully-researched Ford Tot-Guard is one accessory worth having. You can pick up literature at your Mercury dealers that explains why it's one of the experts' top choices in safety seats for children.)

I don't think car advertising should condescend to women. But I think cars should. And I think Comet does.

Comet. The compact car with better ideas.

MERCURY COMET

Certain items illustrated are optional at extra cost

With the rise of Women's Lib, Ford wrote this 1973 Canadian Comet ad from the little lady's perspective, and made mention of Ford's Tot-Guard child seat. (Courtesy Ford Motor Co)

Audi and Volvo were a tad over 180in long, and slightly under 70in wide. This placed Comet four-door slightly closer to the Audi and Volvo in size than the Mercedes. Many observers noted that the new Comet was sized how American intermediates used to be, but had almost the interior space of contemporary mid-size machines, which were much bigger on the outside. Comet four-door brought an invaluable 4.4in of extra rear legroom, versus its coupe counterpart. Indeed, all interior dimensions were mighty amenable.

Front headroom and legroom on the Comet four-door was 37.9in and 41.3in respectively, with rear legroom 36.7in. With size becoming a crucial buying magnet, the Comet was very comely. Although Mercury didn't name its colors fancifully, the deluxe 1972 paint costing $34.66 was denoted 'Glamour Paint.' It seemed like the sound labs, interior studios and fabric designers had pulled quite a number, on what was originally a simple machine. In July 1972, *C/D* described the Comet four-door as "... one of America's most pleasing sedans." The same year, *Motor Trend* added that Comet was "... a value much appreciated by a growing clientele." It couldn't match the Volvo's giant trunk, but in every other measure Comet was a sensible choice.

It seemed that Mercury's Comet four-door had regained the perfect middle ground, once occupied by the '60s Comet. A TV commercial showed one of the specially prepared '63 Comets at Daytona Speedway. Here, Comets had run for 100,000 miles, and the only thing they broke were endurance records. These records still stood at the time of

With the '74 Comet, you could enjoy the small size and luxury of a Mercedes 240D, minus the diesel racket! (Courtesy Ford Motor Co)

the 1973 commercial. A new '73 Comet pulled up alongside, and the ad voiceover said "Today we build a new kind of Mercury Comet. Smaller by almost a foot. Priced right down with the little imports. But we still build Comet to be tough."

The viewer witnessed Comet being subjected to a torture test on Ford's test track and proving grounds. The ad referred to a "solid unibody suit of armor," and concluded with: "Mercury Comet. It's one tough little car. Built better to last longer." And it was looking better still, thanks to 1973's Bronze Age trim option package. The Bronze Age pack was for Mercury Cougar hardtops and Comet coupes, and consisted of a Laguno grain Metallic Bronze vinyl roof over Saddle Bronze exterior paint. However, you could specify six different exterior colors. Inside it was tan seat facings and side bolsters, combined with Ginger tooled vinyl inserts. The remaining interior color scheme was tan. Naturally, earth tones were very popular in this era, both inside and out.

Bronze Age exterior items included deluxe wheel covers, WSW tires and Bumper Protection Group, plus protective side moldings. In keeping with Mercury tradition, the wheel covers were another chance to chrome up. 1973 was a year for big industry sales, and more standard equipment for both Maverick and Comet. Standard bright window and fenderwell moldings came along for the ride. On Comet, you would discover a molded dashboard absorber covering the cowl sides. There was a molded cowl top absorber, and full-width hood to cowl seal, plus a molded package tray absorber and spray-on mastic in the quarter panels.

As further refinements, 1973 saw new shock absorbers and a voided type rear spring front eye bushing. Plus, rubber insulators under the front springs, for no metal to metal contact between spring and upper control arm. What had been optional was becoming standard. It delivered that 'Big Car' feel in a small car. *Car and Driver* said a luxurious Comet was one achieved with an array of options specified. *Motor Trend* noted that, by 1972, it had expected differentiated packs like the Cougar's XR7 assemblage. It's true that even Maverick had the LDO package from late '72 MY. During 1973, Mercury Comet finally, like Maverick, got a glovebox, albeit a small one. However, of greater import was the 1974 model year arrival of Comet's Custom Option.

The 1974 $408 Custom Option was Comet's equivalent to Maverick's LDO ensemble. It

The Comet's role in the Mercury range was largely taken by the mechanically related 1975 Monarch. By the time the '77 Comets shown rolled off the line, model year sales had fallen to 21,545. It was Comet's final year. (Courtesy Ford Motor Co)

represented a combination of the Interior Group and Luxury Exterior Option. Now Mercury Comet had a standalone package, too. It was small car luxury, without having to tick all those option boxes. The TV ads announced and revealed the new goodies. Given the Custom Option coincided with the fuel crisis, the luxury message was blended with an economy claim: "Who says economy only comes in plain little cars?" A cute cougar cub then alighted from a gas can. "For '74, Mercury put a little Cougar in this gas stingy Comet compact with a special Custom Option." Said cub went towards a fancy bronze Comet four-door.

Yes, even though Cougar had moved on to intermediate grazing land, and wasn't really sporty anymore, Mercury kept name dropping to lend a youthful, sporty zest to its product line. And this was literal, the cute cougar cub was now exploring the Comet's interior, and experiencing that Custom Option. In ads for the new pack, a six-cylinder Comet was always shown and spoken of. Given the gas mileage conscious times, the 302 V8 was de-emphasized, as it were. To reinforce Comet's virtue of smallness – an increasingly sought quality worldwide – Comet was paired with Mercury's Capri in ads.

Once again, that little cougar cub was playing

around. This time with a gas pump nozzle, and meowing at the plushness of Comet's Comfort Option. And meow it should. The silver blue metallic exterior was one of three optional "Metallic Glow" shades. The soft touch vinyl interior was colored to match; that is, no tan. The voiceover said: "Coaxing good gas mileage from your car these days can be a battle, but your Lincoln-Mercury dealer can help you fight it …" That help came courtesy of 'The Mileage Cars,' Comet and Capri. The introduction for the gas-stingy six-cylinder Comet went "… with custom options that's got a little cougar in it." The little cub found the glove soft vinyl reclining buckets, extra thick shagpile carpet and steel belted WSW radials.

As an alternative to that Silver Comet coupe, a red '74 Capri coupe with tan vinyl interior was displayed. The Comet with Custom Option came with a silver blue interior. Like Maverick, Comet's special packs were no longer limited to tan. Capri represented "mileage European style with Capri, our sexy European." Here it was a Pinto in-line four, combined with floorshift four-speed stick, rack and pinion steering, power front disk brakes, and steel belted BSW radials, all standard.

Either way, Comet or Capri, "The first place to look for small car gas mileage is your Lincoln-Mercury dealer." By now the little cougar cub was on top of the illuminated Lincoln-Mercury sign. Focusing on Thriftpower Comets may have been a sign of the times, but in its July 1974 issue, *Road Test* evaluated an automatic Comet four-door, with Custom Option, a/c and 302 V8. By now, inflation saw a/c cost $383, with power steering at $106, manual front disks for $34, automatic at $212, AM/FM radio for $222, tinted windows for $38, rear defogger at $30 and Bumper Protection Group a 24 buck steal. Custom Option was priced separately, and all up the Comet sedan priced out at $4553.

The 64,000 dollar question was, could Comet with Custom Option take the parking space of full-size luxury cars? With the price of gas soaring and gas lines lengthening, a new kind of luxury transportation was needed. At the height of the fuel crisis it cost 10 bucks to fill up a big car, and due to the OPEC induced shortages, many gas stations would only sell $5 worth of gas. Of course, industry critics had claimed people bought big cars because that's all Detroit offered. No, it wasn't all it offered, and many buyers chose big because they liked big. The quiet refinement of a large car, that so-called 'Big Car Feel' was both real and desired. Leading the way, Comet with Custom Option, Maverick LDO and domestic rivals soon tried to offer a smaller alternative.

Ads soon appeared informing buyers of many different types of domestic cars. Their base engines were now smaller, and this would yield a gas saving of considerable size. It was a reason to update. Indeed, during this time many much-loved muscle cars from yesteryear sat worn out and unloved on street corners, or at used car dealers for pennies. And of course, you wanted a new car that could pass smog tests and drink unleaded gas without the engine succumbing to VSR (valve seat recession). The feds were phasing out lead as an octane booster in gasoline. Fuel crisis or no, Mercury Comet sedan with Custom Option was a capable and appealing car in its own right. *Road Test* said its well specified four-door, which wanted for nothing in luxury, consumed 14.8mpg. Compared to a full-size land yacht, this represented an $800 saving, for the average driver doing 20,000 miles per annum.

There was no performance penalty for thrift, given the FoMoCo 302 Windsor. *Road Test* said its V8 sedan with C4 automatic nearly matched

Everything a gal, or guy, could wish for! Mercury Comet GT was the sporty counterpart to Maverick Grabber. Largely a trim package, although a standalone model with selective hardware such as HD suspension and V8 could be optioned. (Courtesy Ford Motor Co)

The Comet GT was easy to distinguish from its Grabber relation. Mercury used a single forward hoodscoop, rather than Ford's Dual Dome hood. (Courtesy Greg Holland)

a '74 Capri 2.8 V6 manual for acceleration. More importantly, the Comet V8 provided great low end response, and didn't feel like a smog motor aside from a fast idle under choke, which necessitated brake pedal usage in gear at rest. Beyond this, there was none of the warm-up stumble, nor highway surge, so commonly experienced on contemporary cars.

Indeed, in *Road & Track*'s February 1973 'Three Luxury Sports Sedans' test, its Mercedes 280 Compact displayed atrocious driveability. Ironic, given Ford faced off the Maverick's successor, the Granada, against the very same Mercedes in future comparison ads. Compared to the Comet V8 four-door *Car and Driver* tested in July 1972, *Road Test*'s machine was smogged down to 8.0:1 CR and 140 net horses at 3800rpm. Torque from the two-barrel Motorcraft carb fed 302 was also down to 230lb-ft at 2600rpm.

The performance stats were less than before, but still peppy, and the equal of any V8-powered Mercedes, coupe or sedan. In light of Ford's oft-used Mercedes comparison ads, that's just as well. *Road Test*'s Comet V8 sedan did 0-60mph in 10.9 seconds, plus a 17.84-second $^1/_4$-mile at 76.98mph. In each of the C4 slushbox's gears, it was 42mph, 66mph and 92mph at 3500rpm in top gear. So, flat out cruising was feasible, but not possible in light of the new 55mph national speed limit.

The Comet, with newly available front disk brakes, stopped from 60mph in 167ft, and registered 0.672g on the skidpad. With its 15-gallon tank, Comet's gas mileage suggested a range of 222 miles. For the record *R&T*'s Mercedes did 0-60mph in 11.7 seconds, an 18.5-second $^1/_4$-mile at 76mph, and 14.5mpg. All this on the looser 1973 smog standard. The MB 280 also stopped in 151ft and registered 0.679g on the skidpad. The 1973 Mercedes tested also lacked the heavy impact bumpers that 1974 cars had to endure. Then there was the small matter of price. The 1973 Mercedes 280 automatic with a/c, cost … $8931!

Comet was competent in all respects, and that Custom Option interior was judged second to none. *Road Test* observed six areas rated out of 100, to produce an overall rating also out of 100. The areas were: acceleration, brakes, skidpad, interior noise, tire reserve and economy. The best car the journal had tested to date was the Porsche 914, scoring 74/100. The worst car was the Mercedes 240D, with 58/100. The Comet V8 four-door with Custom Option garnered 66/100. It was fitting that Lincoln-Mercury had trumped its bench mark target, the Mercedes W114/115 Compact. The Mercedes' advantages in build quality, economy and road holding were outweighed by its very pedestrian performance and noise. Ah that diesel clatter!

The Comet's gas mileage would have been better, if the HVAC panel made provision for a fresh air mode, sans a/c. As with many types of car, import and domestic, at all price levels, it seemed you couldn't enjoy fresh air without engaging the a/c and a gas mileage penalty. Sometimes you didn't need a/c, just fresh air. Many companies made no provision for this scenario. Smallness aside, *Road Test* declared in July 1974: "Those having

Resplendent in Bright Yellow, this 1975 Comet GT has had a small bumper conversion.
(Courtesy Greg Holland)

The original 302 V8 now sports an Edelbrock Performer intake painted Ford blue, Holley 600 CFM vacuum secondary carb, tube headers, X-pipe and Mac Flow Path mufflers. (Courtesy Greg Holland)

A Top Loader four-speed has a cruising compliant 3.25 rear axle. The original low back buckets were swapped for high back equivalents, trimmed with cloth inserts. The center console is a modified Mercury Sable unit. (Courtesy Greg Holland)

to give up on big cars quite possibly can find true happiness with the Comet." Sensibly sized, even with 1974 impact bumpers, thrifty, peppy and more responsive at the helm than full-size luxury sleds. Yes, Comet and Custom Option were a match made in Dearborn!

Comet GT, Dealer Specials and Bobcat

Cars are released onto the market long after initial planning. Such planning for the Maverick began in 1967, when engineering and styling work appeared on drawing boards. Maverick's cousin, Comet, was two years in the planning. A strategic release was made in the fall of 1970, for '71 MY. There would be a sporty equivalent to the Maverick Grabber. Like that Ford, there was no intention for the Mercury Comet GT to be a fire breather, even if it did resemble a mini Cyclone!

The Mercury brochure intimated that Comet GT was a sporty trim package, stating "In front, a color-keyed hood scoop and blacked-out grille impart the appearance of performance." That appearance came from a 1971 $178.80 GT pack consisting of: black-out grille, black-out headlamp doors, black-out back panel, body color dual racing mirrors, wheel trim rings, dual body tape stripes with 'Comet GT' front fender script inlays, deluxe door cards, black trim instrument panel, non functional forward hoodscoop, and bright window frames.

For all the sporty touches, The GT's base engine was the humble Thriftpower 170cu in six, just like you got in a Maverick. Stock tires were 6.45-14s on 14 x 4.5in steel rims, and, like any other Comet, the 170cu in motor couldn't be combined with Maverick's

early semi-auto three-speed box. Power teams were consistent with Maverick. That is, manual-only 170 six, manual or automatic 200cu in six, slushbox-only 250 six and manual or automatic 302 V8. It was 2.79 rear gears for all, bar manual 200cu in six, 250 six and all Comets with factory air. These little Mercs received the 3.00 performance axle.

High-performance wasn't standard with Comet GT, but could be optioned, in a fashion. The 302 V8 was a Mercury exclusive, versus Maverick, for the first half of 1971 model year. GT or no, Comet V8 coupe flew off dealer lots for $2387. The GT package was only for coupes, so a 302 V8-powered edition was a good place to tick on the order blank sheet. So too the D70-14 WSW Wide Oval footwear, ditto the 12 buck handling pack. In so optioning, you were now in command of a coupe popularly chosen by sports fans and magazines alike. Nationally, 46.2 per cent of 1971 Comet buyers took the 302 V8 option. This was up to 61.8 per cent in the Golden State. California increasingly displayed a schizoid character between its sporty car mecca past and environmental future.

The V8 one received was no different to that in a '71 Maverick. It was a 9.0:1 hydraulic lifter unit with single point ignition, two-barrel Autolite carb with a 1.56in throttle bore, and single exhaust making 210bhp at 4600rpm. This was accompanied by a useful 296lb-ft at 2600rpm. When it came to Comet GT, all magazines elected to test the V8 version. Tony Grey of *Road Test* magazine said, in its January 1971 issue, that even with the stock 2.79 econoaxle, it was child's play to burn rubber. This was despite 14 x 6in rims being present. The Comet

Comet GT had various Mercury refinements over most Mavericks, like vinyl lined doors and extra carpet inside. This coupe attended the 2015 MCCI Roundup Nationals in Washington, PA. (Courtesy Greg Holland)

GT was well behaved, too. Floored take-offs brought no axle hop.

Road Test made the observation that Comet GT felt like a high-powered light truck with an unloaded tray. Weight distribution for a V8 coupe with manual transmission was 56.8 per cent front and 43.2 per cent rear. As with most domestics, the ultimate handling flavor was understeer. Magazine journal consensus was that the 10in four-wheel drums on Comet GT were oversized for the size and weight of coupe, and therefore perfectly adequate. V8 cars had 'em, so too 250 six motorvated Comets and Mavericks, with D70-14 tires. Swept area for the larger drums was 267.2in^2. This stat improved to 332.4in^2 when the front disk brake option materialized for '74 MY.

As per Maverick, there was no four on the floor option in North America. Three by the knee was the best Comet GT could have, and moving said shifter to the floor cost $13.10. D70-14 tires were $98.90 extra, with *Car and Driver* saying such footwear brought the 14 x 6in rims along for the ride. *Road Test*'s economy figure for the Comet GT was 15.1mpg city and 22.2mpg country, all on regular gas. Acceleration saw a 16.6 $^1/_4$-mile at 75mph. *C/D*'s test subject also sported a floor shifted manual. Its Comet GT managed a 16.3-second pass, at 84.2mph, 0-60mph in 8.2 seconds and 0-100mph in 26.8 seconds.

Both *Road Test* and *C/D* estimated Comet GT's

terminal velocity at 115mph, or a little faster. All cars tested by magazines were without a/c, and therefore came with a standard 2.79 rear end. With the usual options expected on a Comet GT, you would receive a $3500 machine. Yes, it was a long way from that $1995 Maverick stripper, but good value, and the way many would want such cars optioned. 13,677 people bought a Comet GT in 1971. This Mercury occupied a performance middle ground in the market. *Road Test* noted it had no direct rivals.

Mercury Comet GT, and its Grabber counterpart,

Sadly 1975 would prove to be the final year for Mercury Comet GT and Ford Maverick Grabber. (Courtesy Greg Holland)

The Mercury Comet Stabber was a Comet GT V8 based dealer special from Pugmire Lincoln-Mercury. It used to be popular to paint drum brakes an exterior matching color. (Courtesy Todd Rowell)

lived between the peppy imports, small-engined domestics, and the more serious Nova/Demon/Hornet compacts that could have potent optional engines. Of course, the 210bhp 302 V8 was as far as FoMoCo would go. Anything greater would clash with the Ford Mustang and Mercury Cougar. As such, Comet was usefully faster than lower powered four-cylinder jalopies, while skipping the gas mileage and insurance penalties of true hi-po compacts. *Car and Driver* offered some figures for recently tested cars. The popular Mercury Capri 2000, and up-engined Chevy Vega with 110bhp, turned in respective $1/4$-mile times and gas mileage ranges of 17 seconds, 19-22mpg and 17.8 seconds, 18-24mpg.

The 250 six 1970 $1/2$ Grabber that *C/D* sampled was timed at 18 seconds flat, with 155 horses of 1970 descending to 145bhp in 1971. Mercury Comet GT V8, with essential options, was equal in price to the 110-horse Vega. Therefore, Comet GT wasn't only more refined than the vocally awkward Vega, it was also much better value. The '70 $1/2$ Grabber had been a mere $2.5k, with the Capri costing $2.6k, making Ford right on the money. Comparisons of the 250 six with the 302 V8 also showed how a Comet GT V8 took up that middle ground. The Thriftpower workhorse produced 240lb-ft at 1600rpm. The 302 V8 did 296lb-ft at 2600rpm. The in-line six was a real low rpm slugger, in stock form. Next to the six, the 302 looked hi-po, but wasn't really.

The subcompact Comet GT was midway between the high 14-second compact screamers and the 18-second econocoupes. It was unique in the junior supercar ranks for its luxury and prestige. Compared to most Mavericks, Mercury engineers had sneaked in vinyl door liners on Comet. There was also better Lincoln-Mercury trim, in the form of more carpeting, plus front and rear armrests. In the end, the Mercury Comet GT was a Mercury. This implied visiting upscale L-M dealerships. You certainly couldn't say that about Chevy Nova SS 350 owners, regardless of performance. It was a sign of things to come.

Big land yachts didn't sell like they used to, even prior to the 1973/74 gas crunch. Cognizant of this development, Lincoln-Mercury diversified. The Mercury Capri, Pantera and Comet GT, were certainly diversification in action. It was a wider range than Cadillac could offer. Such sporty models definitely brought in a younger, swinging clientele. Were Comet and Comet GT worthy to wear the Mercury badge? According to *Road Test*'s Tony Grey, yes on quality. He said *Road Test* observed the first six Maverick prototypes in January 1969, and subsequent regular assembly line versions. The cars all checked out fine. On this basis, *Road Test*'s January 1971 Comet GT report, saw the coupe score 92/100 for finish. This put the mini Merc in the excellent range. Steering, ride comfort, interior space and cornering were also judged excellent. The

Originally, the Comet Stabber package was largely a cosmetic one. It was available from Midwestern dealers during 1971-72. (Courtesy Todd Rowell)

Pugmire decals were only affixed to complete Comet Stabbers. This is believed to be the only surviving Comet Stabber. (Courtesy Todd Rowell)

lowest element was instrumentation, 78/100 or fair, due to the Comet GT only possessing the basics of speedo, odometer and idiot light for coolant. As for a tachometer, maybe a helpful dealer had one of those Rotunda dash add-on units left over from the '60s?!

Aside from options and color, one Comet GT looked pretty much like another. To steer more

traffic to their particular enterprises, enter the dealer special. Dealership specials weren't unique to Ford, or domestic cars. They were sometimes sold exclusively at one dealership, or at a few dealers within a geographical location: that is, the regional special. Mostly, such cars had cosmetic packages to visually distinguish a model that was ultra popular on the streets. This kind of game seemed more associated with the Comet GT than Maverick Grabber. So, you were already starting out with the rarer of Dearborn's small cars.

The Mercury Comet Stabber was a 302 V8, three-speed floorshift manual coupe, based on the Comet GT coupe. It was the creation of Pugmire Lincoln-Mercury of Marietta, Georgia. Visual changes included a Thrush brand chrome sidepipe exhaust system, slot aluminum rims and lots of dealership insignia. Pugmire decals would only be applied on a full Pugmire L-M car. Dealership owner Richard Pugmire, used a Stabber as personal transportation. The Comet Stabber's sales seemed to reach mid-western states.

Along similar lines, consider the Mercury Comet Bearcat. This once again coupe-only vehicle, was based on a Comet GT V8. Said Bearcat was associated with well-known Knoxville Ford dealer Hull-Dobbs Ford. This dealership had the industry accepted method of selling an automobile, the Hull-Dobbs system, named after it. The dealer was also a sponsor of the subsequent Mustang II related racing car, called Kemp Cobra II. Concerning Kemp Cobra II, there were even plans in the late '70s to build a street available version of the racer. If the plan had come to fruition, you could have bought this coupe from Dobbs Ford, as it was known by then.

The most striking features of the Comet Bearcat were its wheels and tires. Indeed, the Bearcat name was derived from a set of aftermarket rims,

seen on 1971-72 Comet GTs, as a dealer option. The Comet Bearcat may have been a promotional exercise, designed to encourage the sale of the option nationally. Such aluminum rims had deep slots, with the wheels painted black and contrasting with polished cutouts or trim rings. They sported a polished conical chrome cap and chrome lugnuts.

Apart from Hull-Dobbs Ford, the Bearcat was also spotted in 1972 at Morristown Lincoln-Mercury, with one example in red and one in black. The Comet Bearcat was also purchasable from Pugmire and Jacky Jones dealerships. Aside from the fancy wheels, oversize Grand Prix brand F70-14 bias-belted tires were fitted, with rear three-quarter panel and front fender Bearcat chrome badges and Thrush sidepipes also in evidence. The side exhaust system on such dealer specials was an easy route to duals. Usually, tight underside design didn't leave much room for a dual exhaust system on Maverick and Comet 302s. Such specials seemed to end in 1972 model year.

Of course, the Comet GT didn't end in '72 MY. Like the Maverick Grabber, the Comet GT battled bureaucracy's federal regulations, until the end of 1975. Noticeable changes for '73 MY saw the 'Comet GT' decal callout moved from the front to rear fender. There was also the 5mph front impact bumper, joined by a like rear bumper in 1974. Annual revisions saw Comet GT keep pace with Grabber, but unlike Ford, Comet GT kept its special forward hood-scooped hood until the final curtain.

Dealership owner Richard Pugmire had this Stabber coupe as personal transport. It was subsequently sold in 1974, and with an odometer reading of 73,000 miles, went into storage for 37 years. (Courtesy Todd Rowell)

By 1975, the Comet GT's standard rims were the stamped steel, five-lug jobs with trim rings, resembling 14in Magnum 500s. Unfortunately, as with other FoMoCo products, the Comet GT's 302 V8 option had gained a catalytic converter for '75 MY, and was down to 122bhp SAE net in dual cat Californian form. The 49-state version was on 129bhp at 4 grand, 213lb-ft at 1800rpm, and had escaped the cats ... for now.

Compensations for 1975 had seen the adoption of FoMoCo electronic ignition. As with contemporary GM cars, this was for better driveability, emissions and power with economy. To meet the post fuel crisis scenario, Select-Shift auto cars could be had with a 2.79 rear axle. There was even the option of an econometer.

Maverick and Comet had such thrifty items, with the econometer being the usual vacuum device. Drive with a heavy foot and get chastised by a dashboard light. It informed one of more OPEC donations. On the plus side, the 1975 Comet GT came standard with raised white letter steel-belted radials. Softer vinyl trim was claimed for '75 Comet GT's buckets. And of course, Comet in general came with more sound proofing, cut pile carpeting and expected Mercury plushness. It was sourced from the Custom Option package. Your regular Comet was now a nicer place to be!

For 1976, Maverick replaced Grabber with Stallion, and Comet GT gave way to the 1976-77 Sports Accent Group. The Sports Accent Group was basically the GT pack with a new name. The fact it continued through '77 MY, whereas Stallion ended in 1976, was probably because Mercury lacked a Cobra II in its stable. So, Ford Maverick could lose the sporty version by 1977. However, Mercury still needed a little something to complement the Capri, especially with Pantera gone by the end of '74 MY.

In 1970, the intermediate sized cars were the sales ticket. Such machines outpaced both full-size and compact classes. So, Ford was justified in putting most of its eggs in that size basket with the new '70 Torino. However, the small car writing was on the wall. Maverick was gaining on Torino in 1970, just as Nova was eating into Chevelle sales. So, the 1971 *Motor Trend* Buyers Guide asked "what will the new Comet do to the Montego, and Cyclone?" Take sales, was what! In its debut 1971 model year, 83,000 Comets shot out the dealer door. It was a welcome result for the 2689 L-M outlets that gained an additional volume seller. However, as per

The Comet Bearcat originated from Hull-Dobbs Ford. The model took its name from the distinctive aftermarket alloys it wore. (Courtesy Hull-Dobbs Ford)

Torino to Montego sales comparisons, it seemed the Ford version outsold the upscale Merc counterpart three to one.

Based on calendar year totals, Comet went from 27,577 in 1970, to 65,842 in 1971 and 66,236 by 1972. 1972 and 1973 model year sales were a respective 82,359 and 84,691. It made Comet a stable performer. The Ford Pinto wagon's arrival had thrown things for a loop, cannibalizing both Maverick and Comet sales somewhat. As a response, *Motor Trend* expected FoMoCo to bestow a hatchback body variation for both Maverick and Comet by early spring 1973. This would have been consistent with rivals like Nova, Hornet, Duster and Demon. However, it never happened, most likely since the Mustang II was coming to town for '74 MY. That subcompact could feature a fastback hatch.

So, Comet stood its ground. It seemed Detroit had taken a page out of the imported car book; that is, making small annual changes. Gone were the carte blanch annual reworking of sheet metal of the '50s. Comet also proved to be a barometer of auto trends. It exemplified the fall of the performance car and rise of the small luxo sedan. Mimicking Maverick Grabber's steady decline, Comet GT sales descended to 12,221 in 1972 and 8405 units in 1973, neat coupe though it still was.

In October 1970 *Car and Driver* saw Comet as a Lincoln-Mercury hope to boost divisional sales in a new auto landscape, where big cars weren't loved like they used to be. The journal speculated that if this plan didn't pass muster, expect a Pinto with a power dome hood for '72 MY! It nearly got it

A 1975 Mercury Comet GT at the 5th Annual All Ford Car and Truck Show, hosted by Waconia Ford of Minnesota. (Courtesy Greg Gjerdingen)

right. Mercury did release an upscale version of the Pinto subcompact for 1975, '74 MY in Canada. The name of the new ride was Bobcat, and its wagon counterpart, using Mercury-speak, was denoted Villager. Also consistent with naming practice, Bobcat was blessed with plusher trim, more chrome, and Merc styling cues. Yes, Bobcat was brought into the Mercury fold, with 224,026 sales being the reward by the time production wound down at the end of 1980.

Coinciding with the Bobcat's Canuck debut, was a Maverick and Comet sales renaissance. In the wake of the gas crunch, the moment was right for small car luxury. What better exponent of this than Mercury's Comet? As Galaxie and Gran Torino patrons downsized, Comet rebounded to a compact sales zenith of 125,695 cars in 1974 model year. Ford had intended to discontinue both Maverick and Comet at the end of '74 MY to make way for the upscale and much revised, but related, 1975 Ford Granada and Mercury Monarch.

Buoyant small car sales prompted Ford to continue the Maverick and Comet pair beyond 1974. However, the new Granada and Monarch adversely affected sales of the older cars. At Mercury dealers, the premium was 600 bucks, but even so, buyers took the luxury bait and went for Monarch. It reduced the Comet's 1975 model year total to 53,848 cars. Sales fell further to 36,074 and 21,545

in 1976 and 1977 respectively. Comet's calendar year totals for 1973, 1974 and 1975 displayed a similar respective pattern of 82,716, with 90,113 and 37,222 units to come. Walking into a Mercury dealer and being confronted with two small luxury sedans, the result was obvious: one being newer and plusher than the other made Monarch the automatic choice for many. 1978 saw the Comet formally replaced by the Fox platform Mercury Zephyr, itself an upscale Ford Fairmont cousin. So, it was the end of ties with the 1960 Falcon chassis!

This 1977 Mercury Bobcat features the Ford dealer-fitted ground effects and vinyl stripe pack done for Pinto, called the 'Hot-Pants Kit.' (Courtesy Bill Fallert)

From A/FX to funny cars

Due to a mix of history and Ford corporate policy, most Ford Maverick and Mercury Comet racing occurred at the drag strip. Detroit's major automakers didn't really want to have a great deal to do with racing. Selling loaded full-size family cars was where the money was at, and racing was often more trouble than it was worth. The tragic deaths at the 1955 running of the Le Mans 24 Hour race, turned many countries and companies off racing.

Then, too, in America there was the civic responsibility of avoiding the placement of high-powered cars in the hands of young, inexperienced drivers. So there arose rules that the major players adhered to. No active sales promotion of the performance angle, no big engines in smaller size class vehicles, and an arm's-length involvement with racing.

When Ford's era of Total Performance began, with a more active role for the automaker, various models did certain kinds of racing. Stock car racing went to the intermediate Fairlanes and Torinos, and road circuit racing was first the preserve of Mustang, then the Pinto. Of course, the Mustang was a big winner in the SCCA's Trans Am series. When this deflated, the Pinto featured in the SCCA's 2-5 Challenge, and IMSA Racing Stocks. There was some overlap. The Baby Grand cars were NASCAR's pony car tie in, which brought the Mustang. The Mustang and Pinto were in drag racing, too. However, the Ford Maverick and Mercury Comet were largely doing the 1320ft sprint.

The drag racing story of Henry's compacts, is greatly linked to the legends of the sport that built and raced the cars. In the 1960s and 1970s there were few national events. The drag racing scene was local and regional, with match racing as king. This was something individuals and the dealerships they worked out of, or were affiliated with, dominated. In the background, Detroit designed and made the basic hardware, and supplied the same, but kept a safe distance.

Dyno Don and the funny cars

Dyno Don Nicholson was a major force in the sport, and raced cars of the Ford Motor Company continuously from 1964 through 1980. Dyno Don got his nickname from being one of the first racers to make great use of the chassis dynamometer. Indeed, in keeping with contemporaries, he was proficient in

Dyno Don Nicholson at the 1964 Winternationals. He chose the Comet wagon for better weight distribution-induced traction. Fast Eddie Schartman's name, his then employee, was also on the car. (Courtesy Ford Motor Co)

The 1966 Comet Eliminator I's stock appearance kept Mercury management interested in Funny Cars. (Courtesy Ford Motor Co)

most aspects of racecraft, with knowledge in engine tuning and fabrication skills, too. In the lead up to 1964, he alternated between Ford and Chevy.

As a youngster, Dyno Don raced his Stovebolt six-powered Chevy against friends in more popular Flathead Fords, and won! However, Nicholson and brother Harold created a '34 Ford with dual rear wheel setup for greater traction. This Flathead V8-powered vehicle attained a trap speed of 120mph. His wide technical skills saw him sought out by

Ford races...and you win every time!

1. Mario Andretti Ford GT Mark II
2. Connie Kalitta Ford-powered 427 SOHC Dragster
3. Don Peckham Ford-powered Cobra 427 Roadster
4. Skip Scott Ford GT Mark I
5. Peter Revson Ford-powered McLaren Sports Car
6. Don Pike Mustang (Sedan Class) Competition Car
7. Dick Brannan Ford B-Stock Drag Car
8. Gas Ronda Mustang 427 SOHC Exhibition Drag Car
9. Bill Ireland Fairlane 427 A-Stock Drag Car
10. Fred Lorenzen Ford Grand National Stock Car
11. Jerry Titus Ford-powered GT 350
12. A. J. Foyt Ford-powered Championship Car
13. Tom McEwen Ford 427 SOHC Drag Car

Anybody driving a hot, surefooted and tough new Ford is a winner.

The '67s are all of these things because the young engineers at Ford have been staying after school with the 13 teaching machines pictured above. These devices—and people like Mario Andretti and Freddy Lorenzen who operate them—have produced hundreds of solutions to the problems of how to build the strongest, smoothest over-the-road car possible. Solu-

tions that can't be arrived at on anybody's proving grounds . . . including ours. For instance . . .

Want to accelerate an engine and driveline to over 200 mph in a quarter-of-a-mile? What are the aerodynamics required to make a car handle safely at speeds over 200 mph? Find out during the gruelling 24 hours of Le Mans.

All of these machines and drivers—from Connie Kalitta and his National Drag top fuel eliminator to A. J. Foyt's

knee high Indy car—have a lot more to teach Ford engineering. That's why they'll all be going to the line in '67. And whether they win each time up or not . . . you can't lose!

Mustang • Bronco • Falcon
Fairlane • Ford • Thunderbird • Cortina

The Ford Total Performance era was in full swing by 1967. This was the closest a Big Three member got to the action since the 1963 AMA anti racing pact. (Courtesy Ford Motor Co)

dealerships. In the 1950s, he became the manager of Service Chevrolet, and by this stage was already proficient in using a dynamometer to fine tune customer's cars.

Working out of Service Chevrolet, success came at the NHRA's inaugural Winternationals of 1961. Here Dyno Don won with his stock class '61 Chevy Bel Air Bubbletop 409. The location was Pomona, California. Although Nicholson was a Missouri native, he was raised in Pasadena, California. Mr four-speed, Ronnie Sox, was also racing Chevrolets at this time, when Ford was the dominant drag racing brand. Don Nicholson repeated his Chevy triumph at the 1962 Winternationals. However, things turned bad in 1963, when Chevrolet signed the AMA (American Manufacturer's Association) anti-racing pact, and left the racing scene.

This was good news for FoMoCo fans, because Nicholson's reputation preceded him, and Mercury came knocking on his door. So it was that 1964 saw a change to A/FX (A/Factory Experimental)

Mercury Comet. Ronnie Sox also made the switch to Comet. Mercury was looking to rid the brand of its sedate image, much like Pontiac had done

For the 1968 racing season, Dyno Don moved into Super Stock along with other drag racing legends. His first choice was an adapted A/FX 1966 Mustang. (Courtesy Ford Motor Co)

with its fuel-injected Bonneville in the '50s. Drag racing would bring a high-performance image to the marque of the Greek messenger. Well, Dyno Don found success with the Comet, too. He was the first to achieve a 10-second pass in a door slammer in 1964. With one for the crowds, he was also the first to lift his front wheels off the deck when power shifting. But of course, match racing ruled at this time. In this discipline Don Nicholson enjoyed an over 90 per cent success rate during 1964.

So, things were looking good, but the Mopar camp was starting to get restless. To help raise its flag up the pole, it explored a new avenue in A/FX. Mopar moved the axle lines front and rear for better traction, and acid-dipped the steel bodies to cut weight. Then there was that four letter word ... HEMI! Combining the Hemi V8 with Hilborn fuel-injection created a very potent combination, and overall a new kind of racer, the Funny Car. With their wheels relocated, such vehicles did look kind of funny! In 1964, when many were racing A/FX Comets, Dyno Don took a slightly different route. He chose Comet wagon to aid weight distribution and traction. Now, in response to the new style Mopars, Dyno Don was the first to launch a Mercury response.

The NHRA quickly banned the new altered wheelbase Mopars from its events. However, Dyno Don was worried about the loss of match race income from not having a competitive car. Ford followed the NHRA by forbidding FoMoCo-affiliated racing outfits from racing against the new, quicker Mopars. If you can't beat 'em, build a Funny Car. Dyno Don converted his steel-bodied Mercury Comet, to the new style. He went over to a nitro-methane, fuel-injected motor, set back 18 per cent. More crucially, he moved the rear axle 12in forward. By doing all this, in August 1965 Dyno Don defeated a Ramcharger Dodge with a 9.3-second pass at 150mph.

Mercury didn't like what it saw, and wanted to get out of racing. However, help came in the form of the Mercury Racing Department's boss Fran (Francisco) Hernandez, and Al Turner. Hernandez bought time by keeping the Mercury brass on side, while Turner masterminded a new racer, the 1966 Eliminator. This car looked sufficiently stock in appearance, to keep the corporate bigwigs happy. Turner's inspiration came from the Mooneyham and Sharp '34 Ford coupe, of Gene Mooneyham and Al Sharp. This coupe looked stock, but wasn't. It had a tube chassis, central driving position and blown, nitro-injected Hemi V8.

Mercury commissioned the Logghe brothers, Ron and Gene, along with aluminum frabricator Al Bergler, to create the new '66 Comet Flopper. It looked like the '66 intermediate coupe you could

Larry Fullerton's 'The Original Maverick' was a Funny Car Flopper. (Courtesy Rudy Flores Galpin Auto Sports galpinautosports.com)

As a Flopper, The Original Maverick still tried to keep stock touches like chrome trim, tail-lights and ... an antenna! (Courtesy Rudy Flores Galpin Auto Sports galpinautosports.com)

Unfortunately, major racing success wasn't forthcoming for The Original Maverick. However, Larry Fullerton enjoyed a 1972 NHRA World Championship triumph with his subsequent Trojan Horse Mustang Funny Car. (Courtesy Rudy Flores Galpin Auto Sports galpinautosports.com)

The Original Maverick was sponsored by Galpin Ford. It's a famous San Fernando Valley dealership, run by the legendary Bert Boeckmann. (Courtesy Rudy Flores Galpin Auto Sports galpinautosports.com)

the new Flopper was forthcoming, but Dyno Don did indeed flip this much revised machine during match racing back East. What's more, the cars of Jack Chrisman and Colorado's Kenz and Leslie burnt to the ground! However, on a match racing and national event basis, Mercury was competitive once again.

If 1966 was the year of the Flopper and nitro-methane, then 1967 brought Eliminator II, blowers and much improved tire technology. The wins kept coming for Dyno Don and Mercury. Nicholson's blown Comet won the Irwindale held New Year's Day race of 1968. He also won the second annual Stardust National Open, beating Fast Eddie Schartman in the final round. Dyno Don's 7.83-second pass, the lowest ET of the meet, was like a matador going for the kill. As Sox and Martin's Buddy Martin once said of Dyno Don, he did more than just seek a win, he sought an edge.

By the end of 1968, it was apparent that there were a couple of problems with Funny Cars. For one, they bore little resemblance or technical relation, to the cars people could buy. For another, Funny Cars were getting dangerously fast. A couple of well known Ford Maverick Funny Cars illustrate the point. Larry Fullerton's 'The Original Maverick' was a Flopper, sponsored by well-known dealership Galpin Ford. Apart from the expected 427 SOHC 'Cammer' motor, it tried to look stock. The generally believable body carried chrome bumpers, Maverick tail-lights and even an antenna! Unfortunately for Fullerton, this Flopper didn't garner major race wins. Such success came with his next car, the 1971 Trojan

buy, and the Hilborn injectors that you couldn't, were concealed. This rig made its debut courtesy of Dyno Don, the event was the AHRA Winternationals, and the place Southern California's Irwindale Raceway. There were some teething problems. The flip top body, flipped off! The latch mechanism was then redesigned by reversing it. The body also went to Ford's wind tunnel for aero refinement, whereupon a spoiler was placed under the body. Race success for

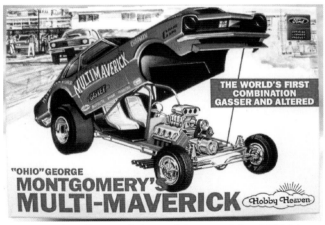

The wheelbase of the Multi-Maverick of 'Ohio' George Montgomery could be adjusted fully 9in for optimal racing traction. It utilized a 429 V8 Shotgun motor. (Courtesy round2corp.com)

Dyno Don Nicholson with his 1970 Pro Stock Maverick, at Orange County International Raceway in 1971. (Courtesy Mr Gasket Co)

Horse Mustang. With this Funny Car, Larry Fullerton won the 1972 NHRA World Championship, and set a new world record-elapsed time into the bargain.

Then there was the very successful 'Multi-Maverick' of Ohio George Montgomery. The 20-year veteran's '70 Maverick Flopper could extend 9in, had a moveable motor (429 V8 'Shotgun'), and many fine engineering touches. It started with a trick Chapman chassis, Chapman coilovers at both ends,

a strengthened and narrowed Detroit Locker lsd with 4.40 rear gears, Zoom cogs and Watts linkage. Rear rubber ran to M&H sized 13.00 x 16in tires on American Racing mag wheels.

At the front of the vehicle was a Moon gas tank, Chapman straight tube axle, and Strange Engineering spindles. Two radius rods attached to the frame. Willard batteries and Simpson harness joined other leading names in the component industry. Indeed, the 429 V8 sported M/T rods, forged True Slug pistons, plus a Crane experimental cam and kit. Crane heads, Hedman Hedders, Hilborn fuel-injection, Chapman oil pan and pickup, Mallory ignition, as well as a blower modified by Montgomery himself. The body was made by Fiberglass Trends, and painted by The 'Vette Shop. The body featured interchangeable fenders. Therefore, the Multi-Maverick could participate in NHRA AA/GS or AA/Altered coupe. This Flopper was featured on the cover of the January 1971 issue of *Hot Rod* magazine.

Super Stock and Pro Stock

In an attempt to get back to simpler times, Don Nicholson organized a group of leading racers Ronnie Sox, Bill 'Grumpy' Jenkins and 'Dandy Dick'

In completing his Pro Stock '70 Maverick coupe for the NHRA racing season start, Dyno Don took a biblical-like seven days! (Courtesy www.mecum.com)

It wasn't a winner straight out of the box, but Dyno Don took this ride to Ford's first NHRA P/S title win, the 1971 Summernationals. (Courtesy www.mecum.com)

Landy to compete in Super Stock match racing. Super Stock machines were closer to production cars, and what had existed in the pre-altered wheelbase/Flopper era. So, they featured four-speed manual gearboxes, carburetors, a normal wheelbase and conventional body. Super Stock cars also ran on pump gasoline, and the racing was heads up, not NHRA handicap style. It was the kind of racing Dyno Don and the aforementioned legends did in 1969.

The problem of Funny Cars bearing little relation to their showroom kin, had seen Chrysler Corp pull out of Funny Cars at the end of the 1967 racing season. Chrysler then got Sox, Martin and Dandy Dick to do Super Stock instructional clinics. This complemented the Super Stock drag racing that they now did. FoMoCo followed suit a year later. Super Stock racing was slower than that of the Funny Cars, but exciting, so the NHRA introduced its equivalent for the 1970 racing season, called Pro Stock. Dyno Don transitioned to the new format by first employing a 1966 A/FX Mustang, modified for A/MP. Once the AHRA and NHRA were on board with Super Stock (S/S) and Pro Stock (P/S) respectively, Don Nicholson built a new '70 Maverick race car in just seven days. Earl Wade was his crew chief.

AHRA playing card promotional material set the scene. Mechanical teething problems with his new Maverick kept Dyno Don on a simmer early on. However, he still won many match races, and enjoyed triumphs at the major meets. At the start of the racing season, many were counting out the 42- year-old Nicholson, due to age. At the start of the year, he was selected as one of eight AHRA Grand

Dyno Don Nicholson's '70 P/S Maverick used the Ford SOHC 'Cammer' 427 V8. Earl Wade was Nicholson's crew chief. (Courtesy www.mecum.com)

American Champions, and one of six '70 AHRA Grand American Professionals in Super Stock. As for the Holley carburetor-sponsored Maverick, it used a 700-plus horsepower 427 SOHC Cammer V8, four-speed and weighed 2880lb, achieving a 9.72-second pass at 141mph on pump gas. Dyno Don's home was stated as being Atlanta, Georgia. This is where Nicholson had moved to in the '60s, given it was the place to be for match racing.

Dick Harrell with his '69 Camaro and Bill Hielscher campaigning a '70 $^1/_2$ Camaro were also in the group of AHRA Grand American Professionals. The AHRA racing organization stressed the down to earth nature of Super Stock. Despite the various makes and models in the series, "... each runs on straight pump gasoline, and is legal weight!" Dyno Don's '70 P/S Maverick was the

Dyno Don maintained his match racing reputation in this P/S Maverick, with 45 consecutive straight round victories. (Courtesy www.mecum.com)

Dyno Don was the first Ford P/S driver to legally do a 9.7-second pass at 140mph. He retired the '70 P/S Maverick at the close of the 1971 racing season. (Courtesy www.mecum.com)

The bespectacled Dyno Don Nicholson had a tremendous '60s rivalry with former employee Fast Eddie Schartman. By the early '70s, both were match racing P/S Mavericks. However, from 1972, Dyno Don walked into short wheelbase, small block P/S Pintos and Mustang IIs. (Courtesy Hot Rod)

subject of a $^1/_{25}$ scale Jo-Han-made kit model. The Jo-Han box stated he was the only Ford P/S driver to legally achieve a 9.7-second pass at 140mph. He did more than that. In its famous Candy Apple Red, orange and white 'Mr Gasket' livery, this Maverick coupe was the first Ford to win a NHRA P/S title.

Initially, Dyno Don had just managed to get the car ready for the 1970 racing season debut event, the February NHRA Winternationals. Nicholson subsequently dominated the match racing circuit with this Maverick. He achieved 45 consecutive straight round wins. It culminated in victory at the 1971 Summernationals, held at Raceway Park in English town, New Jersey. Dyno Don retired his '70 P/S Maverick at the close of the 1971 racing season. Nicholson moved onto a '72 Cleveland 351-powered Pinto, winning the AHRA and NHRA Winternationals, plus the NHRA Gatornationals in 1973. Staying with Ford, Dyno Don campaigned a new Mustang II from 1974 through 1980. In so doing, he won the 1977 Winston Pro Stock Championship, a national tour that contrasted with the regional match racing he usually did.

Fast Eddie Schartman

When it comes to drag racing rivalries, you can't overlook the one between Dyno Don Nicholson and Fast Eddie Schartman. Hailing from Ohio, Fast Eddie was working at Jackson Chevrolet in Cleveland, and racing his '62 Chevy. The dealership's biggest customer was Dyno Don, who met Schartman and became friends. Nicholson offered Schartman a job – come to Atlanta, and build engines for him. So, Eddie Schartman moved to Atlanta in 1964, coinciding with Nicholson's, and others, switcheroo to Mercury. Fast Eddie achieved a Mr Stock Eliminator win at the 1965 NHRA winter drags.

Schartman eventually grew tired of working for someone else. It meant handing over half your winnings! Plus, his relationship with Dyno Don was on the rocks. Mercury regarded the young driver highly. So when Schartman demanded his own car, he got it. It was a Comet with a Wedge motor, and 5 grand sponsorship money from Cleveland Lincoln-Mercury dealers. At the time, factory-affiliated racers got the 427 SOHC Cammer V8. Of course, like other Merc campaigners, Fast Eddie made the move to a Flopper for '66 racing season. The switch proved very illuminating. His first encounter, in December 1965 at Motor City Dragway, saw a 166mph trap speed, and Fast Eddie nearly taking out the finishing line lights!

Fast Eddie Schartman stayed a year longer in Funny Cars than contemporaries. However, he continued his match race winning ways in this '70 P/S Maverick; especially outside national events. (Courtesy www.mecum.com)

This authenticated coupe is the only known survivor of the Boss 429-powered era racers. (Courtesy www.mecum.com)

Super Stock and Pro Stock cars had normal bodies, four speeds, carbs, and they raced on pump gas. This one allowed Fast Eddie a 93 per cent win rate in match racing during 1970-73! (Courtesy www.mecum.com)

The usual A/FX trap speed had been 125mph, but these new Funny Cars were something else. You drove them from the back seat. The Funny Cars were basically dragsters, with a car body on top. They were such a big hit with fans, as drivers struggled to keep 'em in a straight line! Excellent chassis design was key when it came to getting the power down and maintaining control. Fast Eddie

was doing over 80 match race events per year, and was Dyno Don's chief rival. On behalf of Mercury, Schartman attended car shows and boyscout events. In those days, FoMoCo racers were running stock block 427s. Other racers blew the cranks out of their blocks using too much nitro while trying to match Fast Eddie and Dyno Don.

For 1966 racing season, Mercury hired nitro-methane tuning veteran Roy Steffey. Steffey didn't exactly get on with Schartman, and they had different viewpoints on racing. However, the Roy Steffey Enterprises Merc Flopper, emblazoned in yellow, garnered the S/XS trophy with an 8.28-second pass at 174.41mph. What's more, Fast Eddie beat Dyno Don to win the first NHRA Funny Car Eliminator Trophy. Such 1966 world finals were held in Tulsa, Oklahoma. Schartman won with an 8.38-second run at 174.08mph, after Nicholson aborted his second run. Along the way, Fast Eddie had beaten fellow Merc runners Jack Chrisman and the Kenz and Leslie outfit, not to mention Gene Snow's Rambunctious Dodge Dart. Snow had been much slower on Saturday, and red-lighted on Sunday trying to keep up with Fast Eddie's Merc.

Things got bigger with blowers in 1967, and Mercury got Californian supercharger guru 'Famous Amos' Satterlee as crew chief that year. Although Dyno Don made the same claim in 1967, Funny Car history also shows Fast Eddie Schartman as doing the first 7-second run in a stock-bodied car, at Detroit Dragway in April. Timing system accuracy being what it was back in the day, blame the Chrondeks, not the drivers. Then, too, Fast Eddie could claim to have invented the rear spoiler, at least in drag racing. At Maple Grove Raceway in 1967, they added hardware store bought ballast to the tail, and voila! The bolt-on improved straight line stability and top speed. Fast Eddie's trap speed was in the 190mph range, and he had this to say about Dyno Don's reaction: "… and 'Dyno' was still in the 180s, and believe me, he heard about it."

1967 had seen Air Lift picked up as a sponsor.

The Air Lift Rattler Cougar with pedestal rear spoiler took out the 1968 AHRA Winternationals and Great Lakes Dragaway's Night Funny Car Championship. However, Fast Eddie was second to Dyno Don at the 1968 Stardust National Open. There were some notable developments in 1968 concerning Ford and Mercury's racing interrelation, plus attitude to Funny Cars. Prior to 1968 it was understood Ford would do stock car, and Mercury would handle drag racing. Certainly Dyno Don and Fast Eddie had raised Mercury's public profile since 1963. However, NASCAR wins in 1968 at the Daytona 500 and Atlanta 500 by Mercury Cyclones, called into question the status quo.

The Cyclone had a clean aerodynamic shape for high-speed ovals. More than that, showroom Fords and Mercs could now be had in high-performance guise. This removed the former disconnect between FoMoCo's trackside prowess and family-oriented production cars. Plus, in late 1968, Ford and Mercury merged their racing efforts and told teams they would be backing out of Funny Cars at the close of 1968. Dangerous high-speed racing, and limited connection between racers and showroom stock, were once again determining factors.

In spite of the change in corporate policy, Fast Eddie Schartman stayed in Funny Car racing for the '69 season. He had managed to negotiate a low six figure sum from Ford, that allowed him to do so. Not a national event winner in 1969 understand, but still a match racing force. Nevertheless, Fast Eddie still departed Funny Cars at the end of 1969, to do the increasingly popular Super Stock and Pro Stock. Initially he did this in a Cougar, but the subsequent

The Tijuana Taxi Maverick four-door, sharing Gapp & Roush workshop space with the Sudden Death Mustang II big block street racer. (Courtesy Roush Automotive Collection)

The Tijuana Taxi arose from a NHRA weight break concession, granted to long-wheelbase cars for the 1975 racing season. (Courtesy Roush Automotive Collection)

With time running short, Gapp & Roush resorted to Maverick four-door. They based their sedan on a Don Hardy-built '74 Maverick coupe. (Courtesy Roush Automotive Collection)

Wayne Gapp lines up the Tijuana Taxi against Wally Booth's AMC Hornet coupe. (Courtesy Roush Automotive Collection)

'70 Maverick permitted a 93 per cent match racing success rate during 1970-73. The yellow and blue racer was very popular on the match race circuit, and is now the only known survivor of the Boss 429 era racers.

However, the 2012 Drag Racing Hall of Fame inductee had problems with national P/S events. Drivers Bill 'Grumpy' Jenkins, Mr Four-Speed Ronnie Sox and Bob Glidden didn't make the going easy. What's more, Schartman got disqualified from the 1972 Gatornationals because his Maverick possessed Comet tail-lights! So, he was moved from Pro Stock to the tougher B/Gas in the modified eliminator, the modification being those Comet tail-lights! Even so, Fast Eddie nearly won, only losing in the final round to Dennis Grove. And the rulebook

Wayne Gapp raced the Tijuana Taxi to three NHRA final round wins, and was runner-up to Bob Glidden's '70 Mustang in the championship. (Courtesy Roush Automotive Collection)

said modified cars had to run a pro driver. This pushed Fast Eddie out of the national events, and purely towards match racing. However, by 1975 the expensive 'rain-out' fee had made even match racing uneconomic for Schartman.

Fast Eddie Schartman then left racing and got into buying and selling cars wholesale, dealerships and NAPA Auto Parts stores. After the fuel crisis-induced recession, finding money to go drag racing got tougher. Automakers were even more distant, and sponsorship dollars were in short supply. 1975 also saw the disbanding of Sox and Martin. Ronnie Sox continued to race, eventually in a Mustang by 1981. However, Buddy Martin left the sport and successfully entered the car finance business. By the mid '70s, even Gapp and Roush dissolved, with 'Cactus Jack' Roush going into NASCAR as a successful team owner.

The Tijuana Taxi
When Lee Iacocca became Ford President in 1970, he cut Ford's racing budget by 75 per cent. By the end of the 1970 racing season, Ford even withdrew factory support from NASCAR. However, in Super Stock and Pro Stock drag racing, Ford was doing great. In this realm, Iacocca's championing of small cars had worked to Ford's advantage. Car industry observers have said that the Mustang II was the right car, at the right time – never more so than in drag racing, with the Mustang II and Pinto. The NHRA had been trying and succeeding in breaking the Hemi-powered Mopar stranglehold of drag racing. It did this with more favorable weight breaks for short wheelbase, small block V8-powered machines. As a

result, by the end of '74 racing season, NHRA P/S was dominated by Pintos, Mustang IIs and Vegas.

Naturally, Chrysler Corp wasn't too pleased about this, being left high and dry, as it were, with big block Dusters and Demons. It lobbied for more favorable weight breaks, using its Hemi-powered captive import Colt as a kind of nuclear option. Anyway, it got the concession, but before this ... a loop hole. Just months before the '75 racing season, the NHRA announced a great weight break for longer wheelbase cars. That meant the Ford faithful dusting off their vintage '70 Mustang P/S coupes, which were on the edge of a five-year body envelope, to compete for 1975.

Gapp & Roush had no such Mustang, and had been doing Pintos and Mustang IIs. Trying to ready a '70 Mustang from scratch would have taken too long. So, for the 1975 racing season, they turned to a Don Hardy-built 1974 Maverick coupe, removed the body, lengthened the rear of the frame, and added an acid-dipped Maverick four-door body. The result was the Tijuana Taxi! The nickname came from someone remarking that the race car resembled a Mexican taxi. At this time, such nicknames resonated with the public far more than any corporate sponsor logo. After a debut at the 1975 NHRA Winternationals, the Tijuana Taxi made six NHRA final round appearances, winning three times. Wayne Gapp was runner-up to Bob Glidden in the championship thanks to the Tijuana Taxi.

Glidden was campaigning a '70 Mustang. The Gapp & Roush Tijuana Taxi has been an iconic Pro Stock racer ever since, although more in mind than body.

Unfortunately, shortly after the Tijuana Taxi was sold in the '70s, it got wrecked in a pit lane accident. Even worse, it wound up in a salvage yard out East, and just rotted to nothing. The only surviving elements of the original car were the wheels. These rims have been incorporated into a restoration

Formerly with a 351W, but now this 302 sports a Speed Demon 750 CFM four-bbl carb, Keith Black flat top pistons and Hooker headers. A Ford Dura Spark ignition and Motorcraft module came along for the ride. (Courtesy Rick Bond https://youtu.be/_dNIGW8fAnA)

Hotrock is a 12-second, street-driven '72 Comet V8 with a 302cu in roller motor, and painted PPG Black Cherry Metallic. It hails from Pittsburgh. (Courtesy Rick Bond https://youtu.be/kQWAlA_DcPo)

The KA trim code was part of the original factory build, including the black vinyl bench seat interior seen. The coupe is raced at Quaker City Raceway and Thompson Raceway Park. (Courtesy Rick Bond https://youtu.be/QSCGoHnVKZM)

Out back it's Mickey Thompson drag radials, 8in differential with 3.80 rear gears and Traction-Lok lsd, plus Flow Master mufflers, too. (Courtesy Rick Bond)

project, overseen by Jack Roush and his daughter Susan Roush-McClenaghan. The basis of this tribute Tijuana Taxi is a 351 Cleveland parts project car, started by someone out West.

Hot Rod magazine said the success of the Gapp & Roush Tijuana Taxi prompted Don Nicholson to debut his '70 Mustang 351 P/S pronto, to take advantage of the aforementioned weight breaks. The magazine also added that such weight breaks might not be legal into 1975. It also noted the dissolution of the Gapp & Roush partnership, although stated both would continue to race Fords. Earlier on, Larry Lombardo's Bill 'Grumpy' Jenkins built P/S Vega, had beaten Wayne Gapp at the 1974 Summernationals. [36]

Hotrock the Comet

As a road-driven, never-trailered tribute to the Super Stock era, Rick Bond's 1972 Mercury Comet V8 fits the bill. From Pittsburgh, Philadelphia, Bond described his coupe thusly: "It's kinda like a Maverick, but different." [37] With a 1/4-mile time in the 12s at nearly 110mph, this originally 302-powered Comet is something different alright. For one thing, it was a rare factory build. One of 34 '72 Comet coupes with 2B Bright Red paint, Trim Code KA (black vinyl bench seat and black vinyl top). However, of those 34 cars, only one had the handling option and D70-14 Firestone Wide Ovals specified.

That said, Hotrock wasn't originally a Comet GT, but has had a GT hood retrofitted, and made functional. And by the way, that 2B Bright Red color, was the same used on the *Starsky & Hutch* Gran Torino! For many years, Rick Bond's coupe used a 351 Windsor V8. However, it now employs a 1991 302cu in roller motor, and is presently painted PPG Black Cherry Metallic.

A Speed Demon 750 CFM vacuum secondary 4bbl carb, Keith Black flat top pistons, Hooker headers, Flow Master Mufflers and Mickey Thompson drag radials are some of the highlights. However, Ford Dura Spark ignition is used, along with a Motorcraft module. Also, a stock 8in differential houses 3.80 rear gears, and not forgetting Traction-Lok lsd. So, plenty of FoMoCo hardware is present when Hotrock visits places like Quaker City Raceway and Thompson Raceway Park.

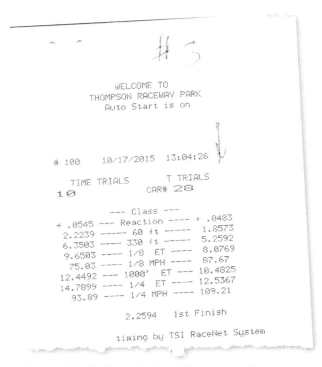

Hotrock's timing slip from Thompson Raceway Park in 2015. A 12.54-second pass at 109.21mph! (Courtesy Rick Bond)

CHAPTER
Seven
Mavericks, South American style

High class Mavericks

The South American car market is very different to the North American one, but Ford Maverick could adapt. Given historical background, it's understandable how in many ways South America is a lot like Europe. Fuel is pricey, there is a great interest in road circuit racing, rather than drag racing, car ownership per capita is much lower, and the condition of roads in general implies that suspension has to be tuned more sympathetically. Then, too, the individual countries of South America are more restrictive in trade. Imported cars and parts attract a high import duty. So, there is an incentive to produce locally as much as possible. The South American Maverick is looked upon in a very different light to its North American cousin.

Mavericks made south of the border, and not just Mexico way, were low volume, high quality cars. They were often purchased by the affluent 35-year-old, professional male buyer. Indeed, far from being The Simple Machine, South American Mavericks were prestige cars, and considered special. With Maverick mostly available instead of the Mustang, the former had an image akin to a well-specified 1964-66 era Mustang 289 V8.

This was certainly the case in Venezuela. Here, the Maverick was around from very early times. A glance at this market's 1975 Maverick brochure gives an idea of the course of business. It was a blend of early and late Mavericks. There were small bumpers, limited pollution controls, and an absence of American federal safety equipment, like head restraints or retractable three-point seatbelts for the front outboard occupants. Locally sourced upholstery was combined with a/c, and the 250 cube Thriftpower six was standard equipment. As compensation for the reduced gasoline octane, South American smog law was looser and provided tuning potential.

Escaping exorbitant import duties, the 1970 Maverick became another in a long line of Fords made in Venezuela. Valencia Assembly was Ford Venezuela's factory, which opened in 1962. (Courtesy Ford Venezuela)

This 1974 Regatta Blue, Brazilian-made Ford Maverick Super Luxo has been owned by the same family since new. It was quickly upgraded from stock 6.95-14s to E70-14 Wide Ovals. Maverick GT HD suspension was also retrofitted. (Courtesy Ernesto Frantzen)

Brazilian Mavericks could have four on the floor. With this coupe, optional recirculating ball steering replaced the antiquated stock Willys Aero hardware. Aftermarket gauges are present. (Courtesy Ernesto Frantzen)

Brazilian Mavericks

This all came together for Brazilian Ford fans at the 1973 Sao Paolo Auto Show, held in May that year. Naturally, the Brazilian Maverick would be made in Sao Paolo and Ford Brazil's Sao Bernardo do Campo facilities. However, before all that transpired, there were earlier Brazilian-built Fords and a customer clinic. For starters, the smallest car: the front-wheel drive Ford Corcel. This was a four-cylinder sedan based on the Renault 12. Next up was the somewhat antiquated Ford Aero. The Aero was an updated 1954 Kaiser-Willys Aero Eagle, and utilized that firm's ancient in-line six. Indeed, from 1976, Ford do Brazil and Willys-Overland do Brazil had merged. The latter was 50 per cent Renault-owned, which explained the product mix in this locale. [38] Finally, the flagship four-door-only Ford Galaxie. Along with the Dodge Dart, the Galaxie represented the only other Brazilian-made car with factory a/c, power steering and automatic available on the one car.

From 1968, GM's local operation had been knocking out Chevrolet Opalas. The Opala, as the name suggests, blended the Opel Rekord with US engines: Chevrolet's 151cu in I4 and 250cu in I6. Like you would find in a Nova. The Opala was very popular, and could be had as a two- or four-door sedan. It should be noted that at this time, and for many years, Brazilians had an aversion to four-door cars, whereas France, South Africa and Australia favored four doors. Car tastes were very country-specific in past times. The Opala put the heat on

Ford do Brazil to replace the aging Ford Aero. Opala's two positives were its locally made 250 six, and having greater rear passenger compartment accommodation than the Maverick coupe.

Back to the aforementioned customer clinic. Four unbadged white cars were put before potential customers: Ford Maverick, Ford Taunus, Opala and Ford Corcel. The German Taunus won out, but then came production realities. No Brazilian-made Ford motor would fit, and the 2.3-litre OHC Lima would, but wasn't planned for local production until 1975. In addition, the Taunus' independent rear and all-coil suspension never got past the bean counters. So, Maverick it was, ancient Willys flathead six and all.

There was glamour aplenty in the lead up to the Maverick's Brazilian launch. Emerson Fittipaldi had just become the youngest Formula One World Champion, and Brazil's first, in 1972. To get some publicity glow from the national milestone, Ford do Brazil teamed up ol' Emmo with an American spec Maverick coupe at the Interlagos circuit. The 1973 documentary was called 'The Fabulous Fittipaldi,' and featured 1972 Formula One races, plus Fittipaldi driving the Maverick at Interlagos. Emmo arrived at the venue by chopper, got out and said, "This is the Interlagos race course, 7960 meters long, 15 turns ... let's go for a ride!" Using a voiceover narrative, he then explained the course. "This turn we take in third gear, 7500rpm ... " Naturally, in a Formula One car with Ford Cosworth DFV V8, you would!

For '74 MY, Brazilian buyers could enjoy a base Maverick six, called the Super 3.0. This had four

Performance fora da rotina.

Potência - O Ford Maverick GT é o carro de maior aceleração no Brasil. Com seu motor 302 de cinco litros e diferencial longo, o Ford Maverick GT deixa a rotina bem para trás.

Segurança - Quem acelera rápido, precisa parar rápido.

Por isso o GT tem freios a disco nas rodas dianteiras e duo-servo a tambor nas traseiras, projetados especialmente para ele.

Com um baixo centro de gravidade, bitolas largas e pneus de banda extra-larga, o Ford Maverick GT oferece uma estabilidade fora de série.

Principalmente para quem não está acostumado com isso.

Estilo - O Ford Maverick GT vai fazer você mudar seu conceito de carro esportivo.

Por fora, você vê o seu desenho esportivo, sua traseira fast-back estilo "rabo de pato", sua frente agressiva e a sua bitola larga.

Por dentro, o equipamento mais atualizado para um GT: console, volante esportivo e painel acolchoado.

Sem dúvida, é o fim da rotina.

Ford Maverick GT

This 1975 Maverick GT shows that in the absence of Mustang, Brazil saw its locally made coupe as a high-performance pony car. (Courtesy Ford do Brazil)

on the tree, allied to front bench seat. Next was the Super Luxo 3.0, which added more chrome, front buckets, deep pile carpeting and AM radio. Super Luxo options were: 302 V8, recirculating ball steering, four on the floor, GT suspension, power steering and Ford three-speed C4 slushbox.

At the Maverick apex, the gentleman racer could avail himself of the Maverick GT. This wasn't a Comet, and featured an imported Windsor 302 V8, four on the floor, handling pack, bigger rims with D70-14 Wide Ovals and recirculating ball steering. Other Brazilian Mavericks endured the old Aero's 6.5 turns lock-to-lock steering! GT's only options were metallic paint and power steering. Like Grabber, the GT had rectangular front grille driving lamps, and matte black hood paint as standard.

The Maverick GT's side stripe decals were standard, came in black like early Grabbers, and had the '302-V8' script inlaid, also like in America. All Brazilian Mavericks came with a glovebox. The country's leading car magazine, *Quatro Rodas* (Four Wheels), supplied the figures. The Maverick 3.0 six managed 0-100kmph (0-62mph) in 20.8 seconds, with a 93mph top speed. This made it slower than the Opala four pot. The Maverick GT V8, with 7.5:1 CR and 380 CFM 2bbl carb, managed 11.6 seconds. In fact, the Maverick six was thirstier than the 302-powered GT above 50mph.

Naturally, most folks wanted the V8, and by late 1973 there was a 12-month waiting list for Maverick

By 1976, Ford Brazil was an amalgam of Henry's local operation and Willys-Overland of Brazil. The latter was 50 per cent Renault owned, which explained the Renault 12-based Ford Corcel II. By 1979, the Brazilian Maverick had a 99bhp 2.3-liter Lima I4, or 199 horse 302 Windsor V8. (Courtesy Vereinigte Motor-Verlage)

Ford Ford Brasil S.A., Av. Rudge Ramos, 1501 São Bernardo do Campo, C.P.8610, São Paulo, Brasilien

Ford Maverick GT 73—147 kW, 148—180 km/h

Ford Brasil entstand 1976 aus der Fusion von Ford Motor do Brasil und Willys-Overland do Brasil, welche zu 50% zur Regie Renault gehörte. Kurz vor der Übernahme von Ford entwickelte Willys-Overland den Vorläufer des Renault 12,

Ford Galaxie Landau 147 kW, 165 km/h

der dann von Ford als Corcel lanciert wurde. Ford Corcel II jetzt mit zwei Motoren zur Wahl; 1,4 Liter mit 56 PS, 1,6

Liter mit 71 PS. Beides Vierzylinder-Reihenmotoren. Zweitürige Stufenheck-Limousine oder als Kombi. Viergang- oder auf Wunsch Fünfganggetriebe, Lenkradschaltung, Frontantrieb. Die zweite Modellreihe, 1973 vorgestellt, der auf dem US-Modell basierende Maverick, gehört ebenfalls zur Mittelklasse. Zwei- und viertürige Limousine und als Coupé mit 2,3 Liter-Vierzylinder oder 5 Liter-V8, 99 und 199 PS. Das Oberklassemodell hat ebenfalls einen US-Vorfahren: Unter der Galaxie 500-Motorhaube arbeitet ein 5 Liter-V8 aus dem Maverick, Viergang oder Automatik auf Wunsch. Auch als LTD und Landau.

Ford Corcel II 41—52 kW, 134—150 km/h

V8s. Using a 3.08 rear axle, the Maverick V8 was good for 111mph. This made it the fastest Brazilian production car in '74 MY. A few months after the Brazilian Maverick's introduction, the coupe was joined by the four-door sedan. However, the most popular version was the two-door Super Luxo. The fuel crisis hit V8 demand adversely. From 1975, you could get a Maverick 4, powered by FoMoCo's 2.3-liter I4. This motor was made at Ford Brazil's new engine factory in Taubate.

1975 Mavericks witnessed a braking system upgrade, ditto the front suspension. The four on the floor gearbox was a new design, and recirculating ball steering was standard across the Brazilian Maverick range. With a 0-100kmph clocking of 15.3 seconds and 96mph terminal velocity, the Maverick 4 creamed the Opala 4 into submission. The new version was well received by the press, and the Aero six was deep sixed! The downside was that the steelwork on the latest Mavericks was of lower quality. The steel that Ford do Brazil was buying contained ore impurities.

Falcon Maverick... otro éxito de Ford que renueva el concepto del automóvil compacto. Fácil de manejar, gracias a su distancia entre ejes —2.62 metros— y a su gran visibilidad —3.5 metros cuadrados de cristales.

Fácil de estacionar, 5.42 metros de radio de vuelta y una dirección tan suave que facilita esta operación y hace un placer el manejo.

Su operación es económica, pues su poderoso motor V-8 269 está diseñado para el consumo de Supermexolina.

Sus suaves y esbeltas líneas son el resultado de muchos años de experiencia de la ingeniería Ford y dan idea de su estabilidad, solidez y ausencia de ruidos.

The 1970 Mexican-made 'Falcon Maverick' was marketed and seen as an adjunct to the Falcon range. (Courtesy Ford de Mexico)

The Brazilian Maverick range was rationalized and updated for 1977, with the 'Phase II' models. Choices were limited to the Maverick 4 and Maverick GT. However, you could now have a four-cylinder GT, which raised the ire of enthusiasts! Factory a/c was newly optional on in-line four and V8 cars. In another development, Maverick 4s could also have a three-speed automatic and power steering as options. There was a new front grille, revised chrome trim and larger tail-lights. In fact, *Car and Driver* had once referred to Maverick's original tail-lights as resembling glowing beer bottles. The US journal preferred Comet's style. Radial tires were standard on all Phase IIs, and the suspension was recalibrated to suit. The local GT's hood was restyled with faux air intakes.

These were times when gas mileage was of rising interest, so Maverick 4 sales were strong. Maverick V8s adapted with a taller 2.87 rear axle, allied to a 7.8:1 CR. As ever, the Maverick was an excellent handler. This contrasted with the tail-happy Opala. 1978 saw the belated arrival of the LDO (Luxury Décor Option) pack, plus a heavily reworked front drive, five-speed Ford Corcel II. This latter Renault-based car contributed to Maverick's Brazilian decline. Corcel II was lighter, more economical, and offered better outward visibility than the Maverick coupe. With over half of Brazilian car buyers now women, this cohort chose Corcel II over Maverick. Not only was Corcel II easier to park, it also avoided the Maverick's machismo. This latter quality didn't sit well with lady buyers. In the aftermath of a second fuel crisis and with recessionary times a reality, Ford do Brazil decided to discontinue its Maverick at the close of 1979.

108,106 Brazilian Mavericks had been built, including 85,654 coupes, of which 10,573 were GTs. Once the 2.3L I4 became available in the GT, most GT buyers took this gas mileage-saving route. One point of distinction between the Brazilian and US Mavericks, was their logo: no cow horns featured on Brazilian Mavericks, as in this country, it was a symbol of marital infidelity!

Another difference was Maverick public perception. In America, classic Mustangs are revered, but Brazil has always been a youthful, forward-looking nation. The people look for the next big thing, even more so. As a result, the concept of a collector classic car tends to be an alien one. So, the once iconic Brazilian Maverick can get overlooked, although a rare survivor is appreciated when one

FORD FALCON MAVERICK, el automóvil familiar deportivo por excelencia, porque ofrece las características de seguridad que usted desea para su familia. Frenos hidráulicos autoajustables, con líneas separadas para las ruedas delanteras y traseras; volante anti-impacto; columna de dirección energiabsorbente; tablero acojinado, manijas no operables con el seguro puesto; perillas de manijas de ventana, botones y perillas del radio y ganchos para ropa, con diseño de seguridad; cristales inastillables; cinturones de seguridad; seguros para los respaldos delanteros; espejos retrovisores, interior y exterior; descansabrazos con diseño de seguridad; indicadores de vueltas de cambio de carril y luces de emergencia con repetidores laterales; espejo interior "día y noche"; viseras acojinadas; cerraduras de puerta de doble quijada; bisagras de dos posiciones; carrocería unitaria de gran resistencia.

Y para el conductor individualista, la oportunidad de personalizar su vehículo con gran cantidad de accesorios, que lo harán aún más bello y más cómodo: Tacómetro exterior, consola con reloj, auto estereo, calefacción con antiempañante, radio o cartuchos FM, tapetes de vinilo y muchos accesorios más que puede elegir con su Concesionario Ford.

Upscale in nature as South American Fords often were, the '70 Falcon Maverick was an early adopter of the Windsor V8. (Courtesy Ford de Mexico)

appears on the street. This is a shame, because from 1975 Brazil even had a four-door wagon! It was a version America didn't get. The roofline was extended further back on Brazilian wagons, and a third side window along with a rear liftback door was added. And yes, the wagon could possess the 302 V8.

As might be expected, Maverick V8s figure prominently in the nation's racing exploits. During 1973-77, Maverick V8s dominated road circuit racing. In 1973 alone, Mavericks won all three major endurance races at the Interlagos circuit: 25 hours, 500km and 1000 miles. For all three events, four of the top five were Mavericks. The Opala was limited by its wayward handling, even though it was a lighter car. Mavericks won all NASCAR style oval circuit races. Chevrolet's retort was the hot Opala 250-S. A problem here was that although the Opala's 250 six was locally made, the 302 V8 and associated hi-po parts were imported, and

hence expensive. Ford's response in such racing horsepower wars was the Quadrijet 302 V8. This premium fuel motor had a Holley four-barrel carb, Iskenderian solid lifter cam and 8.5:1 CR pistons.

In reality, the Quadrijet 302 was something only available to racers. In the popular pastime of night street racing, the attainable Opala 250-S had an edge over normal 302s. Even so, on the track the Maverick continued its success. Unlike in America, there was no reticence concerning Ford do Brazil getting involved in racing. The nation's top selling cigarette brand was the sponsor, and famed Argentine race car builder Oreste Berta's V8 had four Webers, Gurney heads, along with air dams, wings and fender flares to keep the Maverick coupe on terra firma. Driven by Luis Pereira Bueno, it wasn't as reliable as the milder Quadrijet cars, but did win every race it survived!

1975 witnessed a Ford do Brazil sponsored one-make Maverick 4 racing series. It promoted the

This blower kit was the kind of hardware Eduardo Velazquez imported for sale at his Shelby de Mexico operation. (Courtesy Shelby American)

new four-cylinder Maverick. Formula One and Can Am racer Jose Carlos Pace was inaugural champion. 1977 saw a ban on imported performance parts to try and bring balance to local racing. However, you

can't keep a good Maverick down. From 1981, the Tourism 5000 series catered to production cars up to 5.2 liters: the local Dart's 318 V8, that is! Dodge Darts and Ford Galaxies were in there, but it was the Maverick that dominated.

The Chevy Opala didn't participate. It had its own one-make series, given the Opala was still in production. By the late '80s it was hard to find cars and parts for Tourism 5000, so the series faded. That said, the 1992 running of the prestigious Mil Milhas Brasileiras 1000 saw a Maverick close on the heels of the BMW M3 winner, until it sadly DNF'd at the halfway point.

Then, too, a custom 1974 Maverick coupe racer is run by the Baptista family. When it began racing in the '70s, it employed a 351 Windsor V8. Much modification since has seen an aluminum 427 V8 set well back in the chassis, with lightweight body panels used for hood, doors and a trunk lid. However, the base steel unibody is intact. So, too, the basic suspension layout of double A arms front with a live axle out back. On February 2019, this Baptista Maverick coupe set a lap record at Interlagos for Brazilian-made production cars: 1 minute 39.7 seconds.

As an historical legacy, the Maverick joined the Ford Galaxie and Dodge Dart as the only three modern OHV V8-powered cars built in Brazil. The Dart ended in 1981, with the Ford Landau Lincoln Town Car lookalike serving as the final Galaxie vestige into 1983.

The Shelby Maverick was displayed at the 1972 Mexico City Auto Show. It combined visual Maverick and Comet elements. (Courtesy http://mmb.maverick.to)

As in America, the Mexican performance scene was in decline by the early '70s. The Shelby Maverick tried to capture remaining enthusiast interest. (Courtesy http://mmb.maverick.to)

Shelby de Mexico manager Manuel Ortiz on the left speaks to boss Eduardo Velazquez at the Mexico City Auto Show. Note the locally made oversized FR70-14 BF Goodrich radials. (Courtesy http://mmb.maverick.to)

The Mexico City Auto Show was a swan song for Shelby de Mexico. Eduardo Velazquez was transitioning his business into a coachbuilder that transformed local Galaxies into Lincoln Continental-like creations. (Courtesy http://mmb.maverick.to)

Hecho en Mexico

There were some similarities between car production and use in Mexico and other South American countries. Once again, there was encouragement for foreign companies to make vehicles in Mexico along agreed lines. In 1962 the Mexican government sat down with the Big Four and outlined a selective model availability scenario. This was to achieve economies of scale, and hence the commercial viability of Mexican car production.

There would have to be at least 60 per cent local content, and besides the Ford sheet metal stampings traveling by train from America to the Ford factory in Mexico City, the engine, transmission, suspension, seating and interior trim were all made in Mexico. This involved some different materials compared to US Fords, so appearance varied. Even tires were locally sourced. Plus, being a metric country, speedometers could reach 220kmph! Ford also divided countries into zones A or B, depending on the smoothness of road conditions. Being a zone B locality, Mexican Fords rode higher, and with 10 per cent stiffer springs to resist bottoming out.

Pollution and safety laws were also milder compared to America. In spite of such differences, both Maverick bodystyles were offered in Mexico. Plus, unlike Brazil, the 302 V8 motor was made locally. Indeed, Maverick commenced in Mexico as a 1970 coupe called Falcon Maverick. It was as if the Maverick was sold and promoted as a new Falcon bodystyle. By 1971 the local Maverick had replaced all Mexican Falcon versions. There was also a transitional period from 289 to 302 Windsor V8 usage. Early Mexican V8 cars carried '289' fender badging, and all had sidemarker lights, whereas Brazilian cars did not. Due to a free trade agreement between Mexico and Venezuela, Mexican Fords utilized front springs from Ford Venezuela.

Transmissions and differentials were done locally. The gearbox factory Transmisiones y Mecanicos, formerly Tramec now Tremek, made three-speed and four-speed Top Loader boxes in Nuevo Leon. The Mexican Dana Heavy Axle factory supplied the Dana 30 unit for most Mexican Mavericks, with an 8in unit. However, some Dana 44s were done too. 1973-74 marked the Mexican Maverick transition, to 302 V8 fitment. The Mexican 302 V8 block was thicker than its US counterpart, and therefore better suited to performance modification. Some wound up on American Mavericks and Comets too. US cars had central radiator caps, Mexican equivalents were offset.

Among detail differences, if you inspect a Carter ABD 2bbl carburetor, the top part of the housing says "Hecho en Mexico." With an eye to the fuel crisis, towards the end of the Mexican Maverick production the Cuantilan Izcalli assembly plant made Cologne 2.8 V6s. It is also suspected that the 2.3 I4 Lima unit joined the local production portfolio as a Maverick base unit. Initially, the 1970 Falcon Maverick had been limited to the 289 V8 and three on the tree. However, with gas mileage becoming so key, it was a whole new ball game.

Those early Falcon Mavericks had small, chrome US bumpers and Falcon body emblems. By 1974-75, the local car made an impact bumper switch to the 1973 US Maverick's semi-impact bumper. One good thing all Mexican Fords had for the consumer was a 'Calidad Universal Ford' sticker on the lower right part of the rear window. It was a truthful, outward sign of the Universal Ford Quality within all low-volume Mexican production. To combat theft, there were two identification markers concerning vehicle licensing and VIN. Firstly, a licence plate duplicate window tag, usefully inside your locked Ford. Secondly, a heavy metal tag with embossed serial numbers inside the right door pillar.

For performance, a Mexican Ford from 1974 was equivalent to a 1972 American vehicle. So, it was Ford IMCO smog equipment, even though Mexican cars seemed to run better than such theory would suggest. For a Windsor 302 V8 it was a tale of 205 gross ponies at 4600rpm, and 295lb-ft at 2600rpm. The optional four-speed's ratios were 2.78 (1st), 1.93 (2nd), 1.36 (3rd) with a direct top gear. The 3.07 rear axle possessed no lsd, and compression ratio

Ray Parrish's tribute to the Mexican Shelby Maverick features a Shelby-style Maverick hood, custom Shelby influenced front valence and spoiler, plus Shelby dual racing stripes! (Courtesy Ray Parrish)

A 1971 Grabber was the starting point for this Shelby Maverick tribute coupe. Now it has a 347 stroker V8, connected to a Top Loader four-speed. (Courtesy Coast Collision & Car Care Mississippi (228) 762-7781)

was 8.2:1, with a dual going into single exhaust then two mufflers, and ending in one large resonator on the passenger side. A 0-60mph run of 10 seconds, allied to a top speed over 110mph, were all within the Maverick coupe's ken. The magic was performed on 91 octane Gasolmex for the Ford GPD 2bbl carb. Lower 83 octane gas was also available, and unlike expensive Brazil, Mexican car owners paid around the same for gas as US drivers: 60 cents a gallon.

You probably wouldn't miss the federal impact bumpers or retracting seatbelts, but would have been miffed if there was no sport pack. Relax, there was one for Mavericks south of the border, called the GT. Much stuff could be optioned on a Mexican Maverick GT coupe: buckets, glovebox with key (from 1973), body protection and bumper guards, body side molding trim, D70-14 raised white letter radials, AM radio (with antenna), four on the floor, 'Special Vinyl' interior, 'Special Sport Type' aluminum alloy rims, GT graphics, an exclusive Canary Yellow exterior, and even leather trim inside. There were two distinct stripe packages, but no high-performance imported parts. The latter were banned by this time. Even so, the factory delivered all the enthusiast could want, plus ... Calidad Universal Ford!

Shelby – the Mexican connection

The Shelby experience in Mexico was delivered by businessman Eduardo Velazquez. It was 1965, a time when the sole Mustang available to Mexican drivers was a notchback edition made by Ford Motor Co SA. However, the importation and sale of high-performance parts was allowed in this era. That's where Mr Velazquez came in. He had become the

main distributor of Shelby American parts in Mexico. In fact, he was Shelby American's biggest customer in Mexico from 1966 to 1969. Velazquez dealt with Shelby American parts manager Timothy Foraker. In January 1966, a special notchback Mustang was created. It was done in conjunction with Lew Spencer's Hi-Performance Motors of Los Angeles. The idea was to show Mexican enthusiasts what was available as a Shelby American catalog on wheels!

Eduardo Velazquez had dinner at Carroll Shelby's house, and the affable Shelby asked Velazquez about his distribution business. How parts got to Mexican dealers, shipping policies, and incentives to Ford dealer parts managers. Shelby also gave marketing advice. It all culminated in the 1967-69 GT350 Shelby de Mexico. This was a notchback loaded with hi-po goodies! Production saw 169, 203 and 306 units, made in the three respective production years. Subsequently, a 1972 notchback to fastback conversion with fiberglass rear section was available. Predictably, it was called GT351 Shelby de Mexico.

There came success in racing Mexican Shelby Mustangs locally. Ford Motor Co SA Mexico had a new president from 1967: Siffrein Zeb Vass was appointed by Henry Ford II, and had been Comptroller of Ford Division in America. He was introduced to Eduardo Velazquez by Carroll Shelby. Vass was pro racing, attended most races and became a good friend of Velazquez. One 1970 Libre class Mustang with stock 351 V8 won 18 out of 23 races during the 1970 racing season. So, a successful parts importing business, race track results, and enthusiasm for Mexican Shelby Mustangs. However, when writing in the mid 1980s about his experiences in the mid to late '60s, Eduardo Velazquez gave an interesting insight into Carroll Shelby.

At the aforementioned first dinner that Shelby hosted for Velazquez in America, two Swedish college girls were housekeepers for Carroll Shelby's home. They prepared traditional Scandinavian fare. Indeed, Velazquez was invited for a holiday, and it was soon apparent that Shelby was somewhat of a lady killer, as used to be said, but always a professional in business and racing. It transpired Siffrein Zeb Vass and Velazquez were like-minded. However, the fun times were not to last. In Mexico, as in North America, the times were changing. Interest in and money for racing were in decline. Carroll Shelby exited car manufacturing and parts supply by the end of 1971. Plus, automakers in

The 1968 Shelby tail-light panel, is above a Traction-Lok 9in differential. 4.30 rear gears have allowed a 6.90-second ¹/₈-mile at the strip! (Courtesy Ray Parrish)

general were no longer believers in 'win on Sunday, sell on Monday.'

With a view towards product diversification and using up imported Shelby American high-performance parts inventory, Eduardo Velazquez explored new avenues. There were the aforementioned fastback conversion and GT351 Shelby de Mexico. However, these forays were joined by a Shelby Maverick, too! A Shelby Maverick was on display at the 1972 Mexico City Auto Show. By now, the Mexican Maverick was established in local manufacturing. There would be many base cars to serve as Shelby Mavericks, as well as making the most of whatever interest in high-performance vehicles and racing remained.

The Shelby Maverick had a somewhat unusual nature, blending Maverick and Comet elements. Even the standard sports pack was called 'GT' south of the border. More than that, Shelby Maverick de Mexico had a Comet visage and hoodscoop, along with tail-lights! Tach, aluminum slot rims, locally made performance tires and the expected front and rear spoilers were also present. The rear spoiler was a unique molding, and more substantial than a Grabber equivalent. In 1971, the *Ford High-Performance Parts Catalog* could help, and Shelby

American had done an aluminum intake for the 302 Windsor V8.

According to the Shelby American World Registry, around 300 Shelby Mavericks were created.[39] That said, literally the next big thing for '73 MY was luxury. Following American trends, the public wanted plush, not pace. So, Eduardo Velazquez's firm did a fancy conversion of a 1972 locally made Ford Galaxie. It embodied the spirit of the Lincoln Continental Mark II. This auto departure was very successful, even causing US coachbuilders to follow suit. However, Ford USA was displeased. Indeed, Ford Sales Manager Mr Royal Kelly accused Velazquez of making 'Bastard Continentals,' and ordered him to stop. This Eduardo Velazquez did in 1973.

Velazquez remained friends with Carroll Shelby, and still visited his Los Angeles home into the 1980s. Of course, by this time Shelby and Lee Iacocca had moved to Mopar. When visiting LA, Shelby always arranged for the finest Shelby Charger Turbo to be on hand for his old friend. Naturally, having Carroll Shelby's name on the registration papers was of benefit when dealing with traffic cops and speeding. Plus, little had changed since the '60s. Swedish female students still frequented Shelby's home!

Special Maverick packages

Car customizing and coachbuilding were alive and well in the '70s, but it had evolved from past times. One-offs, like Herman Munster's 289 dual quad Drag-U-La, gave way to production car-based projects. The latter could oftentimes be ordered via the dealership network selling the base car. That included the convenience of a warranty. So, being an individual in the '70s was a no fuss, no muss process, with just a little extra tacked onto the monthly payments. Some outfits offered performance upgrades, that claimed to be 49-state smog legal. However, for the most part, increasing power was up to you, using catalog hardware from the '60s.

Eagle Coach Sales Corp of Dallas Texas, offered Ford-related packages in the '70s. T-top conversions for Lincoln Mark V four-door and Mercury Cougar, Comet, as well as Ford Thunderbird, LTD, LTD II,

Phaeton, formerly Eagle Coach Sales, was a Texan coachbuilder that had sporty bodykit conversion in its luxury portfolio. (Courtesy Marc Cranswick)

Maverick and Mustang II, even. All fully welded, with a roll bar 'X'-membered roof. Contemporary Landau roof jobs were also to hand. In tune with

The Maverick coupe based Drag-N-Fly bodykit was available from 1974. It retailed at $995 fully installed. (Courtesy Doug Bauer)

This 1975 Drag-N-Fly was complemented by Phaeton's 'Wild Deuce Sports Car' bodykit designed for the Mustang II fastback. (Courtesy Doug Bauer)

A Drag-N-Fly and '76 Maverick Stallion join a '50s Hudson Jet on Route 66! Aside from an extra 3in of width, the Maverick coupe shared its length and wheelbase with that sensibly sized, family car of yore. (Courtesy Doug Bauer)

Phaeton claimed its rear spoiler had been track tested for functionality. That rear spoiler could be purchased separately for 100 bucks. (Courtesy Doug Bauer)

the increasing desire for luxury, a T-bird could be transformed into a mini Mark V with a Phaeton Town Car transformation. Eagle Coach Sales also did custom Lincoln-based funeral coaches, Landau irons for C pillar decoration and custom desks for front seatbacks.

Then there were the sports car conversions for both Mustang II and Maverick, plus the Mercury sibling Comet. Mustang II could sport the 'Wild Deuce Sports Car' pack, whereas a Landau roof was recommended for notchbacks. This Wild Deuce ran to an aero nose, fashionable quad square headlamps and backboard rear spoiler, to add sleekness to Mustang II's profile. For Maverick and Comet, try the 'Drag-N-Fly' conversion. It buzzed in at 750 bones for the kit, and $995 fully installed. You could buy it direct from Eagle Corp Sales, or affiliated Ford and Lincoln-Mercury dealers. Work included a 12/12 warranty. For new car conversions, it was stated that such subjects may already have had some FoMoCo interplant or *Road Test* mileage.

With a view to sales operations, Eagle Coach's work was promoted as being for the "merchandizing oriented dealership." Distributor discounts were available for orders of three or more of a single design, even sans an official Distributor Franchise Agreement. For sports fans, Drag-N-Fly was billed as

The sporty Stallion package was in the spirit of FoMoCo's 1972 Sprint trio. It also took the place of Maverick's previous Grabber. (Courtesy Ray Parrish)

The Maverick Stallion was complemented by Ford's Pinto and Mustang II Stallions. It was a cosmetic package limited to coupes. (Courtesy Coast Collision & Car Care Mississippi (228) 762-7781)

Decals, murals and graphics were increasingly all the rage on sporty domestics. This front fender decal was Maverick Stallion's calling card. (Courtesy Ray Parrish)

an inexpensive sports car conversion for Maverick and Comet that had "proven a real traffic draw." Ads said, "Join the Winner's Circle … Go … DRAG-N-FLY." Plus, "The Silhouette Of A Winner." Drag-N-Fly had styling elements of NASCAR's Ford Torino King Cobra, and the very popular Datsun 240Z. It was a sleeker than factory look, for sure.

Drag-N-Fly elements encompassed: aero nosecone with letterbox intake and faired-in headlight tunnels, integrated impact bumpers, hood release mechanism, conversion bracketry, turn signal lighting, track tested rear spoiler and louvered opera windows. Drag-N-Fly emblems and decals included a rear spoiler backboard 'DRAG-N-FLY' script on a black background. Kit elements could be purchased separately, like the racing hood/nose section for 515 clams, opera windows/louver decor panels for a C-note and rear spoiler for 100 bucks, also.

Eagle Coach Sales had a name change to Phaeton Sales Corporation by 1977 model year. The company sold and marketed Drag-N-Fly from 1975 through 1977 model years. While Phaeton Sales Corp converted a coupe into a sports car, Ford was content with its Maverick coupe. Through 1975, Henry's sporting option was Maverick Grabber, which gave way to Maverick Stallion for 1976 model year. Grabber had been allocated the sports sedan code 'Code 62D' from 1971 through 1975.

However, for 1976 this sports sedan code was reserved for the Ford Granada.

The Maverick Stallion was a cosmetic follow up to the Sprint package of 1972. So, you could get a Pinto Stallion, Mustang II Stallion and, as it eventually transpired, 5527 Maverick Stallion coupes. The Stallion pack was only for the Maverick coupe, not the four-door sedan. It consisted of an all-black car, with sides painted in a choice of colors: Silver Metallic, Polar White, Bright Red, Bright Yellow, or Silver Blue Glow. Trim pieces were also in black, given contemporary fashion dictated that chrome was out on sporty rides. Front grille, moldings, wiper arms and tail-light bezels were in black.

The Stallion also came with a front fender horse graphic as standard. Stallions were often shown with aluminum slot rims and D70-14 RWL radials in publicity material. These items were options. So, too, the 302 V8, which was now rated at 134 honest net ponies, which arrived at 3600rpm with 247lb-ft at a tractable 1800rpm. Stallion was a one-year only package. Indeed, the Grabber/Stallion role, was largely taken by the Mustang II Cobra II. This subcompact could also feature the Windsor 302. Also ending in 1976 was the once-popular LDO luxury-oriented Maverick ensemble. Once again, the new Ford Granada had superseded the Maverick's role. LDO had lost its tall, Mercedes-style headrest

This Maverick Stallion was a ground up restoration of a Tennessee barn-find with 32,000 miles. The discovered coupe was originally Polar White. (Courtesy Coast Collision & Car Care Mississippi (228) 762-7781)

This Stallion was ordered in Bright Red. Unlike the aluminum slot rims often seen in promotional pictures, this coupe has the Magnum style stamped steel 14in rims. (Courtesy Wes Notovitz)

A rare car worth celebrating. Just 5527 Maverick Stallions were built in 1976. As per Grabber, the top 302 V8 was optional. (Courtesy Wes Notovitz)

by '75 MY, and was further decontented for 1976. That said, with its standard handling pack, it had been a domestic pioneer in combining luxury and handling European style in one small car. LDO's success certainly inspired management to go to that next level with the 1975 Granada.

On a fleet car basis, Maverick was also there for taxi owners and police forces to some degree, emulating its rivals the Chevy Nova and Dodge Dart. In 1977, the Maverick taxicab package was in the 1977 *Ford Taxicab Brochure*. The Ford LTD and LTD II were also included. For Maverick, expect the following: Automatic 1st gear Lock-Out, auxiliary external transmission oil cooler, five-strand roof light wiring (holes in roof on request), HD 60 amp battery (with heat shield), HD alternator (60 amp), HD suspension, power steering and engine oil cooler, coolant recovery system, 2in-wide flared rear drums (as per Maverick V8), Extra Cooling Package, Transistorized Voltage Regulator, accessory feed connection, rear door courtesy lamp switches, Deluxe Sound Package, HD front and rear seating, assist straps on both center pillars, black carpeting, C78-14 bias-belted BSWs, 14 x 6in steel rims with dog bowl hubcaps, 250cu in Thriftpower Six and 2.79 rear axle.

The Maverick police package, which was listed as a "Non-pursuit police package," was mostly the same as the taxicab. As stated, you could get a Dart as a taxi and a cop car, albeit with a hi-po 340 V8 for the latter. In practice, the Maverick police package wasn't heavy-duty enough. NYPD bought a few for use as detective vehicles, but quickly sold them. Similarly,

the Boston police force purchased the Maverick police package just for patrol car duty. Here as well, the sedans were offloaded at a police auction. Although, that act in itself wasn't unusual. Indeed, even the Blues Brothers picked up their Dodge Monaco cop car at a police auction.

Even Dodge Dart V8s didn't exactly make it while trying to protect and to serve. Too many cracked K frames. For serious police work, you really needed a full-frame, full-size job with a big block V8. This kind of sedan could ride kerbs and median strips sans breakage, although in the South there was some variation. Here, the police force desired really fast cars to

The 2B Bright Red color was shared with the Torino range ... and the *Starsky & Hutch* Gran Torino! By 1976 it was limited to a fleet car choice, concerning Torino. (Courtesy Wes Notovitz)

By 1977, the Maverick Stallion's job was being done by the Mustang II Cobra II shown. Once again, the 302 V8 was an option. (Courtesy Mike Baker)

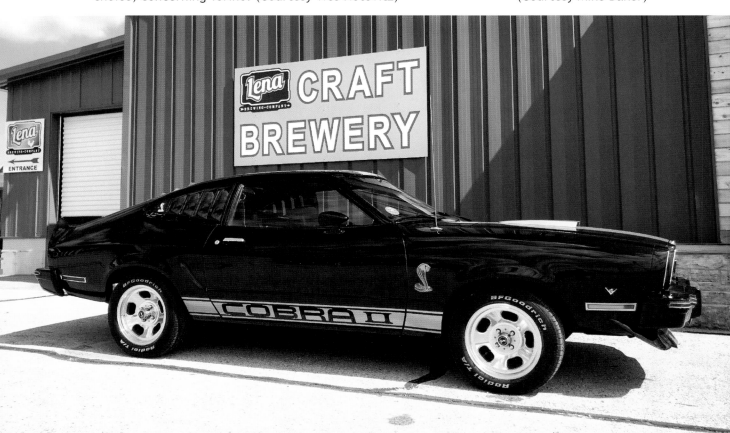

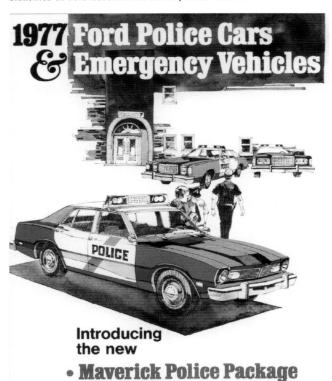

1977 Ford Police Cars & Emergency Vehicles

Introducing the new

- Maverick Police Package
- LTD II Police Package

Similar to the Maverick's taxi cab package, the Maverick's police pack had a number of upgrades that appeared useful for basic patrol work. (Courtesy Wes Notovitz)

Maverick's cop car package was front and center on FoMoCo's 1977 special agency brochure! (Courtesy Ford Motor Co)

Usually, Ford offered police packages from the sedate Sentry to fire and brimstone Interceptor. However, the new '77 Maverick cop car was a 'Non-pursuit police package.' (Courtesy Wes Notovitz)

In common with Ford's serious Interceptor pack, the Maverick cop car brought 1st gear lockout for its automatic, plus oil coolers for the power steering pump and engine oil. (Courtesy Wes Notovitz)

Power for the police Maverick was limited to the one-barrel 250 cube six, shared with the Torino's Sentry package. (Courtesy Wes Notovitz)

There was no built-in donut detector on the cop Maverick. That task was left to the officer! (Courtesy Wes Notovitz)

In keeping with the Torino Interceptor package, the rear drums of police Mavericks were also flared. Tires were C78-14 BSWs. (Courtesy Wes Notovitz)

The fuel crisis, inflation and ensuing recession meant that law enforcement came under increasing financial pressure from 1974. The success of the 1975 Chevy Nova 9C1 package, specially designed for police duty, got law enforcement thinking that a smaller car could do the job cheaper. It's possible some police departments overestimated the Maverick police package's ability, despite Ford's warning that using it beyond its design scope would bring disappointment. Given the Nova was a Maverick market rival, some may have thought that carried to the police package as well. In all, approximately 400 Maverick four-door sedans, were ordered with the police package in 1977. (Courtesy Wes Notovitz)

In its 1973 buyers guide, *Motor Trend* rued that an imaginative exclusive like the Cougar XR7 shown hadn't been forthcoming in the Maverick/Comet range. (Courtesy Lee Rehorn)

apprehend moonshine runners. This explained the popularity of the AMC Javelin AMX 401s, plus some custom jobs with 160mph potential. As for the 1977 Maverick police package, it's believed around 400 units were sold.

1974-77 – Good to be a Maverick

In 1974, *Car and Track* took a look at the Mercury Cougar XR7 in relation to the Olds Cutlass Salon. It was the battle of the personal luxury cars. *Car and Track*'s host, Bud Lindemann, liked a car with firm suspension, and always advocated HD (heavy-duty) suspension as an option. It was an inexpensive box to tick back then, and greatly improved vehicular control. Lindemann was always disappointed by poor handling cars. In this regard, the Cougar XR7 emulated the '74 Camaro Type LT that *Car and Track* had already sampled.

Bud Lindemann was also critical of Ford's badge engineering approach to the mid-size Gran Torino, Montego clan, and the price associated with high-end versions. The Cougar XR7 was loaded with an interior likened to Cleopatra's chamber. Then there was the FoMoCo 460 four-bbl V8 underhood. When it came to road-insulating luxury, you could want for no more than the XR7 offered. However, the sporty side of things had been allowed to slide, since the Cougar commenced as the Mustang's upscale cousin in the '60s. The Cougar had gone mid-size for '74 MY, just as the Thunderbird had gone full-size

As observed by *Car and Track*'s Bud Lindemann, it did seem the case that many Ford offerings were upsizing. The Thunderbird downsized to mid-size for 1977. (Courtesy Ford Motor Co)

for 1972. Lindemann was left wondering whatever happened to the posh, jazzy little pony car that Dan Gurney drove in the Trans Am series? He answered that by saying it "fell into the Ford calorie tank and fattened up …"

There was no doubt Ford had been making the correct commercial decision in the various market segments. Buyers were now more into luxury than sport, and loved that 'big car' feel, which the Cougar XR7 and its ilk provided. However, observing its predecessor, the mid-size '70 Merc Cyclone that *Car and Track* tried, the older car seemed like a better deal. The older Cyclone was plush, and out-accelerated the latest XR7, even though it had a mere two-barrel 351 V8. That Cyclone even out-handled the XR7, in spite of the younger car possessing Merc's Cross Country HD suspension,

The Maverick, Pinto and Mustang II showed that Henry was wise to the growing demand for small cars. (Courtesy Jeff Thomas)

Ode for a glovebox, the wait was long but eventually worthwhile concerning Maverick and Comet. (Courtesy Jeff Thomas)

The 250 cube Thriftpower six in this 1974 Maverick coupe has proved a trusty performer in FoMoCo vehicles the world over. (Courtesy Jeff Thomas)

With the original Mustang gone, Ford permitted Maverick the latitude of a $34 front disk brake option. (Courtesy Jeff Thomas)

with the earlier Cyclone passing on said option. Naturally, the older car cost less, and who ever willingly signed up for impact bumpers?

The average buyer was indeed questioning how today's car, in 1974, cost more while delivering less than previous counterparts. It was an industry-wide problem. Of course, you had the four horses of the apocalypse to thank for that, namely insurance companies, OPEC, the Federal government and tree

huggers. Ford gave buyers a choice; the government did not. There were big cars for those that wanted them, and smaller cars for consumers desiring compact dimensions and better gas mileage. *Car and Track* faced off a Pinto Runabout against a Vega wagon in 1974, and the little Ford subcompact aced the handling test. This included a J-turn worthy of Jim Rockford! The Pinto even drew the Cougar XR7 460 in 30-50mph and 50-70mph passing times,

This '74 Maverick coupe has had the small chrome bumpers retrofitted, reducing vehicular length from 187in to 179.4in. (Courtesy Jeff Thomas)

The Maverick's styling harked back to a time when fastbacks and all things sporty were in vogue. (Courtesy Jeff Thomas)

using the modest Lima 2.3 I4 and C3 automatic. It was 6.6 seconds versus 7.2 seconds, and 9.8 seconds against 9.5 seconds for the Pinto playing Cougar scenario.

Even more shocking was the loaded Pinto's price of $3918! There was a time when that kind of foldin'

stuff bought a brand new muscle car. Searching for value in challenging times, full-size and mid-size buyers found it in the 1974 Maverick. Just as the 1974 Mustang II sold handsomely, as the right car for the times, Maverick was also automotively topical. Indeed, the Maverick posted its best sales result since its very long debut model year: 301,048! For buyers looking to downsize – and there were many –economy sedans like Maverick and Valiant made out like bandits during the gas crunch. Meanwhile, dust gathered on the roofs of large cars at dealership lots, from sea to shining sea.

It was success for Maverick, in spite of newly mandatory 5mph bumpers, front and rear. This made new design, rear-quarter panel end caps necessary. It was a one-year only modification for such extra securing side bolts on the rear bumpers. By 1974, Maverick finally received a standard glovebox, plus a front disk brake option. Emissions law got stricter for 1974, but was still bearable, with the peppy 302 V8 making 140bhp at 3800rpm, and 230lb-ft at 2600rpm. More importantly, it didn't feel like a smogger when tuned right. The only fly in the ointment was the much stricter pollution laws coming for 1975. That implied the 302 V8 making

This is a 1974 Maverick four-door sedan, with 250 cube Thriftpower in-line six. (Courtesy Paul D Parsons)

129bhp at 4 grand and 213lb-ft at 1800rpm. In California it was 122hp, the 302's lowest ebb. This two-barrel V8's bottom end was still strong, but it ran out of steam past 50mph. However, there were compensations.

The 1975 Maverick featured a new grille, nameplates relocated to the hood and trunklid, plus 'FORD' script in block letters. To meet emissions requirements, Ford 302 V8 cars had the efficiency of dual cats in the Golden State. 49-state cars escaped the cats, for now … This was a boon, since early pellet-type, two-way catalytic converters were powerless over nitrogen oxide, and the EPA was getting stricter on Nox.

For grams per mile concerning hydrocarbons, carbon monoxide and nitrogen oxides, 49-state Mavericks received exhaust gas recirculation and a smog pump to reach a respective legal limit of 1.5/15/3.1. For California, those figures changed to a respective 0.9/9/2. The latter necessitated dual cats, EGR and a smog pump. For comparison, Ford's 1974 302 V8 was putting out a respective 3.2/39/2, on an 8.0:1 CR. The laws would only get stricter, and lack of technology caused poorer running, thirstier cars for the consumer, which were more prone to overheating. However, Washington DC didn't care; it

In the wake of the Yom Kippur war-induced OPEC oil embargo, sales of economy sedans like Maverick and Valiant skyrocketed. (Courtesy Paul D Parsons)

was only listening to the environmentalists.

The improvements kept coming, though. 1976 witnessed another front grille amendment and standard front disk brakes. The rather antiquated, under the dash, T-shaped park brake handle was

Car magazines and consumers alike now expressed greater interest in both downsized cars and engines. They were bypassing entry level V8s for straight talkin' sixes! (Courtesy Paul D Parsons)

With 1974 model year sales of 301,048 units, the Maverick was almost as big a hit as *Tie a yellow ribbon round the ole oak tree*! (Courtesy Paul D Parsons)

given the heave ho in favor of a foot-operated equivalent. And the advertising was confident. 1976's TV ad showed all previous six Maverick model years morphing into the new '77 Maverick! Ford made the claim, "In the last three years scheduled servicing costs of six-cylinder Mavericks have been reduced 40 per cent.". To this it added "The family compact, economical to operate and service," plus "Dependable Ford Maverick." Not to mention "Honed, refined and improved." It was that

5mph rear impact bumpers necessitated a redesign of the Maverick's quarter panel end caps. (Courtesy Paul D Parsons)

Maverick's monster sales caused Ford management to reconsider its original plan to replace the Maverick/Comet with the new Granada/Monarch. You hadn't seen the back of the Simple Machine yet! (Courtesy Paul D Parsons)

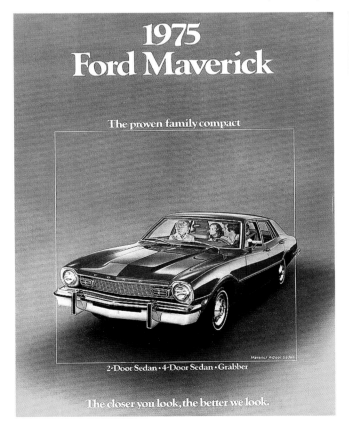

The LDO package continued with Maverick, slightly decontented into 1975. However, its sales and thunder were taken by a new luxo bird called Granada. (Courtesy Ford Motor Co)

With small luxury cars on the rise, little wonder this 1976 Maverick 250 sedan was specified with an automatic, and factory a/c. (Courtesy Craig Selvey)

Once again, the 302 Windsor V8 was eschewed in favor of the Thriftpower six for better gas mileage. It was an era of thrifty luxury! (Courtesy Craig Selvey)

old "The Simple Machine" message, first heard way back in 1969.

Bill believed the ad. His purchase of a '77 Maverick four-door sedan was the subject of a

1977 TV commercial that involved his inquisitive neighbor, who had just bought a 1977 Plymouth Volare Premier. And no, Bill's neighbor wasn't Dean Martin! Even at this late stage, the comparison ads

Front disk brakes were standard in 1976; the grille was new, as was the foot-operated parking brake. (Courtesy Craig Selvey)

On TV, Ford referred to the '76 Maverick as being "Honed, refined and improved." (Courtesy Craig Selvey)

kept coming, with the disclaimer of "comparably equipped vehicles," and mention of both cars having vinyl roofs, tinted windows and whitewalls. However, Maverick trumped Volare with front reclining buckets rather than a mere split bench, plus the kind of soft touch vinyl found on the aforementioned Cougar XR7 and in Maverick's former LDO pack. Yes, LDO was gone, but you could still option a plush Maverick, if that was your wish.

The '77 MY 302 Windsor V8 had smaller intake passages and a comp ratio raised from 8.0 to 8.4:1. It benefited from Ford transistorized Dura Spark ignition. Peak power was made at lower rpm, and the motor felt torquier. Annual re-ratings had seen the 302 climb to 134bhp at 3600rpm and 247lb-ft at 1800rpm for 1976. 1977 ratings were 129bhp at 3400rpm and 242lb-ft at 2000rpm.

Bill probably bought a Thriftpower six Maverick to save gas, so all that V8 goodness was lost on him. In any case, Bill had the winning edge, with

In size and economy, the Maverick sedan was a prelude to the mid-size American family car of the 1980s. (Courtesy Craig Selvey)

This Portland, Oregon coupe's spec showed how luxury was in by the late '70s: originally with a sparkly cinnamon brown exterior and white vinyl roof, automatic, power steering, power brakes and faux wires. The optional vinyl interior, was like that of earlier LDO packs. (Courtesy Richard Rome)

As this coupe shows, the Maverick was still going in 1977. Like an import, there had been no change for the sake of change. (Courtesy Richard Rome)

Maverick costing "A couple of hundred less" than a comparable Volare. "I'm going for a new lawnmower tomorrow, will you come with me Bill?" Sure, said Bill, and Mr Volare then kicked the Premier's back tire in disgust!

The larger Maverick four-door was more appropriate in such value 'show and tells' than the smaller Maverick coupe, concerning GM and Mopar rivals. However, it was a value that convinced fewer and fewer prospects. For 1975, FoMoCo had introduced the upscale Ford Granada and Mercury Monarch compacts to replace Maverick and Comet.

Ford retained both older cars beyond 1974, and through 1977

model year. The company feared another gas crunch was imminent, so it was wise to keep more small cars on hand. In actuality, OPEC dropped its second bombshell for 1980 model year. However, once the Granada and Monarch came out, buyers had fewer reasons to purchase the older Maverick and Comet. Maverick sales in 1975, 1976 and 1977 model years fell to a respective 162,572, 139,687 and finally 98,506 units. During 1975 to 1977, only the Kansas City and St Thomas assembly plants were making Maverick.

Before the end, the Maverick made a cameo on the silver screen, in the 1977 movie *In Hot Pursuit* (aka *Polk County Pot*

Clockwise from top left: Contemporary ads de-emphasized the 302 V8 in favor of the Thriftpower in-line 6 shown. (Courtesy Richard Rome) Sliders, pull out knobs and longhand script used to be domestic car de rigueur. This coupe came with the rare rear window defogger option. (Courtesy Richard Rome) Like that Timex watch, Fords took a licking but kept on ticking! (Courtesy Richard Rome)

Plane). The film starred real life stuntmen the Watson Brothers, and was a B movie for the Southern drive-in circuit. During a payroll robbery of an armored car, the brothers used a '68 Camaro 350 as a getaway vehicle. The Camaro got pretty trashed, and while out of sight of the law, the brothers purloined a brand new Maverick four-door sedan from a lady's garage. The Ford had just been picked up from the dealership.

The lady Ford owner when opening her garage door, to show neighbors her beautiful new car, only found the trashed Chevy in its place! The Watson Brothers had driven off sedately in said sedan. One

This Canadian spec sedan is a 1977 Maverick LDO 250 six. (Courtesy J LaLonde)

A visual mod involves a blacked-out hood complemented by painted custom striping. (Courtesy J LaLonde)

For stealth, a blacked-out grille, recessed front bumper and tinted glass are joined by an antenna free passenger fender. (Courtesy J LaLonde)

doned a lady's scarf, looking like, but not driving like Jan and Dean's little old lady from Pasadena. However, this wasn't Pasadena, it was Jonesboro, Georgia. What's more, the dark blue Maverick four-door with black vinyl roof, whitewalls and wires, was purchased from dealer Handshaker Ford. The other Watson brother hid out of sight, with the loot!

The police just drove past, that was the kind of low profile performer that Maverick was. Over 2 million sales, no controversy, and no falling apart like a Vega. However, that wasn't the end of the story. In spite of Ford's advertising for the new Granada, inviting Mercedes comparisons, there was an awful lot of Maverick in the new Ford compact.

In spite of its luminous appearance, the drivetrain is all original, and so, too, interior seating trim. (Courtesy J LaLonde)

With 2,099,263 Mavericks and 487,212 related Comets, this small Ford family was an unqualified success! A 1977 sedan is shown. (Courtesy Ford Motor Co)

Custom painted Cragar S/S 15 x 7in rims are wrapped in front 215/60-15s and rear 245/60-15s. Paint, vinyl top and carpet have been renewed. (Courtesy J LaLonde)

Granada and Monarch – Play it again Lee!

Lee Iacocca was on the cover of Fortune business magazine. He was standing between FoMoCo's two new luxury compacts, the Ford Granada and Mercury Monarch. A guy wasn't going to buy a car anymore just because it had a long hood, said Lee. He was right; the final year of Mustang One sales were dismal, but Mustang II went through the sunroof! Being ahead of the game, Ford broke the domestic correlation between size and luxury. Henry popularized small luxury American cars. That's where the 1975 Granada and Monarch came in. Planning began around the time Maverick came out, 1969.

Lee Iacocca and Ford could see that small size class cars would be increasingly important to mainstream buyers as time went on. To this end, the Granada and Monarch were originally intended as premium compacts, rather than direct Mercedes and BMW competitors. Ford research predicted the rise of luxury compacts, as increasing gas prices, multiple family car ownership and urban congestion would all bring change to pre-1970 buying patterns. At first, the European 1972 Ford Granada was evaluated as a captive import. However, federalization costs, a strong Deutschmark and lack of suitable engine choices dictated otherwise.

Early US Granada and Monarch thinking concerned downsized domestic buyers, as well as those wishing to trade up from plain compacts. However, the fuel crisis brought a change in game plan. The Maverick and Comet would be kept. The Granada and Monarch would be pushed upscale of the older pair, and priced more at the European import level. The latter group had garnered considerable attention in the press and on the street.

The engineering connection between the Maverick and Granada was a strong one. The basic chassis of the new car: front SLA suspension, a leaf sprung live axle, the same 109.9in wheelbase of Maverick four-door, the front part of Maverick's floorpan, and elements of the recirculating ball steering. Indeed, base Granadas were little different in

What looks like the newest Cadillac and is priced like the newest VW?

Ford Granada. 1975's best-selling newcomer.

Ford Granada 4-Door $3,756*

Cadillac Seville $12,479*

VW Rabbit 4-Door $3,800*

Ford Granada—with Cadillac's $12,000-look at a price like VW— is a real engineering achievement. But it's only one of the reasons Granada is 1975's best-selling newcomer.

What so many people like about Granada is the efficient way it brings together features they are looking for today. This distinctive new-size design provides full-scale room for five. Granada combines a smooth, quiet ride with precise, sure handling and a high level of elegance. The engine choice ranges from a 200 CID Six to an action-packed 351 CID V-8. There's lots more you'll like about Granada. Check it out at your Ford Dealer soon.

*Base sticker prices excluding title, taxes and destination charges. Dealer prep extra on Granada and VW. Price comparison based on sticker prices excluding title, taxes and dealer prep which may affect comparison in some areas. Granada shown with optional WSW tires ($33) and paint stripes ($24).

Look close and compare. Ford means value. And your local Ford Dealer can show you.

FORD GRANADA
FORD DIVISION *Ford*

Unlike the Rabbit or Seville, the new 1975 Granada could be an economy car, luxury car, or both. It all depended on ticked option boxes. (Courtesy Ford Motor Co)

substance to the Maverick. It was a manual three on the tree, and no power assist for steering or brakes. The Thriftpower 200cu in six was familiar, but there were exclusives. Maverick never got the 351 Windsor V8, nor a four-speed. From 1976, Granada even enjoyed a four-wheel disk brake option.

The first 1970 Granada prototype benchmarked the Mercedes W114 Compact 280. True enough, the '75 Granada avoided Maverick's Coke bottle styling in favor of a squared-up Mercedes roof and grille headlamp visage. This was accentuated with the 1978 restyle, which also incorporated elements of the recently introduced Ford LTD II, itself a reworked Gran Torino. As ever, interest was in the high-end versions; for example, the European Sport sedan-oriented 1976-77 Granada Sports Coupe and Monarch S. All Granadas and Monarchs utilized

11in front disk brakes as standard. However, the Sports Coupe had larger front brakes, standard HD suspension and floor shift.

The 1978-80 Granada and Monarch ESS (European Sports Sedan) took the game even higher, targeting the much-vaunted Mercedes W123 in comparison ads. Top Ghia luxury versions brought the expected vinyl roof, optional leather interior and wood trim dashboard. In this respect, the 1975-76 Merc Grand Monarch Ghia was unique, for there was no Granada counterpart. Henry Ford II had a Monarch Ghia as personal transport. One could say it coincided with the spirit of the 1975 Caddy Seville. Cadillac was anxious as hell – Mercedes was taking their sales. In addition, existing clientele, to use *MotorWeek*'s John Davis' turn of phrase, were being buried by the cemetery's worth!

USA Lincoln
Lincoln-Mercury Division, Ford Motor Co.,
300 Renaissance Center, Detroit, Michigan 48243, USA

Lincoln Versailles   97 kW, 195 km/h

Lincoln Continental   119 kW, 170 km/h

Lincoln Continental Mark V   119 kW, 175 km/h

Neben Cadillac bleibt der Lincoln die Prestigemarke auf dem amerikanischen Markt. Interessant dabei ist, daß der ehemalige Cadillac-Präsident Leland 1917 die Firma Lincoln gründete, die dann fünf Jahre später von Ford erworben wurde. Der Lincoln Continental als Top-modell ist der Dienstwagen des US-Präsidenten.

Lincoln Versailles
Leicht modifizierte Version des Ford Granada, aber die äußerliche Identität des Versailles wurde für den jetzigen Jahrgang durch ein neues Dachhinterteil betont. Neu auch sind Halogenscheinwerfer, die gemäß einem neuen Gesetz die doppelte Beleuchtungsstärke leisten, und ein vollelektronisches Quadrosonic-Radio, Vierrad-Scheibenbremsen, Automatik, Servolenkung, automatische Klimaanlage, Cassettenspieler serienmäßig. Ab $ 13 206.

Lincoln Continental
„Letzter der Dinosaurier." Dieser riesige Familienwagen, als Limousine und Coupé angeboten, war der letzte ungeschwächte amerikanische Big Car und verkaufte sich noch im vorletzten Produktionsjahr sehr rege: mehr als 93 000 davon! Dann im Juni 1979, als die Bevölkerung in Benzinschlangen wartete, wurde die Produktion eingestellt. Neue, abgemagerte Modelle erscheinen im Herbst 1979. Preis für die letzten Exemplare: ab $ 11 252.

Continental Mark V
Auch mit diesem Riesencoupé geht eine Ära zu Ende. 5,85 Meter lang, 2,13 Tonnen schwer, 6,6 Liter V8-Motor. Die Collector's Series feiert sein letztes Jahr in „fullsize", die Designer Series bietet noch immer Versionen von Bill Blass, Emilio Pucci, Givenchy und Cartier. Preise ab $ 13 334.

Mercury
Lincoln-Mercury Division, Ford Motor Co.,
300 Renaissance Center, Detroit, Michigan 48243, USA

Mercury Bobcat   66–76 kW, 150–165 km/h

Mercurys sechs Modellreihen, im wesentlichen mit entsprechenden Ford-Modellen identisch, weisen im jetzigen Jahrgang zwei Neuheiten auf: den Capri und die großen Marquis/Grand Marquis.

Mercury Bobcat
Mercury-Version des Ford Pinto; nur als dreitüriges Kombicoupé und Kombi erhältlich. In seiner aktuellsten Fassung weist der Bobcat ähnliche Änderungen wie sein

Ford-Zwillingsbruder auf: neue Frontpartie, Stoßstangen und Interieur-Details, verbesserte Leistung beim V6-Motor. Neue Extras: MW-UKW-Stereo-Radio mit Cassettenspieler, Leichtmetallräder. Ab $ 3797.

Mercury Capri
Seit Anfang August 1978 wird der europäische Ford Capri nicht mehr nach den USA exportiert. An seine Stelle trat Ende 1978 ein neuer, in Ame-

144 auto katalog 23/1980

The ultra luxury 1977-80 Lincoln Versailles could trace its engineering origins to the Ford Maverick. (Courtesy Vereinigte Motor-Verlage)

Cadillac used the very humble Chevy Nova as the engineering basis for the original Seville. It utilized an injected Olds 350 V8. Placing Caddy sentiment to one side, sales did rocket like the proverbial Olds V8. From May 1975 to April 1976, 44,475 Sevilles were delivered. This nearly matched the entire North American Mercedes total of 45,353. [40] It was Cadillac's smallest car, but carried the marque's biggest price tag. That's a helluva lot of value added, heaped onto a Nova

base! This achievement probably inspired the most lavish Maverick ever created, the 1977-80 Lincoln Versailles.

The Lincoln Versailles representatively took the Mercury Grand Monarch Ghia to the ultimate level. It had styling elements of the Continental and Mark V, standard V8, four-wheel disk brakes and halogen headlights. It was also the first US vehicle to feature clearcoat paint. Inspiration came from the Mercedes W116 S class and BMW 3.0Si. It also certainly took a leaf from the Caddy's book, by being the smallest Lincoln in that brand's history. But it also had the highest price! The Versailles had a strict quality control regimen, matched and balanced driveline, reinforced unibody chassis areas, and even a Ford 9in differential. That last item, along with a rear axle coming with disk brakes attached, has made the 50,156 Versailles sedans popular vehicles for car modifiers to raid.

The price tag was considered stratospheric for a domestic, but was in fact cheaper than a BMW. The Monarch had been originally planned as a new Comet to take on the Mercedes 280 Compact. Still, buyers mostly considered the Versailles too visually close to a Grand Monarch Ghia. Plus, at nearly twice the price, it was a hard sell given the shared showroom. Sales of the Versailles more than doubled after a '79 MY update, but always trailed the Seville. The Versailles lacked Seville's development budget. However, Cadillac suffered a reversal of fortune with its ill fated GM J car-based 1981 Cimarron.

Fortunately, sales of the Granada and Monarch were hardly disappointing. From the Mahwah and Michigan assembly plants, 2,006,276 Granadas and 575,567 Monarchs were made. So, 1980 was the final curtain for Falcon's engineering blueprint. It made Lee Iacocca and Ford the ultimate recyclers! For 1981, such designs were completely superseded by the Fairmont-based cars that had commenced in 1978 as the Maverick's direct replacement.

Appendix A - Ford's transition into the '80s

In the post fuel crisis world of increasing foreign competition, Detroit would try and reconcile tradition with the future. This balancing act was seen in the Ford Granada TV commercials. A 1976 ad showed two silver Granadas on a banked test track, and two silver Mercedes 280s. Ford made the statement that Granada went further than merely resembling Stuttgart's W114 Compact, it also had the great gas mileage and sub 4-grand base sticker the American buyer expected. A second 1976 ad showed three silver sedans: a Granada, Caddy Seville and Mercedes 280. These cars were track-test subjected to the usual Detroit yardsticks of luxury evaluation.

At steady speed, the three posted respective decibel readings of 67.5dBa, 66dBa and 68.5dBa. In a ride test over rough surfaces, with an interior vibration recorder at 20, 30 and 40mph, Granada came either first or second on test. It was mentioned the Mercedes cost 12 grand. Along similar lines, the Ford Granada Sports Coupe, costing $4189, was value-compared with the Mercedes 450SLC. The West German car retailed for $23,976, and was acknowledged internationally as one of the finest automobiles money could buy.

Ford titled the ultimate coupe clash ad "A remarkable achievement," but steered clear of getting out the test equipment to measure anything.

The statement was simply made that the Granada came with HD suspension, buckets and a floor shift as standard equipment. Then there was the lady that got a parking ticket from a traffic cop, who mistook her new Granada for a Cadillac, to which she replied "I don't own a Cadillac!"

In real life, at least one lady has mistaken the front of a silver '80s aero Thunderbird for that of a Mercedes W126 S class. Given the color and headlamp framing, it's a mistake the casual passer-by could understandably make. However, all of the above definitely showed that while yardsticks and benchmarks of excellence had changed, the Big Three still had to appease their mainstream core buyers.

For genuine change within, veteran Ford designer Jack Telnack steered Henry Ford II towards European design. It had been agreed to that point that new Fords would be boxy and possess upright grilles. Telnack, as was normal with the Big Three, had done sojourns overseas at Ford subsidiaries during his career. This began with Ford Australia in the '60s. In the '70s, Telnack was with Ford Europe. He wished to show Henry Ford II the proposed European Ford Granada MkII sketches. It was a sedan to be released for '78 MY. Henry Ford II said he was uncomfortable with the sedan's slant grille.

(Courtesy Christelynn Teed)

(Top and bottom) Ford had its finger on the small car pulse. Hidemi Aoki is with the Fresh Cherries Mustang II and Granada. (Courtesy www.nepoeht.com)

For 1977 some car makers narrower, lighter full-size cars.

Ford LTD. The full-size car that kept its size.

The trimmer, sportier LTD II at a trimmer price.

FORD

FORD DIVISION *Ford*

will offer you only shorter, Ford has a better idea. Choice:

Ford LTD. The full-size car that kept its size.

This year some car makers are making their full-size cars smaller. But Ford believes that people who want the traditional full-size car they're used to should have that choice. So the 1977 Ford LTD hasn't been reduced by a single inch!

You'll find Ford LTD has a longer wheelbase than cars like the downsized Olds 98 and Buick Electra and about the same size wheelbase as Cadillac de Ville.

And Ford LTD now has a longer wheelbase than Chevrolets (both Impala and Caprice) which have come down to the same wheelbase as the mid-size Chevelle.

Ride, room and trunkspace—unchanged

Ford LTD has retained its traditional smooth, quiet ride. Interior spaciousness, deep-well trunk, road-hugging performance, long wheelbase and 3½-ton rated towing capacity (with optional trailer towing package) are all unchanged. Keep all this in mind when you go shopping for a new car this year.

Will "down-sized" cars have "down-sized" prices?

As this magazine goes to press, 1977 prices are not available. When they are, compare LTD's value to its down-sized competitors. Compare with test drives. What you may really want is the quiet ride and roominess of Ford's full-size 6-passenger car, the 1977 Ford LTD.

SIZE COMPARISONS		
Cars with full-size wheelbase		
4-DOOR MODELS	1977	1976
Ford LTD	121.0"	121.0"
Cadillac de Ville	121.5"	130.0"
Cars with mid-size wheelbase		
Ford LTD II	118.0"	—
Caprice	116.0"	121.5"
Impala	116.0"	121.5"
Chevelle	116.0"	116.0"

Stylish Ford LTD Country Squire, LTD Landau 2-Door

And the new trimmer, sportier LTD II.

If you prefer a 6-passenger car that's trimmer in size and price than LTD, Ford gives you that choice, too. Ford introduces a sporty new line of cars for 1977—2-doors, 4-doors, station wagons—called LTD II.

A new idea that's a better idea

Ford's new quiet-riding LTD II combines LTD's traditional high-level of workmanship with a unique sporty spirit that's all its own. The result: a comfortable new car that's trimmer in size and price than LTD.

A new kind of value

Ford will price LTD II to strongly challenge all competitors. So as soon as 1977 prices are announced, compare LTD II value not only with other mid-size cars, but even with GM's cut down "full-size" cars.

And you should know that all

Trim LTD II Squire, Sporty LTD II Brougham 2-Door

LTD II and Ford LTD 1977 prices include V-8, automatic transmission, power steering, power front disc brakes, steel-belted radials, Dura Spark Ignition system, and more.

Shop where you get a choice

Full size or trim size? Some car makers won't give you this choice of car sizes in 1977. But Ford will: full size Ford LTD or trim size LTD II.

So this year, before you decide on the car size that's best for you and your family, take a comparison test drive. And compare prices at a dealer who offers you a choice: your local Ford Dealer.

When America needs a better idea, Ford puts it on wheels.

Slow to downsize its large cars, Ford tried to convince buyers that the LTD II offered full-size value at a mid-size price. (Courtesy Ford Motor Co and Scott Goodrich)

Jack Telnack said to Mr. Ford, could they do some alternative sketches while he considered the restyle? Henry Ford II agreed to think it over. On a subsequent trip to London, he was in agreement with the European restyle and said, "Boy, I've got to tell you, it really works. Let's go with this." The concession from the Ford family paved the way for the European-influenced 1979 Fox platform Mustang. Jack Telnack was very relieved that Mr Ford said yes, because he wasn't so hopeful concerning the alternative Mustang. That proposal was boxy, and in Telnack's words, "very, very American."

Jack Telnack feared that if they had gone with the 'Boxstang,' Ford would have been into a major restyle after just a few years. He was concerned the boxy proposal wouldn't have the market longevity,

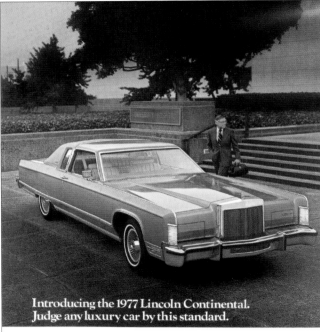

Introducing the 1977 Lincoln Continental.
Judge any luxury car by this standard.

The 1977 Lincoln Continental sets a high standard for luxury cars. Full-sized, full-luxury, to give you the pleasures of space, of comfort, of superb handling on the highway. That's because it's a Continental. Unmistakable from its redesigned front end to its winning Lincoln ride.

For 1977, some luxury cars are smaller than last year. For 1977, Lincoln Continental retains its traditional luxury car size. We believe it's a luxury car that meets your standards.

Lincoln Continental. A standard by which luxury cars are judged.

LINCOLN CONTINENTAL
LINCOLN-MERCURY DIVISION · Ford

The Lincoln Continental Mark V was the real 'Big Car' deal that no downsized Caddy could match! (Courtesy Ford Motor Co)

in a world where Japanese sports coupes were changing every few years. The Land of the Rising Sun had learnt well the old Detroit lore, that there was nothing older than last year's model. *Road & Track*'s August 1978 issue had the new '79 MY Mustang and Capri on the cover, with the headline: "New Capri-Mustang. European bred, American built." What's more, the Mercury version was displayed in the foreground, with the Mustang in the background. The Capri was perceived the more European of the two. To use industry parlance, the Mustang was de-emphasized in this era.

In a March 1979 owner survey, *Road & Track* said the 1975 BMW 530i possessed all the flat panes and sharp styling creases that had since become a styling fad: "If you don't believe it, take a look at the 1979 Mustang." In June 1983, the same magazine ran a 'Three American Eurosedan' test. Here, it observed the front drive trio of the Buick Century, Dodge 600 and Pontiac 6000. The subtitle was "Arriving refreshed, with a lot less wallow." *Road & Track* said it was unfortunate the term 'Euro sedan' had to be coined at all, for it was just good design. It took the words right out of Jack Telnack's mouth.

Telnack proved to be correct. The Foxstang did last a very long time, 1979-1993. In many ways, it was the most successful Mustang generation of all time. Speaking of the coupe's acceptance, he said "today, it's normal design. I like to think of it as normal good design, but you don't hear anybody refer to it as 'European' anymore." Well, almost. In *R&T*'s February 1993 'War Horses' piece comparing the Camaro Z28, Firebird Formula and Mustang Cobra, Patrick Bedard said that, sitting in the Mustang, "The mood is BMW." The upright seating position, black interior and relatively vertical windshield, led him to that conclusion.

Indeed, the 1970 $^1/_2$ GM F body had started life in similar fashion: declared European on debut, but then becoming so popular it was seen as normal. The new Camaro and Firebird did make '60s muscle cars look awfully boxy. The Mustang might have followed, the unsuccessful path of the 1980-82 Boxbird Thunderbird. It was a coupe that didn't stray far enough from its Kellogg's cereal box-like Fairmont basis. Jack Telnack said they went to the expense of custom inner front fender aprons and radiator supports, versus Fairmont, all so that the Foxstang could have a faster sloping hood that pivoted over the air cleaner. [41]

A 1976 Mustang sketch proposal. Jack Telnack facilitated the European design move at Ford.
(Courtesy Ford Motor Co)

With aerodynamics going hand in hand with performance and fuel savings post gas crunch, Ford made the move to flowing shapes in timely fashion. Ford VP of Design, Donald Kopka, said how important aerodynamics, embodied in the Ford Probe show cars, had been in allowing Ford USA to meet its CAFE obligations, and avoid a gas guzzler tax. GM had shown in the late '70s that boosting economy through downsizing and weight cutting was a costly exercise. FoMoCo had been behind the eightball with downsizing, and aerodynamics allowed Henry to play catch-up in obtaining those crucial MPGs for the '80s. Indeed, Donald Kopka predicted cars would have no grilles by the year 2000. [42]

Underhood, Donald Petersen got things revved up with Ford's Modular V8 family. Petersen became President of Ford in 1980. He regarded Ford's existing OHV V8s as in need of replacement. With a view to achieving improved performance, economy and emissions, the solution was OHC, DOHC and multivalve. The 4.6 V8 was the result, first seen in 190-horse form in the 1991 Lincoln Town Car. The Romeo V8 took its name from the Romeo, Michigan engine plant it was built in. So, when Lexus and Infiniti were there with their modern V8s, so was Ford.

Then again, tradition is important. You don't know where you're going, if you don't know where you've been. A big part of the Fox platform Mustang's success came from offering a speedy V8,

rear-drive package at an affordable price. Change the word speedy to comfy, and you have the reason for the Panther platform's success. America still wanted cars like this, as evidenced by the experiences of Joe Sherlock. In his automotive blog *The View Through The Windshield*, Sherlock recounted his pleasurable experience owning a 1979 Lincoln Williamsburg Edition Town Car.

This 233in long, 400M (Modified) V8-powered, separate chassis leviathan offered the long distance, insulated cruising experience that used to be considered normal luxury fare. Faux dashboard wood and 12mpg highway perhaps, but a 127.2in wheelbase and 4600lb curb weight produced a ride no VW Rabbit could have. Town Car sales rose greatly in 1977 partly due to defections from GM, which had downsized its full-size cars that year. Regardless, it seemed many Americans still liked the refinement of a rear-drive V8-powered, body-on-frame sedan. Ford obliged with its downsized Panther platform cars, taking over completely from older mid-size and full-size body on frame Fords by 1980. In the smaller size class, Fairmont kept rear-drive and a V8 option with a unibody design. This maintained what the Maverick had done before 1978.

With Ford USA's smallest car, the Pinto, replacing Escort, Henry went front-wheel drive with transverse in-line four power. At first this 'World Car' shared an engineering basis with the European front drive Escort. It subsequently switched to being related to the third generation Mazda GLC/323. Indeed, Mazda

The Foxstang couldn't have happened without Jack Telnack convincing Henry Ford II to accept a sloping grille. (Courtesy Vereinigte Motor-Verlage)

The Panther platform satiated big Ford demand from 1980 to 2012. (Courtesy Vereinigte Motor-Verlage)

had become Ford's small car partner from 1980. It was a help dealing with fuel efficient projects outside Ford's wheelhouse. Future successful results were the Ford Festiva and Probe coupe.

All the while, Ford resisted the move to go full-scale front drive, and without V8s. GM had gone front drive with a vengeance in the '80s, much to the enthusiast's chagrin. Chrysler was fully into K car related jobs for economic survival, so aside from aging V8-powered M cars, offered little choice. Apart from Jeep and Eagle, AMC was with Renault, so it seemed like front drive there, too. However, the customer was king, and the old ways still had appeal. In its January 1974 report "Measuring the Mid-Sized Machines," *Motor Trend* tested the Torino Brougham 460 and said "Ford's edge in sound deadening is very hard to overcome."

Fast forward a decade, and Jim Dunne wrote a piece for *Popular Science* in August 1985, called "Rear-drives retained." It stated that Ford was cautious concerning total changeover to front-wheel

drive. FoMoCo felt it prudent to retain rear-drive for its large cars, at least through 1990 model year. However, a Ford insider confided that "These decisions could change tomorrow." The price of gas was a determining factor, and of course that went into freefall in 1986. The Reagan administration relaxed CAFE in 1986, feeling the full 27.5mpg requirement to be an unnecessary burden on automakers. [43]

Dunne wrote that Ford executives knew many buyers liked the smooth ride, quieter interior, and more imposing appearance that traditional rear-drive automobiles offered. How long for? Well, the separate chassis, rear-drive, V8-powered Panther platform Fords lasted a record 33 years, ending in 2012! The Mustang carried on, but like the returning 5th gen Camaro, reverted to 'old skool,' pre-Telnack styling for modern, niche market muscle cars. Dodge joined in, too, reviving the classic Charger and Challenger look from bygone days. Then, too, there's the pickup truck market. It's hard to see anyone giving up their trusty, V8-powered Ford F150!

Appendix B – The Road Warrior Falcon

Imagine if, in a parallel universe, Ford hadn't stopped making the Falcon in 1970. If it carried on, what would have happened? In Mexico, the Maverick was originally called Falcon Maverick, but that's not quite the same thing. No, you need a scenario where the Falcon itself just continued. That's indeed what occurred with Ford Australia. Back in what was 1961 model year, the Aussie Falcon was simply a RHD CKD version of America's most popular compact. Yes, 144cu in Thriftpower six and all! By the end of the '60s, there was still a strong visual and mechanical kinship between US and Australian Falcons. A larger, boxier, V8-powered sedan compared to the 1960 econoriginal. The ultimate example of this kind of sedan was the 1971 Falcon GTHO Phase III with Cleveland 351 V8, Top Loader four-speed and 385bhp gross. It was an homologation special, which won the legendary local Bathurst endurance race.

In 1972, it was a whole new ball game, with the XA Falcon range. This included a two-door GT hardtop, which in size and looks greatly resembled a contemporary US Mustang. Thanks to an anti performance, alarmist media campaign, that got the public scared of a swarm of pending 160mph supercars terrorizing the streets, planned homologation specials never transpired. However, Ford's Falcon Phase IV hardware did get fitted to the 1972 XA Falcon GTs, using the RPO83 option code. This brought a large gas tank, winged sumps and 15 x 7in Globe alloys. Australia tended to prefer four-door sedans, but all three local subsidiaries of the Big Three had coupes with V8s. AMC was there, too, with a local AMX 401 coupe.

Ford Australia made the Cleveland V8 in 302 and 351 cube forms at its Geelong foundry. In 1973, the coupe used in the Road Warrior, post apocalyptic *Mad Max* movies came out. This was the XB Falcon GT 351 coupe. Only slightly restyled from the outgoing XA, the Falcon range was still available in a multitude of body types, two-door hardtop, four-door sedan, wagon, pickup Ranchero style two-door and luxury, long-wheelbase versions called Fairlane and LTD. Yes, Australia was Henry's second home for many years.

The Road Warrior coupe saw the first 211 XB Falcon GT 351s, with 351C big port head V8s, imported from America. The XB model range was billed as "The Great Australian Road Car," with GT

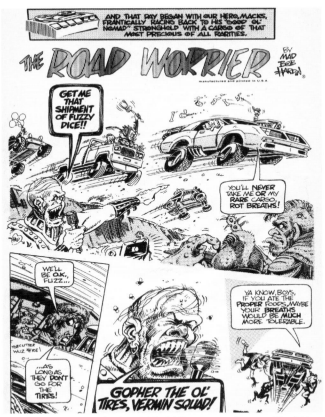

Artist Bob C Hardin's 1983 CARtoons take on *Mad Max 2: The Road Warrior*, featuring the Australian Falcon coupe! (Courtesy Bob C Hardin)

The 1972 XA Ford Falcon GT 351 V8 coupe was one real hot performer. (Courtesy Ford Australia)

Mad Max painted his Falcon coupe a stealthier shade! (Courtesy Ford Australia)

featuring color contrasting paint schemes like Blaze Yellow, and even a psychedelic purple, against matte black paint, along with stenciled GT 351 front fender callouts. Rear tail-lamps weren't dissimilar to the units *Car and Driver* called "glowing beer bottles" on Maverick. You could get the GT variant in two or four-door forms. Emission controls saw the 1974 GT 351 coupe automatic good for a 16-second flat 1/4-mile. The Australian-made two-barrel 351 now had closed combustion-chambered quench heads. That said, the GT's four-wheel disk brakes were still present.

There was no GT version in the lightly restyled XC Falcon of July 1976. However, there was a milder GS (Grand Sport) edition. Like America and South America, the public's appetite for muscle cars and high-performance was waning. Of course, most family guys bought four-door Falcons, with automatic transmission and a locally built 250cu in crossflow version of the Thriftpower six. The final XC Falcon coupe was a Cobra version, liveried like the 1976 white and blue Mustang II Cobra II.

Local hot Chrysler Charger and GM-Holden Monaro coupe rivals had already left the building. By the time of the 1979 *Mad Max* movie, the reskinned XD Falcon four-door, wagon or two-door pickup had arrived. This reworking of the Falcon resembled a larger version of the European Ford Granada MkII, which had come out for '78 MY. Both Fords featured Mercedes W116 S class styling cues.

The XD Falcon retained the local 302 and 351 Cleveland V8s, with the 351 making 200 net DIN horses. Such choices ended with the 1982 XE Falcon, where said 351 could still be teamed with four on the floor. V8 engines for the Australian Falcon returned in the 1992 EB Falcon. However, this time it was a fully imported Mustang 5.0 unit from America. Ford Australia stayed loyal to the 302, until the Modular 5.4 V8 was introduced in 2003. The supercharged 'Miami' 5.4 V8 was a local special. Stricter smog law saw a switch to the Coyote V8 in mid 2010. The final Aussie Falcon, a blue XR6, rolled off the line on October 7 2016. The Falcon was a victim of rising interest in SUVs. [44]

Appendix C – Specification tables and Ford items of interest

1970 Ford Maverick Coupe

Base price: $1995, as tested; $2427, options fitted: 200cu in I6 ($26), Select-Shift auto ($174), Accent Group with 6.45-14s ($39), AM radio ($61)

Engine: 200cu in (3.3 liter) in-line six (Thriftpower), OHV, cast iron head (with integrated intake manifold) & block, 1bbl Carter carburetor, 8.7:1 CR (regular gas), 120bhp @ 4000rpm, 190lb-ft @ 2200rpm

Gearbox: three-speed Select-Shift automatic (1st) 2.46 (2nd) 1.46 (3rd) 1.00 (rear axle: 2.83)

Suspension front: SLA independent, 0.69in front swaybar, drag strut, coils, tube shocks

Suspension rear: Leaf sprung live axle, tube shocks

Steering: Recirculating ball (manual) 5.2 turns lock to lock

Dimensions: Length 179.4in / width 70.6in / height 52.3in / wheelbase 103in

Weight: 2535lb

Weight distribution: 54.8/45.2 per cent

Brakes: 9.0 x 2.25in drums (front), 9.0 x 1.50in drums (rear) – non boosted

Wheels & tires: 14 x 4.5in steel four-bolt rims / Goodyear Polyester Power Cushion 6.45-14

Performance: 0-60mph 13 seconds

¹/₄-mile: 19.4 seconds at 73.8mph

Top speed: 99mph

Economy: 20mpg on test (regular gas)

Source: *Car Life*, October 1969

This is where it all started for Ford's Simple Machine, and America's first subcompact. The options were limited, but the Mini Mustang looks hinted at the performance potential. And there was nothing small about Maverick's 451,081 1970 model year sales!

1971 Mercury Comet GT

Base price (two-door V8): $2387, as tested; $2859.20, options fitted: HD battery ($12), floor shift ($13.10), Handling Pack ($12), GT pack ($178.80), power steering ($95.40), AM radio ($60.80)

Engine: 302cu in (4.9 liter) V8 (Windsor), OHV, cast iron head & block, 2bbl Autolite carburetor, 9.0:1 CR (regular gas), 210bhp @ 4600rpm, 296lb-ft @ 2600rpm

Gearbox: three-speed all synchro (1st) 2.99 (2nd) 1.75 (3rd) 1.00 (rear axle: 2.79)

Suspension front: SLA independent, drag strut, coils, tube shocks. 0.85in front swaybar with HD suspension fitted.

Suspension rear: Leaf sprung live axle, tube shocks

Steering: Recirculating ball (linkage booster for power steering) 3.9 turns lock to lock

Dimensions: Length 181.7in / width 70.6in / height 52.6in / wheelbase 103in

Weight: 2935lb

Weight distribution: 56.8/43.2 per cent

Brakes: 10 x 2.2in drums (front), 10 x 1.80in flared drums (rear) – non boosted

Wheels & tires: 14 x 6in steel four-bolt rims / Goodyear D70-14

Performance: 0-60mph 8.2 seconds

¹/₄-mile: 16.3 seconds at 84.2mph

Top speed: 115mph

Economy: 13-17mpg on test (regular gas)

Source: *Car and Driver*, July 1971

The Grabber and Comet GT V8s were limited in their optionable hardware. Mustang sales had to be protected. However, buyers not wishing to arm wrestle their Allstate Insurance guy saw the value in these junior supercars. For those that wanted a V8 pony, but couldn't stretch to the sticker price ... this was it!

Maverick/Comet forums

http://mmb.maverick.to
A forum and informational resource site for 1970-77 Ford Maverick and Mercury Comet owners. An itrader parts section is included.

www.maverickcometclub.org
An international Ford Maverick and Mercury Comet club devoted to America's first subcompact. Organizing membership, club meets (including Roundup Nationals) and with a product store.

www.fordmaverick.com
An owner registry and information sharing site for Ford Maverick and Mercury Comet owners. Plus product store with T-shirts!

www.roushcollection.com
Preserving the historical timeline of the achievements of Cactus Jack Roush. Includes the

Pro Stock days of Gapp & Roush, and NASCAR exploits through the years.

www.gapponline.net
A website started by son Jeff Gapp, which shares and seeks information and pictures concerning Wayne Gapp's racing career. It was a career which involved the Gapp & Roush partnership, plus well-known Ford Maverick (Tijuana Taxi), Mustang II and Pinto Pro Stock drag racing cars.

www.fordmuscleforums.com
Billed as the "Ultimate Ford Performance Community," the site offers discussion and help, concerning classic enthusiast postwar Fords. It has Maverick and Comet subforums.

www.mustangii.org
Established 1997, this online group shows owner cars, Mustang II activities, information, member mailing list and forum links. Join the Mustang II online revolution!!

www.fordpinto.com
With a Ford Pinto and Mercury Bobcat register, online store, classifieds and forums, this is HQ for Pinto and Bobcat devotees.

Appendix D – Bibliography and Footnotes

Bibliography

Bean, David, "Spurs For The Maverick" *Car Life,* May 1969

Bentley, John, *All The World's Cars 1954*, New York: Cornell Publishing Corp, 1954

Brennan, Brian ed. "Roddin' At Random," *Hot Rod* October 1974

Brown, Bob ed. "15,000 Mile Comparison Test: Chevrolet Vega Versus Ford Pinto," *Car and Driver,* November 1971

Dunne, Jim, "Detroit Report Rear-drives retained," *Popular Science*, August 1985

Evans, Don ed. "Hot Stuff For Mavericks," *Hot Rod,* January 1970

Ford, Jeff, "What If?" *Legendary Ford*, March/April 2010

Freund, Klaus ed. *Auto Katalog 1980*, Stuttgart: Vereinigte Motor-Verlage, 1979

Gillies, Mark, "Design for Today," *Autocar,* December 10, 1986

Given, Kyle, "And Now A Word From Our Sponsor," *Car and Driver,* September 1969

Gross, Ken, *BMW Illustrated Buyer's Guide*, Wisconsin: MBI, 1984

Grove, Noel, "Swing Low, Sweet Chariot!" *National Geographic,* July 1983

Hamilton, Jim, "Hot and Cold Running Mavericks," *Car Life,* October 1969

Jennings, Gordon ed. "Maverick Grabber," *Car and Driver,* August 1970

Kilpatrick, Bill, "Maverick Versus The Mob," *Popular Mechanics,* August 1969

Koch, Jeff, "Buyer's Guide 1971-'75 Ford Maverick Grabber," *Hemmings Muscle Machines,* September 2009

Mandel, Leon, "Maverick and the mini space race," *Car and Driver,* May 1969

Mandel, Leon ed. "Preview Test: AMC Hornet," *Car and Driver,* September 1969

Mandel, Leon ed. "The Great Imported Car Invasion," *Car and Driver,* September 1969

Morley, Dave, *Six Decades of Holden versus Ford,* Melbourne: Hardie Grant Travel, 2018

McGough, Peter ed. "Real-World Supercars," *Car Craft,* February 2001

Robson, Graham, *The Illustrated Directory of Classic Cars*, London: Greenwich Editions, 2004

Sanders, Bill, "Continental Mark III First Driving Report," *Motor Trend,* March 1968

Schilling, Robert, "Detroit's Economy Car Gap (Part 2)," *Motor Trend,* April 1967

Stone, Matt, *Mustang 5.0 & 4.6 1979-1998*, Wisconsin: MBI, 1998

Wakefield, Ron, "Ford's New Maverick," *Road & Track,* May 1969

Whipple, Jim ed. *All The 1964 Models Popular Mechanics CAR FACTS*, New York: Popular Mechanics Co, 1963

Wilson, Quentin, *Great Car*, New York: Dorling Kindersley Publishing Inc, 2001

Footnotes

[1] Graham Robson, *The Illustrated Directory of Classic Cars* (London: Greenwich Editions, 2004): p220

[2] John Bentley, *All The World's Cars 1954*, (New York: Cornell Publishing Corp, 1954): p112

[3] Quentin Wilson, *Great Car*, (New York: Dorling Kindersley Publishing Inc, 2001): p264

[4] Jim Whipple ed., *All The 1964 Models Popular Mechanics CAR FACTS* (New York: Popular Mechanics Co, 1963): p16

[5] Ron Wakefield, "Ford's New Maverick" *Road & Track* (May 1969): p28

[6] Leon Mandel ed. "The Great Imported Car Invasion" *Car and Driver* (September 1969): p74

[7] Leon Mandel, "Maverick and the mini space race" *Car and Driver* (May 1969): p37

[8] Ron Wakefield, op cit. p32

[9] Leon Mandel, "Maverick and the mini space race" *Car and Driver* (May 1969): p37

[10] Robert Schilling, "Detroit's Economy Car Gap (Part 2)" *Motor Trend* (April 1967): p80

[11] Ron Wakefield, op cit. p29

[12] Ibid. p30

[13] Ibid. p30

[14] Leon Mandel ed., "Preview Test: AMC Hornet" *Car and Driver* (September 1969): p57

[15] Ibid. p83

[16] Ron Wakefield, op cit. p32

[17] Ibid. p32

[18] Bill Kilpatrick, "Maverick Versus The Mob" *Popular Mechanics* (August 1969): p73

[19] Ibid. p73

[20] Noel Grove, "Swing Low, Sweet Chariot!" *National Geographic* (July 1983): p13

[21] Kyle Given, "And Now A Word From Our Sponsor" *Car and Driver* (September 1969): p72

[22] Ibid. p78

[23] Ken Gross, *BMW Illustrated Buyer's Guide*, (Wisconsin: MBI, 1984): p132

[24] Leon Mandel ed., "Preview Test: AMC Hornet" *Car and Driver* (September 1969): p57

[25] Bob Brown ed. "15,000 Mile Comparison Test: Chevrolet Vega Versus Ford Pinto" *Car and Driver* (November 1971): p25

[26] Ibid. p88

[27] David Bean, "Spurs For The Maverick" *Car Life* (May 1969): p49

[28] Jim Hamilton, "Hot and Cold Running Mavericks" *Car Life* (October 1969): p74

[29] Don Evans ed. "Hot Stuff For Mavericks" *Hot Rod* (January 1970): p92

[30] David Bean, op cit. p50

[31] Gordon Jennings ed., "Maverick Grabber" *Car and Driver* (August 1970): p40

[32] Jeff Koch, "Buyer's Guide 1971-'75 Ford Maverick Grabber" *Hemmings Muscle Machines* (September 2009): p51

[33] Jim Whipple ed., op cit. p3

[34] Ibid. p8

[35] Bill Sanders, "Continental Mark III First Driving Report" *Motor Trend* (March 1968): p66

[36] Brian Brennan ed., "Roddin' At Random" *Hot Rod* (October 1974): p34

[37] Peter McGough ed., "Real-World Supercars" *Car Craft* (February 2001): p37

[38] Klaus Freund ed. *Auto Katalog 1980*, (Stuttgart: Vereinigte Motor-Verlage, 1979): p57

[39] Jeff Ford, "What If?" *Legendary Ford* (March/April 2010): p74

[40] Quentin Wilson, *Great Car*, (New York: Dorling Kindersley Publishing Inc, 2001): p110

[41] Matt Stone, *Mustang 5.0 & 4.6 1979-1998*, (Wisconsin: MBI, 1998): p15

[42] Mark Gillies, "Design for Today" *Autocar* (December 10 1986): p55

[43] Jim Dunne, "Detroit Report Rear-drives retained" *Popular Science* (August 1985): p11

[44] Dave Morley, *Six Decades of Holden versus Ford*, (Melbourne: Hardie Grant Travel, 2018): p285

1974 Mercury Comet sedan. (Courtesy Ford Motor Co)

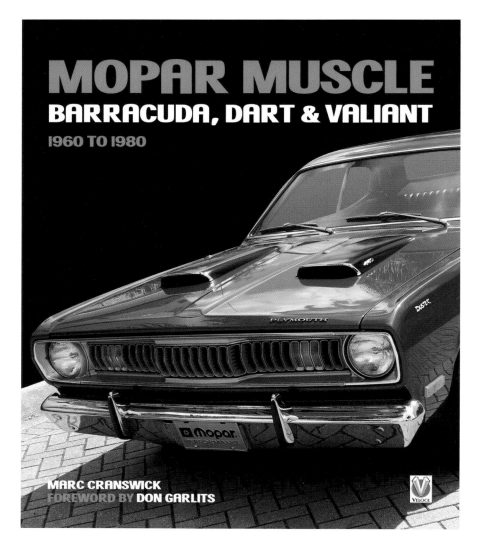

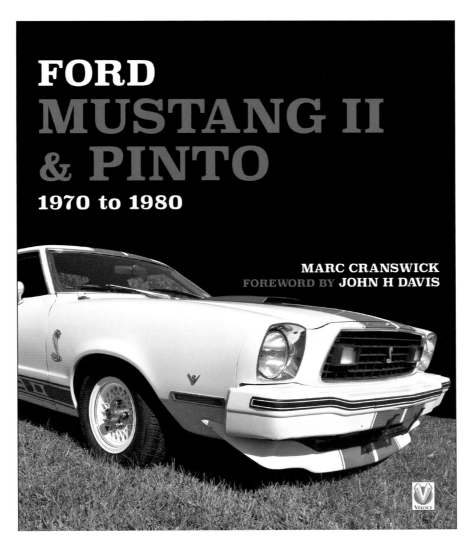

FORD
MUSTANG II
& PINTO
1970 to 1980

MARC CRANSWICK
FOREWORD BY **JOHN H DAVIS**

The history of Ford's first American-designed and built subcompacts. Following the Mustang II and Pinto through a challenging decade, as they competed with domestic and imported rivals in the showroom, and on the racetrack. This book examines icons of the custom car and racing scene, as Ford took Total Performance into a new era.

ISBN: 978-1-787112-67-4
Hardback · 25x20.7cm · 128 pages · 201 pictures

For more information and price details, visit our website at www.veloce.co.uk · email: info@veloce.co.uk · Tel: +44(0)1305 260068

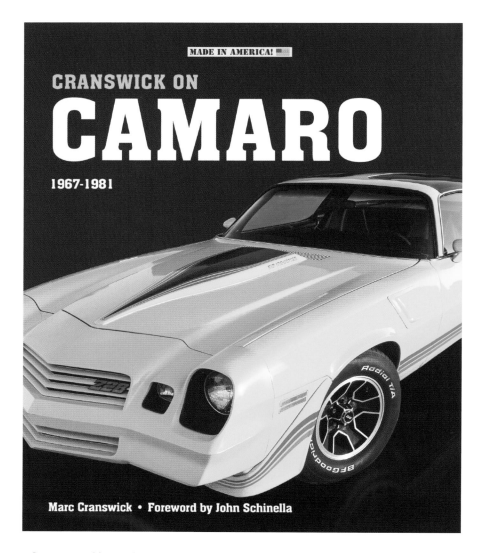

MADE IN AMERICA!

CRANSWICK ON

CAMARO

1967-1981

Marc Cranswick • Foreword by John Schinella

Covering Chevrolet's specialized sport coupe, during the classic 1967-81 era. Relive those outlandish hi-po Camaros, from legendary speed shops Baldwin-Motion, Dana, Nickey and Yenko. Fuel crisis, insurance and the EPA? Don't worry, the Bowtie boys had your back in the showroom, and on the track.

ISBN: 978-1-787116-68-9
Hardback · 25x20.7cm · 184 pages · 223 pictures

For more information and price details, visit our website at www.veloce.co.uk · email: info@veloce.co.uk · Tel: +44(0)1305 260068

Index